The Ultimate Dictionary of Dreams

Eili Goldberg

This is the most up-to-date dictionary of dream symbols and interpretation in existence. We can use this comprehensive list of old and new symbols that appear in our dreams to understand why we dreamt what we dreamt, and what it means. Many of the symbols have a psychological connotation, while others are patently predictive of the future. Our emotions and state of mind are often revealed in the symbols in our dreams. With the clear explanations in this dictionary at hand, we need no longer worry or puzzle over the meaning of our dreams.

Eili Goldberg has published numerous books on mysticism and psychology, and is an authority on dream interpretation.

Eili Goldberg

The
Ultimate
Dictionary
of
Dreams

Astrolog Publishing House

P. O. Box 1123, Hod Hasharon 45111, Israel
Tel: 972-9-7412044
Fax: 972-9-7442714
E-Mail: info@astrolog.co.il
Astrolog Web Site: www.astrolog.co.il

ISBN 965-494-096-5

Published by Astrolog Publishing House 1999

Printed in Israel
10 9 8 7 6 5 4 3 2 1

Since the dawn of human culture, when primitive man, crouching on animal skins in his dark cave, produced wall drawings of a sleeping figure, with huge mammoths inside a cloud emerging from the figure's head, the phenomenon of dreams has occupied man's thoughts. Is there anything more wondrous than a dream – a person deep in sleep, unaware of his surroundings, yet at the same time seeing before his eyes images, active pictures of his life? Here is his long-lost lover; she hasn't aged at all. And what's this? He is standing in a green field of corn... And what is the meaning of that python twined around a branch?

While man has always been fascinated by the phenomenon of dreams as a whole (Why do we dream? Are dreams merely a memory embedded in the subconscious? Can we recall dreams when we wake up? Can we channel our dreams toward a specific subject?), he has been equally preoccupied with the much more pressing question: What is the meaning of our dreams?

A person dreams that the plane in which he is traveling crashes, killing all aboard. He decides to cancel the business trip he had planned for the next day and not to take the flight. Two days later he opens the newspaper... and the plane really did crash! Was the dream a warning to him? Can we guess the future through our dreams?

Several weeks before the maiden voyage of the famous *Titanic*, a London author wrote an article describing his dream – a dream in which the *Titanic* had sunk. The article was roundly criticized; everyone saw it as a cheap attempt to jump on the bandwagon of publicity generated by the *Titanic*'s maiden voyage. When word arrived of the sinking of the luxury liner, many asked themselves: Could the disaster have been prevented if the dream had been believed?

In ancient cultures, there were two approaches to dreams: The first approach saw dreams as a journey of the astral body, which is the part of the personality that is primeval matter, capable of leaving the physical body and embarking on a journey over the face of the earth and on through space. This astral body witnesses scenes of the past, present and future and brings what it has seen to the eyes of the physical body. The second approach sees dreams as instructions and messages sent to the dreamer by the gods or by dead people who wish to communicate with him. Such messages are often statements related to the future. In other words, both approaches stress one thing: dreams have meaning. They are brought/sent to the person in order to tell him something, to warn him, to inform him... Thus a person must understand the meaning of his dreams in order to comprehend the messages that are being sent to him from the extrasensory world.

A person who does not understand English will not comprehend an English-language sign even if it is staring him in the face; in order to know what the sign is saying, he must know the language. So too with dreams: in order to interpret our dreams, we must become familiar with the language, with the meaning of each symbol or figure that appears in a dream.

Another point to bear in mind is that it is not only the symbol appearing in the dream, within its appropriate cultural context, that has bearing upon the correct interpretation of a dream; the backdrop, or the action, appearing in the dream is also important. Is the window open or closed? Is the bird flying toward you or away from you? Do you see the woman from a point above her head or below? Such details, as we shall explain later, help us to reach the correct interpretation of the dream.

In the past, dream interpretation was the province of sages, soothsayers and religious figures; as such, it was linked not only to the culture of the dreamer, but also to his religion. In the twentieth century, the study of dreams has, for the most part, passed to the psychologists, who have their particular interpretation that consists of theories divorced from a specific culture.

Although dreams, like sleep, are little understood by man, almost everyone knows what we mean when we speak of a "dream." Even a young child knows that a dream state exists which is different from that of reality. But the widespread acknowledgment that dreams do exist contributes nothing to their interpretation. Since ancient times, dreams have remained an unsolved mystery. No one can state with precision just what purpose dreams serve, and at what level of consciousness they occur.

The accepted definition of a dream is: "pictures or experiences during sleep, which the dreamer believes are real."

Dreams can be identified by a number of characteristics: a dream, during a sleep state, is "realistic"; it is marked by extremes, excess, a loss of boundaries – anything is possible in a dream; the power of events or feelings in a dream escalates; it is very difficult to channel a dream during sleep; a dream usually presents an event, or chain of events rather than an isolated, static scene; a dream is erased from the memory.

The study of dreams and, more so, the interpretation of dreams, is a broad and fascinating field of interest. Let us mention only a few of the topics touched on in this dictionary:

1. The interpretation of dreams.

2. The psychological interpretation of dreams.

3. The dream as a bridge between distant worlds and the individual.

4. The study of dreams for purposes of therapy.

5. Self-interpretation of dreams – a way of recording and utilizing the information gleaned from dreams.

To help you make the best use of this book, let us briefly explain how to record a dream. First, write down what you've dreamt, even in outline form, immediately upon awakening. Every minute that passes wipes out parts of your dream! Prepare writing utensils next to your bed, or – better yet – keep a tape-recorder nearby that has been set up in advance, so you can record the story of your dream.

After writing down your dream, go over your notes and add various details that occur to you as you read. These details can "pop up" throughout the day. Make sure to add every detail to the original dream.

In addition, jot down your overall feeling upon awakening (sad, depressed, full of energy and anticipation, and so forth). Also, make a note of any special activities on the preceding day (I attended a wedding, went to the income tax office, quarreled with my mother, etc.) as well as on the day following your dream.

A day or two later, combine all the material in an orderly fashion, without insertions or deletions, and you will have a "dream" ready for interpretation.

This book, *The Ultimate Dictionary of Dreams,* is the most modern and extensive dictionary of dreams ever compiled. Over 12,000 dream symbols appear in its 400 pages. Eili Goldberg collected the material for this book – the most up-to-date dream dictionary in existence – during the course of 1999, and made use of 270 dream dictionaries in various languages from all over the world in order to prepare the broadest and most accurate list ever.

The symbols that appear in the dictionary were examined in two stages: During the first stage, the symbols that appeared in at least 20 of the various dictionaries were collected. During the second stage, the symbols were classified into groups (for instance, animals, historical figures, flowers, vehicles, and so on), and fifty percent of the symbols that occurred most frequently in the other dream interpretation dictionaries were selected.

This dictionary presents the dreams in alphabetical order, of course, along with hundreds of illustrations. At the end of the book, there is an article about dreams from Eili Goldberg's book, *The Dictionary of Dreams* (Astrolog, 1998).

Abandonment — If the **dreamer is abandoned**, this signifies a quarrel with a friend. If the **dreamer abandons another person**, it means that he will renew a contact with a friend. If **he abandons his sweetheart**, he will not find valuable items he has lost. **Abandoning a mistress** predicts sudden wealth for the dreamer. **Abandoning children** means drastic financial losses because of errors of judgment. If the **dreamer abandons his home**, he will gamble and lose. If **he abandons his business**, there will be troubles, disputes and accusations.

Abbey — A ruined **abbey** indicates failed plans and dashed hopes. If a **young woman goes into an abbey**, it signifies that she will become very ill. A **priest denying the dreamer entry into an abbey** means that the dreamer will be spared embarrassment at the hands of his adversaries.

Abdomen — **Seeing one's abdomen** in a dream indicates high hopes. A **shrunken abdomen** indicates betrayal and persecution by false friends. A **swollen abdomen** is a sign of hardships which the dreamer will overcome. **Blood flowing** from the abdomen warns of a tragedy in the dreamer's family.

Abhorrence — **Dreaming about abhorring someone** means that the dreamer's dislike of that person is justified. If **others abhor him**, his well-meaning feelings toward them will become selfishness. A **woman who dreams that she is abhorred** by her lover has chosen the wrong man.

Abode — If a **dreamer cannot find his abode**, it means that he will no longer believe in other people's integrity. If he **has no abode**, he will have bad luck in financial matters.

Changing one's abode is an indication of urgent news and journeys. A **young woman who dreams of leaving her abode** means that she is the topic of gossip and slander.

Above — Something **suspended above the dreamer** is a sign of danger; if **it falls on him**, it means ruin or disappointment. If **it misses him**, it indicates a narrow escape from financial losses. Something **suspended securely** means an improvement after the threat of a loss.

Abroad — Dreaming about being abroad predicts a pleasant journey to another country with other people in the near future.

Abscess — This is a prediction of great troubles and difficulties for the dreamer, who will be called upon to sympathize with those of other people.

Absence — If the dreamer is happy about the absence of friends, he will soon be rid of an enemy.

Absinthe — If the dreamer becomes drunk from drinking absinthe, it means that he is acting irresponsibly with innocent people, and he will squander his inheritance.

Abundance — This is a clear indication that the dreamer will have a life filled with prosperity and wealth.

Abuse — If the **dreamer abuses someone**, it is a sign of financial losses. If **he himself is abused**, he will suffer at the hands of enemies. **Abusive language directed at a young woman** means that someone is jealous of her. **Her use of abusive language** means that she will be rejected, making her regret her bad behavior toward her friends.

Abyss — Looking down into an abyss is a sign that the dreamer is about to encounter danger.

Academy — If the **dreamer visits an academy**, he will regret opportunities missed as a result of inertia. **Being a member** of an academy indicates the inability to apply knowledge acquired. **Returning to an academy** signifies impossible demands made on the dreamer.

Accepted — If a **businessman dreams of a proposition being accepted**, it is a sign of success following signs of failure. If the **dreamer's sweetheart accepts** him, it forecasts a life of happiness with her.

Accident — A **road accident** signifies that a bad decision will lead to an unsuccessful deal. If one dreams about an **accident occurring in an unknown place**, it indicates an unsuccessful love life. Dreaming about **being involved in a railroad accident** is an indication of exaggerated self-confidence. If the **dreamer is in a plane crash**, it is a warning against bad business deals in the near future. If an **accident occurs with cattle**, he will battle to acquire something just to see a friend who is helping him lose something similar.

Accordion — When the **dreamer is playing the accordion**, it is a sign that he will soon marry. If the **sound of the accordion** is heard and not seen, disappointment can be expected. **Off-key music** or notes indicate depression and despondency.

Accountant — **Dreaming about an accountant** is connected to the dreamer's financial problems. A **conversation with an accountant** means that the dreamer has a strong desire to raise his standard of living.

Accounts — **Dreaming about accounts** to pay is a sign

of a dangerous situation. **Paying them** means that a dispute will be resolved.

Accuse — If the **dreamer accuses** someone of a base action, he will quarrel with people subservient to him and make a fool of himself. If the **dreamer is accused**, he may be guilty of spreading vicious gossip.

Aches — **Dreams about aches** indicate that by hesitating in business, other people are benefiting from the dreamer's ideas. A **heartache** is a prediction of distress caused by a lover's indifferent behavior. A **backache** signifies illness. A **headache** is an indication of the distress caused by ridding oneself of a rival, or of big worries. **Aching jaws** indicate health and financial troubles caused by illness.

Acid — **Drinking acid** in a dream is a sign of anxiety. **Toxic acids** indicate the discovery of treachery against the dreamer.

Acorns — **Dreaming about acorns** symbolizes success in love and business, and pleasant things. **Rotting or broken** acorns denote hardship and disappointment.

Acquaintance — **A pleasant conversation with an acquaintance** is a sign of smooth business dealings and domestic life. **Belligerent or vociferous behavior on the part of an acquaintance** means that the dreamer will be humiliated and embarrassed. **Shame at meeting an acquaintance** means that the dreamer is hiding something illicit which will soon be revealed. A **young woman who dreams of having numerous acquaintances** is very much in demand. The **opposite** is also true.

Acquittal — If the **dreamer is acquitted** of a crime, he is about to receive property, but may have to engage in a legal battle first. If **others are acquitted**, the dreamer's friends will bring joy into his life.

Acrobat — An **acrobat** signifies that the dreamer has a dangerous enemy of whom he is not aware. If an **acrobat falls** in the dream, it indicates that a plot has been foiled. If the **dreamer himself is the acrobat**, it means that he needs reinforcement from his surroundings.

Actor/Actress — An actor on the stage signals two-faced behavior on the part of one of the dreamer's friends.

Adam and Eve — Such a dream signifies a person seeking the virginal or primal aspect of life, or an individual who lives a full life, in harmony with himself.

Adder — **Dreaming about an adder** indicates the misfortunes of the dreamer's friends and his own threatened losses. A **young woman who dreams of an adder** is in danger of trouble from a treacherous person. If **the adder flees**, she will triumph against this attack.

Addition — **Struggling with addition** predicts trouble overcoming problematic situations — especially in business. Discovering **errors in addition** means that the dreamer will become wise to his enemies' evil intentions before they can implement them. An **adding machine** indicates that the dreamer has a powerful ally.

Adieu — **Happy adieux** are a sign of a happy and good social life, whereas **sad ones** are a prediction of loss and bereavement.

Admire — If the dreamer is admired, it means that he will be loved by former colleagues whom he has overtaken in rank.

Adopted — If the **dreamer sees his adopted child or parent**, he will experience great financial gains through the schemes of strangers. **A dream of adopting a child** means that the dreamer will make a mistake when moving house.

Adulation — **Seeking adulation** indicates that the dreamer will be granted an unmerited position of honor. **Giving adulation** means that the dreamer will give up a prized possession in order to benefit materially.

Adultery — This indicates a guilty conscience regarding the dreamer's sexuality.

Advancement — If the **dreamer advances**, it is a sign of professional or romantic success. If he dreams of **others advancing**, his friends will succeed.

Adventurer — If the **dreamer is the victim of an adventurer**, it means he is gullible and unable to manage his affairs. A **young woman who dreams of being an adventuress** is being exploited and compromised.

Adversary — **Seeing an adversary** means that the dreamer will defend himself from attacks. **Overcoming an adversary** means escaping disaster.

Adversity — If the **dreamer is caught in adversity**, he will experience failure and bad luck. **Others caught in adversity** are a sign of gloom and failed plans.

Advertisement — If the **dreamer advertises**, it signifies that he will be forced to do physical labor in order to advance. **Reading advertisements** means that the dreamer will be defeated by his rivals.

Advice — **Receiving advice** indicates a rise in moral integrity. **Seeking legal advice** hints at something fishy in the dreamer's transactions.

Advocate — Being an advocate of a cause means that the dreamer is loyal and honest both in his public and in his personal dealings.

Affliction — A **dream of affliction** predicts impending disaster. **Other people's affliction** means that the dreamer will be surrounded by hardships and misfortunes.

Affluence — Dreaming about affluence indicates success in business and good contacts with wealthy people.

Affront — **Dreaming of an affront** will cause the dreamer to weep. A **young woman who dreams of being affronted** will be exploited and placed in a compromising situation, and her interests will be jeopardized.

Afraid — **Feeling afraid** in a dream signals domestic problems and business failures. Dreaming of **others who are afraid** means that people will not be able to help the dreamer because of their own worries.

Afternoon — If a **woman dreams of an afternoon**, it means that she will form enduring friendships. An **overcast, rainy afternoon** is a sign of discontent and disappointment.

Agate — The appearance of agate in a dream signifies some progress in business.

Age — If the **dreamer himself or others** close to him **appear older** than they are in reality, or if in the dream the **dreamer is worried about his age**, it means that he will become ill in the near future. If the **dreamer or others close to him appear younger** than in reality, it means that it is advisable for the dreamer to avoid coming into conflict with those around him.

Agony — A **dream of agony** predicts a mixture of

pleasure and anxiety, with anxiety predominating. If the dreamer is in **agony about financial losses,** he is suffering from imaginary fears about his business affairs or a close relative's health.

Ague —A **dream of suffering from ague** often indicates the dreamer's poor state of health, or business failure resulting from indecisiveness. If **others suffer from ague,** it means that the dreamer's arrogance will be offensive to others.

Agreement — This suggests that the dreamer's problems will be solved and his worries will disappear completely.

Air — **Dreams of air** do not bode well: **Hot air** hints that the dreamer will do evil as a result of oppression. **Cold air** indicates business irregularities and a lack of domestic harmony. **Humidity** indicates destructive misfortune.

Air Force Officer — A **dream about an air force officer** is a prediction of a short journey or an unexpected visit. Dreaming of **being an air force officer** foretells a promotion.

Airplane — **Seeing an airplane** fly over and disappear indicates that the dreamer will get out of a restrictive, bad situation. A **moving airplane** is a sign of an upcoming journey. An **airplane crash** is a sign of disappointment and failure.

Alabaster — **Alabaster** predicts success in legal matters and marriage. **Breaking an object** made of alabaster means regret and sorrow.

Alarm Bell — If the dreamer hears a bell, it means that he will have reason to be anxious.

Albatross — The dreamer will overcome obstacles and reach his desired objective.

Album — Dreaming about an album is a good dream, signifying success and true friendship. If a **young woman dreams about looking at photos in an album**, it means that she will soon have a new and delightful lover.

Alchemist — Dreaming about being an alchemist who strives to turn base metals into gold indicates that the dreamer has good ideas, but can never accomplish his objectives. He will be disappointed in business and love.

Alcoholic Beverages — If the dreamer is drinking alcoholic beverages, it means that he must beware of being misled.

Alien — A **dream about friendly aliens** (strangers) indicates good things. An **unpleasant alien** signifies disappointments. **Dreaming about aliens from outer space** predicts the dreamer's meeting with very peculiar people who make him feel uncomfortable at first, but afterwards influence him positively.

Alley — The dreamer's luck will decrease if **he sees an alley in a dream**. He will have more worries. A **young woman who dreams about being in a dark alley** is warned of bad company and a ruined reputation.

Alligator — This is a warning dream which only bodes ill, unless the dreamer kills the alligator.

Alloy — An **alloy** is a sign that the dreamer will be troubled by business embroilments. A **woman dreaming about an alloy** will experience pain and sorrow.

Almanac — **Seeing an almanac** means that the dreamer's luck will vacillate. If **he studies the signs**, it means that insignificant details are bogging him down.

Almonds — Eating almonds predicts a journey to distant places.

Alms — This is a good dreams, unless reluctance is shown in the giving or receiving.

Altar — If the **dreamer sees a priest at the altar**, there will be friction in business and domestic matters. **Dreaming about a marriage** predicts sorrow for friends, and death for the elderly.

Aluminum — **Dreaming about aluminum** indicates satisfaction with one's lot. **Tarnished aluminum** objects are a sign of loss and sorrow.

Amateur — An **amateur actor** signifies the fulfillment of hopes. If he **plays in a tragedy**, the dreamer's happiness will be undermined.

Ambulance — **Dreaming about a siren-blaring ambulance** portends bad luck. If the **dreamer is the patient**, it means that he will become ill in the near future.

Ambush — If the **dreamer is attacked in an ambush**, it is a sign of danger that will beset. him if he is not careful. If the **dreamer lies in ambush**, it indicates that he will stop at nothing to deceive his friends.

America — If the dreamer is a high official, this dream warns of trouble and danger to himself.

Amethyst — A **dream about an amethyst** represents fair business dealings. The **loss of an amethyst** indicates a broken engagement.

Ammonia — This is a symbol of the dreamer's displeasure with a friend's behavior, which will lead to the breakup of the friendship.

Amorous — This is a warning against indulging in one's personal desires and pleasures, as this carries a risk of scandal. Basically, it warns against immoral behavior.

Amputation — If **part of a limb** is amputated, it is an indication of small business losses. The **amputation of an entire limb** represents unusually bad luck in business. This is a warning dream. A **leg amputation** means the loss of dear friends and a bad domestic life. An **arm amputation** signifies separation or divorce, and warns of falseness and deception. **Loss of fingers** denotes financial loss brought about by enemies.

Amusement — **Being amused or in a good mood** in a dream means that the dreamer will soon have good luck. **Dreaming about some kind of entertainment event** means that an opportunity is about to present itself, and it would be a shame to miss it.

Amusement Park — **Seeing an amusement park** is a sign that the dreamer will soon go on vacation. If **he is on a ride**, it means that he will learn how to enjoy life more.

Anchor — This symbolizes stability, security and earthiness. The dreamer has both feet firmly planted on the ground. A good dream for sailors.

Anecdote — A dreamer who relates anecdotes seeks light-hearted, superficial company, and this tendency will be reflected in his business dealings.

Angel — **An angel** is an indication of the dreamer's

strong belief in a superior power; he makes no attempt to alter his own destiny. **Dreaming about an angel also signifies** a successful marriage.

Anger — A **dream about anger** portends good and significant news for the dreamer. **Anger at a person known** to the dreamer indicates that the person does not merit the dreamer's trust. **Anger at an unknown person** indicates that the dreamer's life will soon change for the better.

Animals — The meaning changes according to the type of animal. (Refer to the name of the particular animal.)

Animal Young / Cubs — If **animal young** appear **with their mother** in a dream, it indicates maternal feelings. **Wild animal cubs** symbolize a longing for happiness. **Domesticated animal young** are indicative of the dreamer's childish personality. An **animal corpse** signifies an unhealthy situation, both in business and physically. Cages containing **wild animals** mean that the dreamer will overcome his enemies and hardships.

Angling — **Dreaming about catching fish** is positive. The **opposite** is true if no fish are caught.

Ankle — If the **dreamer's ankle** appears in the dream, it means success and the solving of problems. If his **spouse's ankle** appears, it indicates that the dreamer is being unfaithful to her, or the **opposite**.

Annoy — Being annoyed by or with someone in a dream is a sign of having enemies.

Annoyance — If the dreamer expresses annoyance or anger, it is a sign that his life will be happy and successful.

Antelope — If the dreamer sees an antelope, it signifies that if he makes a great effort, he will accomplish his objectives.

Antenna — **Seeing an antenna** is an indication of uncertainty or curiosity about a relationship. **Putting up an antenna** means that the person who the dreamer is uncertain about will come forward with answers.

Antibiotics — This warns the dreamer that he is going to be ill soon, but briefly, if he sees to himself immediately.

Ants — A **dream about ants** suggests that the dreamer reorganize his professional life and make changes in it. **Ants that are particularly tiresome** indicate an imminent period of frustration and disappointment.

Anvil — **Anvil** signifies fruitful work, or abundant crops for a farmer. The dreamer will be rewarded with success if he works hard. **Broken anvil** means that an opportunity has been thrown away.

Anxiety — Sometimes **anxiety in a dream bodes well**, indicating success after negative situations. However, if the **dreamer experiences anxiety about something really important**, something catastrophic is liable to happen.

Apes — **Dreaming about apes** is a sign of humiliation and ill-health of a good friend. A **small ape** clinging to a tree is a warning of deception and treachery.

Apparel — The interpretation of this symbol depends on the type, condition, color and style of the apparel. For example: **Fine but unfashionable apparel** means that the dreamer will be fortunate, but scoffs at progressive ideas. **White apparel**, except in young women and girls, is a sign of sadness. **Black** predicts disputes, business failure, and the wrong friends. **Blue** symbolizes success and loyal support by friends. **Green** is a sign of prosperity and joy. **Yellow** is a sign of imminent financial gain and fun. **Dreaming of yellow cloth** is lucky.

Apparition — This dream warns of impending catastrophe concerning property and people. The dreamer is warned to take special care of his family.

Appetite — A large appetite for food and drink is a sign of great sexual passion.

Apple — **Eating an apple** in a dream predicts a rosy future. If the **apple is sour**, it is a sign that the dreamer will soon be disappointed or experience failure.

Apprentice — This dream indicates that the dreamer will have to struggle to gain status among his peers.

Apricot — Dreaming about apricots or about eating them indicates a good future and success in most areas of life, with the exception of romance.

April — A **dream about April** is a good dream, signifying happiness and prosperity. If the **weather is bad**, it signifies bad luck that will soon pass.

Apron — This dream carries moral implications, especially for young women.

Arch — **Seeing an arch** indicates that the dreamer will attain recognition and wealth through hard work. A **fallen arch** indicates misfortune and dashed hopes.

Archbishop — Seeing an archbishop in a dream means that the dreamer will encounter many obstacles in his path to success.

Architect — If an **architect draws plans in a dream**, it means that changes will occur in the dreamer's business, and not necessarily positive ones. A **dream about an architect** can also predict disappointment of a woman's hopes for a suitable marriage.

Arm — A **strong arm** signifies unexpected success. A **weak arm** means a great disappointment in the life of the dreamer.

Aroma — If a young woman dreams of a sweet aroma, it is a sign that she will soon receive a pleasant surprise or gift.

Arrest— The **arrest of a respectable-looking stranger** in a dream is a sign of the dreamer's desire to make changes, but he is afraid of doing so. If the **stranger resists** arrest, the changes can be accomplished successfully.

Arrow — **Seeing an arrow** is a dream which predicts pleasure in the form of entertainment, trips and festivities. A **bow and arrow** in a dream means that the dreamer will profit from the inability of someone else to do something. An **old or broken arrow** indicates misfortune in love or business.

Art Gallery — This portends badly in the domestic arena, where the dreamer will pretend to be happy in his present situation, while actually longing for something else.

Artichoke — This suggests a breakdown in communication with one's partner, as well as disagreements and the lack of ability to understand him / her.

Artist — Dreams about artists, painters or other creative people actually indicate the contrary: the dreamer does not have artistic talent and would do better to pursue other avenues of development.

Ascending — If the **dreamer succeeds in ascending to the highest point** of whatever he is ascending without stumbling, things will go smoothly. If **he fails**, he will have to contend with obstacles.

Asceticism — The dreamer who dreams about asceticism will adopt all kinds of weird ideas which strangers will find fascinating, but those close to him will find revolting.

Ashes — This is a very bad dream, signifying nothing but trouble, unhappiness, loss and failure.

Asia — This dream indicates change, but promises no material benefits.

Asp — This is a very bad dream, predicting loss of honor for females, the plots of enemies, and quarrels between lovers.

Asparagus — This signifies correct and good decisions taken by the dreamer. He should continue to follow his heart and not listen to the advice of others.

Ass — **Seeing an ass** promises annoyances and delays for the dreamer. Being **chased by an ass** means that he will be the object of ridicule and gossip. **Riding an ass** unwillingly predicts quarrels. The **braying of an ass** in a dream signifies bad or unwelcome news.

Assassin — If the **dreamer is assassinated**, it means that he will not overcome his difficulties. If he sees **someone else being assassinated**, with blood all over, it predicts trouble for the dreamer. Any **dream in which an assassin appears** is a sign that the dreamer is liable to be harmed by secret enemies.

Assistance — **Dreaming about giving assistance** means that the dreamer's attempts to progress will be rewarded. If the **dreamer is assisted**, it means that he will be in a comfortable situation, with good, loving friends.

Astral — **Dreaming about the astral plane** predicts that the dreamer's plans and efforts will be rewarded with success and recognition. However, if the **dreamer sees his astral self**, it is a sign of extreme trouble.

Astronomer/Astrologer — This shows that the dreamer is facing the future with hope and positive expectations.

Asylum — This is a dream which indicates illness and misfortune. The dreamer will be able to overcome these only by making an enormous effort.

Atlas — If the dreamer is consulting an atlas, it means that he will not make changes or go on trips without considering all the implications.

Atomic Bomb — The **mushroom cloud** created by an atomic bomb is a sign that the dreamer will soon experience a catastrophic event in his life and that of his loved ones. **Dreaming about nuclear war** means that the dreamer is nursing a lot of anger, which is liable to burst out destructively.

Atonement — A **dream about atonement** portends well — the dreamer will have excellent relationships with friends, lovers will be successful with their sweethearts, business will boom. If **others are atoning** for the dreamer's bad behavior, it is a sign that the dreamer or his friends will be humiliated.

Attic — **Dreaming about being in an attic** is a sign of hopes that cannot be fulfilled. **Dreaming about sleeping in**

an attic is an indication of dissatisfaction with one's job.

Attorney — **Attorneys** symbolize serious disputes concerning material things. The dreamer is being threatened by the claims of enemies. If the **dreamer sees an attorney defending** him, it means that his friends will try to assist him, but will prove to be more trouble than they are worth.

Auction — If a **man dreams about an auction**, it is a sign that his business will flourish. If a **woman dreams about an auction**, it means that she will be wealthy and lead a life of affluence.

August — A **dream about August** is a sign of unsuccessful business deals and misunderstandings in love. A **young woman dreaming of marrying in August** should know that sorrow awaits her in her early married life.

Aunt — A **woman who dreams about an aunt** can expect to be severely criticized for something she has done. If the **aunt is smiling**, things will be smoothed out and everyone will be happy.

Aura — If the aura encircles the dreamer himself, it is a warning of a threat to his status and image.

Author — If the **dreamer is an author** who dreams that his manuscript has been rejected, it is a sign that his work will ultimately be accepted. If the **dreamer dreams about an anxious author**, it means that he is worried about his own or someone else's literary work.

Automobile — **Dreaming about an automobile** reveals that the dreamer is restless even when things are good for him, and this can result in dire consequences. A **breakdown** indicates failure to achieve the pleasure the dreamer had hoped for. If the **dreamer escapes being run over**, it means that he should avoid a rival.

Autumn — If a **woman dreams about autumn**, it means that she will come into property through the efforts of other people. An **autumn marriage** in a dream is a good sign.

Avalanche — If the **dreamer is caught in an avalanche**, it means good things are coming his way. If **other people are caught in an avalanche**, it is a sign that the dreamer is longing to move to a different place.

Avenue — An **avenue of trees** symbolizes ideal love. An **avenue of trees shedding their leaves** signifies a difficult life full of obstacles.

Avocado — Dreaming about an avocado signifies economic success and an improvement in the dreamer's status in the workplace.

Awake — Dreaming about being awake means that the dreamer is on the verge of strange experiences that will make him feel bad.

Ax — **Dreaming about an ax** signifies the end of a family feud, fight or struggle. A **sharp ax** symbolizes progress; a **blunt ax** means that business will become slow.

Baby — Dreaming about an especially happy baby indicates that the dreamer will enjoy true love. **Dreaming about a pretty baby** predicts true friendship. **Dreaming about a sick baby** is a sign that the dreamer has treacherous friends. **Dreaming about a bald baby** means a joyful and harmonious home.

Baby Carriage — This is a sign of good friends who do things to surprise you pleasantly.

Bachelor — A man who dreams that he is a bachelor is being warned to stay away from women.

Bachelorhood — If a married person dreams about bachelorhood, it means that he secretly desires to betray his spouse.

Back — **Dreaming about a naked back** means a loss of power and warns against lending money or giving advice. If **someone turns his back** on the dreamer and walks away, he is envious and can do the dreamer harm. If the **dreamer dreams of his own back**, it is not a good sign.

Back Door — If the **dreamer sees himself entering and leaving through a back door,** it indicates an urgent need to effect changes in his life. If he sees **another person leaving though the back door**, he can expect a financial loss, and it is not advisable to enter into a business partnership.

Backgammon — A **dream about playing backgammon** indicates that the dreamer will be treated unhospitably during a visit, but the situation will improve until friendships are formed. If the dream is about **losing the game**, the dreamer will not have luck in love or in financial matters.

Bacon — If the **dreamer is eating bacon** with someone, and his hands are clean, it is a good sign. **Rancid bacon** indicates that the dreamer's perceptions are not clear, and that he is worried.

Badger — This indicates the fear that someone else is harvesting the fruits of the dreamer's labors.

Bag/Handbag — This predicts the advent of good tidings and significant news concerning the dreamer's future.

Baggage —**Dreaming about baggage** means that the dreamer is worried. If he is **carrying his own luggage**, it means that he is so engrossed in his own misery that he cannot see that of others. **Losing luggage** signifies a bad business deal or domestic quarrels.

Bagpipe — If the player is angry and playing harshly, the bagpipe is not a good sign.

Bail — A dream in which the dreamer seeks bail indicates unanticipated troubles, accidents and bad relationships.

Bailiff — This shows that the dreamer is striving to advance, but lacks intellect.

Baker / Cook — This suggests that the dreamer does not have a clear conscience or is involved in some kind of scam; it reveals a desire to conceal a situation into which the dreamer is being coerced.

Bakery — This warns the dreamer to be careful of pitfalls if changing careers.

Baking — If a woman dreams about baking, it is a sign of poverty, too many children and ill health.

Balcony — A **dream about lovers parting sadly on a balcony** indicates a long and possibly final separation. A **balcony** can also mean bad news about faraway friends.

Bald — If a **woman dreams that her hair is falling out** to the point of baldness, it means that she will have to support herself. If a **bald man** appears in a dream, it warns the dreamer to watch out for con artists. A **bald woman** appearing in a man's dream means that he will have a shrewish wife. If a **woman dreams about a bald man**, she should not accept the next offer of marriage.

Ball (game) — If the **dreamer is playing ball**, it is a sign that he will soon receive good news. If the **dreamer sees other people playing ball**, it is a sign that the dreamer nurses an unhealthy jealousy toward one of his friends.

Ball (dance) — Participating in a ball indicates that the dreamer will have a happy and joyous life, full of love.

Ballet — This signifies infidelity, betrayal, envy and quarrels.

Balloon — **Seeing balloons** indicates severe disappointments in the future. A **large-than-usual balloon** suggests ambitiousness. A balloon that **falls from a very great height** above signifies regression.

Ballpoint Pen — This indicates that the dreamer will soon write a letter to a long-lost friend.

Bananas — **Seeing a banana** suggests that the dreamer is bored at work and is not exploiting his talents. **Dreaming about eating a banana** indicates a health problem. **Trading in bananas** means wasting time on peripheral, unprofitable matters.

Bandage — Wearing a bandage is a sign that the dreamer has loyal friends on whom he may depend.

Banishment — **Dreaming about being banished** means

that the dreamer is pursued by evil, and that he will die at an early age. **Dreaming about banishing a child** is a dream of fatality and treacherous business allies.

Banjo — This indicates entertainment and amusement.

Banking — If the **dreamer dreams about being in a bank**, it indicates business problems. If the **dreamer meets the bank manager**, it hints at bankruptcy. **Seeing silver and banknotes** in a dream mean financial prosperity.

Bankrupt — This signifies a business crisis and cerebral deterioration. The dreamer should refrain from speculations.

Banner— A **banner floating** in a clear sky symbolizes victory of the dreamer's country over its enemies. A **tattered banner** means defeat and loss of military honor.

Banquet / Feast— **Dreaming about a banquet with many participants** predicts a quarrel with one's partner. If the **dreamer is single**, it indicates marriage in the near future, but one that will end in failure.

Baptism — A **dream about baptism** indicates that the dreamer needs to temper his mockery of his friends and strengthen his character. **Being baptized** means that the dreamer humiliates himself to win public acclaim.

Bar (for drinking) — **Seeing a bar** indicates insecurity and a yearning for a better future. A **bar with a bartender** signifies that the dreamer longs to have a party.

Barbecue — This signifies that the dreamer is under extreme emotional pressure and is doing nothing to change the situation.

Barbershop / Beauty Parlor — If the **dreamer sees himself getting his hair cut**, it means that he is an ambitious person. A **dream about a barbershop** is also indicative of a strong character and a person who relishes upholding his rights and principles.

Barefoot — If the dreamer is barefoot, it is a sign that his path will be fraught with obstacles, but he will overcome them all.

Barking Dogs — This predicts bad news and difficulties.

Barley Fields — **Fields of barley** foretell great success and the realization of the dreamer's desires. However, **decaying barley** indicates loss.

Barn — A **barn full of grain and corn**, surrounded by plump cattle, predicts great prosperity. An **empty barn** indicates poverty.

Barometer — A **barometer in a dream** indicates positive changes in the dreamer's business affairs. A **broken barometer** is an indication of unwanted and unexpected incidents in business.

Baseball — **Playing baseball** indicates that the dreamer will be easily pleased, and that he is popular with his peers. If a **young woman plays baseball**, she will derive a lot of enjoyment but no security or profit from it.

Basement — A dream about a basement means that good opportunities fade away, and enjoyment becomes trouble and worry.

Basin — If a woman dreams about washing in a basin, it means that she will win true friendships and advancement by means of her feminine graces.

Basket (woven) — An **overflowing, woven straw basket** is a sign of social and financial success. An **empty basket**, however, symbolizes disappointment, sadness and depression.

Bass Voice — If the **dreamer has a bass voice in his dream**, it means that one of his employees has been cheating him. **Hearing a bass voice** is a bad sign for lovers, foretelling quarrels.

Baste (meat) — The dreamer will ruin his own objectives by stupidity and selfishness.

Baste (sewing) — This is a sign that a woman will experience a lot of aggravation because of her extravagance.

Bath — **Dreaming about taking a bath** indicates success in business. If the **water is not clear**, there might be problems and difficulties in the near future.

Bat (animal) — **Dreaming about bats** is a dire warning about the advent of bad news: grief and catastrophe, bereavement, accidents. A **white bat** almost definitely means death, often of a child.

Bathroom — Dreams about bathrooms signify a tendency toward frivolity and superficial pleasures.

Batter — The dreamer is fortunate in love, and he will inherit a home.

Bazaar — See **Fair**.

Battle — **Seeing a battle** indicates a struggle with difficulties, cultimating in victory. A **defeat in battle** means that the dreamer will suffer from other people's bad deals.

Bay Tree — A dream featuring a bay tree means pleasurable leisure. It is a very good dream.

Bayonet — The dreamer will be held by his enemies, unless he gets the bayonet in the dream.

Beach / Shore — This means that the dreamer needs some peace and quiet, some respite from the intensive life he leads.

Beacon (light) — A **lit beacon** is a good sign for sailors, for people in distress, and for the sick. It bodes well for business. If the **light goes out**, the dreamer will no longer have good fortune.

Beads — When the **dreamer sees beads**, it means that important people will pay attention to him. **Counting beads** is a sign of joy and happiness. If they are **scattered**, the dreamer goes down in the estimation of his acquaintances.

Beans — This is not a good dream. **Growing beans** are an indication of illness in children. **Dried beans** mean increasing disappointment in global affairs. They also indicate the possibility of epidemics. **Eating them** signifies that a good friend will get ill or suffer misfortune.

Bear — When a **bear appears** in a dream, the dreamer will have to work hard before he sees the fruits of his labor. **Killing a bear** symbolizes overcoming obstacles on the path to accomplishing a certain goal.

Beard — A **beard in a dream** attests to the fact that the dreamer has a strong character and plenty of self-confidence (particularly a **white beard**).

Beat — **Being beaten** in a dream is an indication of family disputes and quarrels. **Beating a child** reveals the dreamer's tendency to take wicked advantage of other people, usually weaker than himself.

Beauty — Any form of beauty is a good sign. A

beautiful woman in a dream indicates pleasure and profit. A **beautiful child** means a happy relationship.

Beauty Parlor — See **Barbershop**.

Beaver — **Seeing a beaver** means that if the dreamer is works steadily and patiently, he will reach a comfortable state. **Killing a beaver for its skin** indicates fraudulent and improper behavior toward the innocent.

Bed — Almost any situation in which a **bed is seen in a dream** predicts good things. **Making the dreamer's bed** indicates marriage in the near future. **Making a stranger's bed** symbolizes a new and surprising turning-point in life. An **unmade bed** indicates that the dreamer has problems with sexuality and marriage.

Bedbugs — These indicate disease and complications. A **lot of bedbugs** indicate death. **Anything to do with bedbugs** is connected to illness and often death.

Bedfellow — **Dreaming about not liking one's bedfellow** means that someone is trying to make the dreamer's life miserable. A **strange bedfellow** will cause the dreamer to bother everyone around him with his own unhappiness.

Bed-linen / Sheets — **Clean bed-linen** means that the dreamer will soon receive good news from far away. **Dirty bed-linen** indicates financial losses or health problems.

Bedroom — This is usually connected to eroticism and sex. At times, it speaks of a positive turning-point in life.

Bedwetting — If a **mother dreams that her child wets the bed**, it is a sign of exceptional worry and the protracted recovery of people from illnesses. If the **dreamer wets the bed**, it is a sign of illness or a disruptive tragedy.

Bee — A **bee or bees in a dream** are a sign that a joyous occasion is soon to take place in the family. **Seeing a bee** means that the dreamer has good friends. If the **dreamer is stung by a bee**, someone close to him will cause him injury.

Beef — If the **dreamer sees raw, bloody beef**, it is an indication of malignant, cancerous tumors. It warns the dreamer to watch out for any blemishes or injuries. **Seeing or eating cooked beef** foretells unbearable suffering, and gory death. **Well-cooked and served beef**, however, is a sign of harmony in love and business.

Beehive — This indicates a wedding, birth or engagement in the near future.

Beeper — **Dreaming about hearing a beeper** means that a crisis is imminent. **Dreaming about using a beeper** means that someone close to the dreamer will soon become a burden, requiring constant attention and care.

Beer — A **dream about beer** is an indication of disappointment. **Seeing people drinking** beer at a bar means that people are planning to undermine the dreamer's hopes.

Beet — When **beets grow abundantly** in a dream, there will be peace in the country. When **beets are eaten in the company of others**, they are harbingers of good tidings.

Beetle — The dreamer can expect a brilliant future. He will become important and famous.

Beggar — If the **dreamer helps a beggar**, it means that he should expect good things in all areas of life. If the **dreamer refuses to help the beggar**, a future loss is predicted.

Beheading — A **dream about being beheaded** presages devastating defeat or failure in some venture in the near future. If **others are beheaded**, with a lot of blood, it is a sign of violence, death and exile.

Bell — The ringing of a bell in a dream portends bad news concerning a distant acquaintance — such as death.

Belladonna — **Dreaming about belladonna** is a prediction of commercial success following strategic moves. **Women** will experience competition when setting their sights on men. **Dreaming about taking belladonna** indicates failure to acquit one's duties, and misery.

Bellman — If a **dreamer sees a bellman**, it means that he will have good fortune, and disputes will be settled amicably. If the **bellman looks sad**, some sad event will occur.

Bellows — The **bellows in a dream** represents a struggle, but energy and perseverance will eventually prevail over poverty. **Seeing a bellows** means that distant friends miss the dreamer. **Hearing a bellows** means that knowledge of the occult will be acquired.

Belly — A **dream about a distended belly** is an indication of illness. A **healthy belly** is a sign of irrational desires.

Belt — The dreamer will soon receive a large sum of money unexpectedly.

Bench — If the **dreamer sits on a bench**, he should not trust confidants. If **others sit on a bench**, it is a sign of joyful reunions and reconciliation with friends.

Bequest — **Dreaming about a bequest** predicts that the dreamer will derive pleasure from duties well done. A **dream about a bequest** is also a sign of healthy children.

Bereavement — A dream about the death of a child means that the dreamer's plans will be promptly frustrated, and he will meet with failure rather than success.

Betting — If the **dreamer is betting on races**, he is warned to beware of undertaking new ventures, as his enemies are waiting to embroil and entrap him. **Betting at gaming tables** means that the dreamer will be the victim of extortion.

Bhagavad Gita — Rest and seclusion are foretold for the dreamer. A pleasant trip is arranged by friends, but with little material profit involved.

Bible — A **dream about the Bible** foretells innocent pleasure for the dreamer. If the **dreamer denigrates the Bible**, it means that he is about to fall victim to immoral temptations offered by a friend.

Bicycle — **Dreaming about a bicycle** indicates a frenzied lifestyle and the need to slow down. **Riding downhill** warns of danger in the near future. **Riding uphill** signifies a rosy future.

Bier — A **dream about a bier** is an indication of devastating losses and the deterioration of a close relative. If the **bier is strewn with flowers** in a church, it is a sign of a bad marriage.

Bigamy — **Dreaming about bigamy** is an indication of loss of virility and mental powers in a man. A **woman** can suffer dishonor unless she acts with the utmost discretion.

Billiards — A **billiard table with people around it** indicates unexpected problems. An **isolated pool table** indicates that the dreamer should beware of those conspiring against him.

Bills — If the **dreamer himself is paying bills**, it is a sign that his financial concerns will disappear shortly without a trace. Worrying about **not having paid bills** means that the dreamer's enemies are spreading malicious gossip about him.

Billy-goat — This is the symbol of a demon, the devil or an evil spirit.

Binoculars - See **Eyeglasses**.

Bird's Nest — An **empty bird's nest** indicates future problems and sorrow. A **nest containing eggs** indicates a rosy future.

Birds — If a **rich man dreams about birds** in flight, it is a sign that he will suffer financial losses. If a **poor man** or one with financial problems dreams of birds, it is a sign of economic abundance. A **wounded bird** means that a member of the dreamer's family will cause him harm. A **flying bird** is a sign of great prosperity. If a **bird is shot**, it predicts a bad harvest.

Birth (of animals) — This indicates that the dreamer has enemies who are acting behind his back; however, he will overcome this obstacle and succeed in accomplishing his goals and objectives.

Birth — If a **single person dreams about birth**, it signifies that certain problems will soon be solved. If a **married person dreams about birth**, it is a sign that he will soon get pleasant surprises.

Birthday — If a **young person dreams about a birthday**, it is sign of dishonesty and poverty. For an **old person**, it means trouble and loneliness.

Birthday Presents — This is a good dream, one of happy surprises, advancement and accomplishments.

Biscuit / Cookie — This indicates that the dreamer tends to blame others for his own mistakes and deeds.

Bishop — If the **dreamer is a teacher or an author**, he will suffer mental torment brought about by the intricacies of the material he deals with. A **tradesman who dreams about a bishop** is liable to lose money because of senseless transactions. **Seeing a bishop** in a dream predicts hard labor accompanied by fever and chills. If an **admired bishop** gives the dreamer his approval, this will result in success.

Bite — This dream does not bode well. The dreamer will unsuccessfully attempt to undo something that cannot be undone. He will also suffer at the hands of an enemy.

Blackberries — These warn of financial disappointment or loss of economic status.

Blackboard — **Seeing a blackboard** is a forecast of imminent bad news about the illness of an acquaintance of the dreamer. The **dreamer's financial situation** is unstable because of the whims of commerce.

Blackout — A dream about an electricity blackout indicates that the dreamer will forget something very important.

Blacksmith — It is quite rare to dream about a blacksmith. However, it indicates a spirit torn in two.

Bladder — This dreams warns of neglecting health problems which can lead to trouble in business.

Blame — If the **dreamer is being blamed** for something, it suggests that he will be involved in a quarrel in the future. If the **dreamer blames someone else**, it means that the dreamer will have a quarrel with his associates.

Blanket — **Dreaming about a blanket** indicates good times and a happy life: **the thicker and more elaborately decorated the blanket**, the happier the dreamer's life will be.

Blasphemy — This warns the dreamer against false friends who can do great harm.

Blaze — A **dream about flames** or a blaze indicate the eruption of bottled-up rage. **Overcoming a blaze** means that the dreamer will soon receive unexpected good news.

Bleating — Hearing the bleating of animals predicts that the dreamer will soon have new cares and responsibilities, not necessarily negative ones. The dreamer will be called upon to be generous.

Bleeding — This warns of health problems which must be attended to.

Blind — A **dream about being blind** indicates a sharp transition from affluence to poverty. If the **dreamer sees others as blind**, it means that he will be called upon to assist someone who deserves his help.

Blindfold — A blindfold suggests that the dreamer has been greatly disappointed by himself and by those around him.

Blind Man's Buff — Dreaming about this game indicates that the dreamer is about to do something that will cause him humiliation and financial loss.

Blindness — If the **dreamer appears blind** in a dream, he is not totally satisfied with his choice of a spouse. If a person dreams about **leading someone who is blind**, it is a sign that he is too dependent on someone who does not actually deserve his trust.

Blood — **Seeing blood** indicates an unwanted relationship, a quarrel, anger, disagreements or disappointment (particularly in emotional contexts). **Bloodstained clothes** indicate that the dreamer's enemies wish to destroy his successful career. The dreamer should exercise his discretion in his choice of friends. **Blood on the dreamer's hands** or a bleeding nose signifies immediate misfortune if the dreamer does not act with great caution. **Blood flowing from a wound** is a sign of illness and anxiety, as well as business setbacks.

Bloodstone — This means that the dreamer will be unlucky in his relationships.

Blossom — **Trees and shrubs in blossom** indicate that enjoyable and profitable times are in store for the dreamer. **Walking through blossoming orchards** with one's sweetheart means that the relationship will be filled with physical pleasure.

Blows — A **dream about blows** is a warning of injury. If the **dreamer receives a blow**, he will suffer from damage to the brain. If the **dreamer defends himself**, his business will prosper.

Blushing — A **woman who dreams about blushing** will experience embarrassment and worry as a result of unfounded accusations. **Seeing others blush** means that she is behaving in a way that her friends dislike.

Boa Constrictor — A **dream about a boa constrictor** is an indication of trouble and misfortune. **Dreaming about killing a boa constrictor** is a good sign.

Boarding House — This is an indication of complications and troubles in business, as well as of a change of abode.

Boasting — If the **dreamer boasts to a rival**, it means that he will employ unfair methods to beat his rival. To **hear boasting** in a dream means that the dreamer will live to regret an impulsive action which caused problems for his friends.

Boat — **Seeing a boat** heralds changes for the better in the dreamer's life. A **boat on calm waters** indicates a change in workplace or residence. A **boat on stormy waters** is an indication of worries and changes for the worse. **Rowing a boat** is a sign of social success as well as recognition from professional colleagues. If a **boat overturns**, it is a sign that the dreamer will soon receive important news. A **grounded boat** means significant financial losses. If a **dreamer is swept out of a boat during a storm**, he will have bad luck.

Bobbin — This indicates that the dreamer will be responsible for doing some important work, with dire consequences if the work is not done.

Bogs — This indicates oppressive and unbearable burdens and worries. The dreamer may become ill.

Boiler — A **non-functioning boiler** signifies mismanagement and disappointment. **Checking on a boiler** is a sign of illness and loss.

Boiling — A **boiling pot** is a good sign for a woman, indicating pleasant social duties. A **boiling kettle** means that the dreamer's troubles are at an end and good times lie ahead.

Boils — A **pus-filled, bleeding boil** is an indication of immediate bad things, such as insincere friends. A **boil on the dreamer's forehead** predicts the illness of someone close to him.

Bolts — **Seeing bolts** is a sign of tremendous obstacles in the dreamer's path to progress. **Old or broken bolts** mean that failure awaits the dreamer.

Bombshell — This is not a good dream, as quarrels and lawsuits follow it.

Bones — If the **dreamer sees his bones protruding** from his flesh, it means that he will be the victim of treachery. A **heap of bones** indicates famine and evil influences.

Bonnet — **Dreaming about a bonnet** is a sign of gossip and slander. **Black bonnets** mean that friends of the opposite sex are not trustworthy.

Book — **Dreaming about a book** signifies great success connected with reading or studying, which will lead the dreamer to a fulfilling and financially rewarding profession. **Reading a book** in a dream means that the dreamer will go on a trip which will have great significance in his life.

Bookcase — **Seeing a bookcase** indicates that the dreamer's occupation and leisure will be connected to knowledge. **Empty bookcases** mean that the dreamer is unable to work.

Bookstore — This signifies that the dreamer will have literary aspirations that will obstruct his regular work.

Boots — If the **dreamer sees someone else wearing his boots**, it means that his sweetheart will be taken from him. **New boots** are a sign of an improved financial situation. **Old, worn boots** indicate illness and troubles.

Borrowing — To **borrow from someone else** is a sign of financial troubles. If **someone borrows from the dreamer**, it means that the dreamer will be offered assistance by friends in time of need. **Dreaming of spending borrowed money** means that the dreamer's dishonesty will be exposed and a friendship jeopardized.

Bosom — An **injury in the bosom** is a warning of trouble. A **full, white bosom** is a sign of good fortune, while a **shrunken, blemished bosom** is an indication of disappointment in love. If **a woman's lover is secretly examining her bosom through sheer clothing**, it means that she will come under somebody's unsavory influence.

Boss — See **Manager**.

Bottles — **Seeing a bottle filled with a clear liquid** is a good sign, as it portends success in love. **Empty bottles** signify sinister embroilments from which the dreamer will be able to extricate himself only by means of his wits. **Broken bottles of wine** indicate excessive sexual passion. **Bottles of whisky** indicate careful husbanding of financial resources.

Bothering — See **Pestering**.

Bouquet (of flowers) — This indicates that the dreamer feels that his talents are not appreciated.

Bow and Arrow — The dreamer is aware of his talents and has great self-esteem. He knows how to rely on himself and his powers of judgment.

Bowl — A **full bowl** predicts quarrels or disagreements with a partner. An **empty bowl** is a sign of tranquillity, quiet and rest.

Bowling — A **dream about bowling** foretells a scandal that will be harmful to the dreamer's reputation, finances and friendships. **Seeing others bowling** means that the dreamer's preference for superficial people will lead to the loss of his job.

Box / Chest — A **closed box** means financial problems. An open box signifies that a secret, which the dreamer has jealously guarded until now is about to be revealed. A **box that has been broken into** indicates licentiousness. A **sealed box** is a sign of morality. An **empty box** is a sign of disappointments.

Bracelet — **Wearing a bracelet** on one's wrist predicts marriage in the near future. **Losing a bracelet** is a sign of troubles and annoying losses. **Finding one** means that the dreamer will receive possessions.

Brain — **Seeing one's own brain** in a dream means that the dreamer will become unpleasant as a result of his surroundings. **Animals' brains** are a sign of mental illness. **Eating brains** is a sign of profit and knowledge.

Brambles — **Seeing brambles** is a bad dream, signifying unsuccessful lawsuits, and illness in the family. To be **caught in brambles** in an orchard is an indication of bitter rivalry or of a domestic quarrel.

Branch — **Rich, green, leafy branches** indicate rich friendships. **Withered, dry branches** will bring sad news of faraway friends and relatives.

Brandy — Dreaming about brandy means that although the dreamer will achieve status and wealth, his lack of refinement will preclude friendship with those he most wants to win.

Brass — The dreamer will rise high in his profession, but will be haunted with fears of a downfall.

Bray — The **bray of an ass** is a sign of bad news. The **bray of a donkey** means that the dreamer will be publicly insulted by a disgusting person. **Distant, sad braying** is the signal of inheritance from someone close to the dreamer.

Bread — **Seeing bread** signifies that the dreamer is satisfied with himself and derives pleasure from his family. **Eating bread** predicts good health.

Breakage — **Any manner of breakage** in a dream — no matter who is doing the breaking — portends bad things, mainly health and domestic problems. **Breaking limbs** means mismanagement and failure.

Breakfast — A dream about breakfast indicates that the individual is going to face a difficult test, and that he fears failure.

Breath — If the dreamer encounters a person with **fresh, sweet breath,** he will enter into profitable business deals and will behave well. **Bad breath** indicates illness and troubles. **Losing one's breath** means unexpected failure.

Brewing — **Dreaming about brewing** predicts that after being persecuted by the authorities, the dreamer will be proved innocent. Generally, **dreams about brewing** mean success after initial anxiety.

Briars — Being **caught in briars** means that enemies have entrapped and embroiled the dreamer. However, if he succeeds in **extricating himself from the briars**, he will receive the assistance of good friends. **Walking in briars** is a sign of business problems and lack of communication.

Brick — **Seeing bricks** is an indication of unsettled business and rough patches in love. **Making bricks** is a sign of failure to make money.

Bride — **Dreaming about a bride** is an indication of virginity, and a lack of maturity and experience of life. For a **woman to dream of being a bride** is a sign of an imminent inheritance. **Kissing a bride** is a sign of friends making up after a quarrel. If the **dreamer is kissed by a bride**, it means that he will be healthy, and that his beloved will inherit.

Bridge — **Crossing a bridge** indicates exaggerated concerns which will soon pass. A **bridge that collapses** is a warning of economic problems. An **endless bridge** signifies unrequited love. **Passing underneath** a bridge means that the dreamer must be patient if he is ever to solve his problems.

Bridle — **Seeing a bridle** means that the dreamer is involved in a difficult project that will end in success, profit and pleasure. If the **bridle is old and worn**, it is a sign of difficulties that will defeat the dreamer.

Brimstone — This is a warning to the dreamer to be more careful and circumspect in his actions; if he is not careful, they could cost him friendships.

Bronchitis — The dreamer's plans will be disrupted because of illness at home. He will be faced with failure to attain his objectives.

Bronze — The **metal, bronze, indicates** a lack of certainty and satisfaction with one's fate. A **woman who dreams of a bronze statue** will not marry the man she has set her heart on. A **moving bronze statue** indicates a love affair, but not marriage. Dreaming of **bronze insects or snakes** means that envy and ruin will haunt the dreamer.

Brood — **Dreaming about a hen with her brood of chicks** means a lot of difficult children. A **dream about a brood** can also mean wealth.

Broom — If the **dreamer is sweeping** with a broom, it indicates a professional turning-point. A **broom lying on the ground** portends imminent separation from a close friend.

Broth — **Seeing broth** is a sign of faithful and caring friends who will help in any way, including financially. **Broth** is also the sign of enduring love. If the **dreamer prepares broth**, he will responsible for the fate of others.

Brothel — This is a warning that the dreamer will face disgrace because of his profligacy in material matters.

Brother /Sister — A **dream about a sibling** must be interpreted according to the character traits of the dreamer's family. A dream about a **dead brother** means that the dreamer will soon be called upon to give financial or other aid.

Brush — **Seeing various brushes** in a dream signifies that the dreamer earns money in a variety of ways — rather enjoyable and profitable. **Dreaming about using a hairbrush** means mismanagement resulting in financial loss.

A **clothes brush** indicates hard work ahead, which will be lucrative.

Buckle — This foretells a lot of pleasurable invitations as well as chaos in business matters.

Buffalo — **Seeing buffaloes** is a sign of powerful but stupid enemies who can be outwitted and fended off by the dreamer. If **buffaloes are killed** by a woman in her dream, it means that a difficult project she undertook will be successful and will win her esteem from men.

Bugle — **Dreaming about a bugle** is a good sign. **Hearing joyous bugle notes** means great happiness and harmony. **Blowing a bugle** means success in business.

Building — If the **dreamer is standing next to a luxurious building**, it predicts good and pleasant times. If the **dreamer enters the structure**, it means a loss of control, as well as nervousness and impatience. **Old, dilapidated buildings** are a sign of illness and losses in love and business.

Bull — If a **woman dreams about a bull**, it is a sign that she is not sexually satisfied. If a **man dreams about a bull**, it means he relates brutally to women. If a **bull chases the dreamer**, it means that he will be plagued by the attacks of rivals. If a **young woman encounters a bull**, she will reject one offer of marriage in favor of another, better one. If a **bull gores someone**, the dreamer will suffer for having misused someone else's possessions. A **white bull** is a sign of moving up from the mere material realm.

Bulldog — Being **attacked by a bulldog** in strange premises means that the dreamer will embroil himself with the authorities because of deceit. A **friendly bulldog** means success despite obstacles and enemies.

Bullock — This is a sign that good friends will surround the dreamer in times of trouble. It also means good health.

Bundle — This warns the dreamer of a great disappointment in the near future.

Burden — Burdens are an indication of serious worries and injustices caused by a conspiracy of the authorities and the dreamer's enemies. However, the dreamer will prevail and reach pinnacles of success.

Burglars — This is a sign of dangerous enemies who are out to destroy the dreamer if he is not cautious.

Burglary — Dreaming about a break-in or burglary means that someone whom the dreamer has trusted explicitly is not worthy of such trust. This dream may be followed by accidents.

Burial — Contrary to what it seems, **burial in sunny weather** predicts good health, birth or marriage. A **rainy burial** indicates bad news and illness.

Burn — If the **dreamer gets burnt**, it means he will soon win a large sum of money. If he **sees another person getting burnt**, it means he will soon make a new friend. A **burnt hand** means that the dreamer's quest for wealth and fame is out of control, and he will fail. If the **dreamer walks through a bed of burning coals**, it means that he is capable of accomplishing anything, no matter how difficult. If **he succumbs to the flames**, it means that he is being harmed by treacherous friends.

Burr — This symbolizes the dreamer's struggle to liberate himself from a burden and to change his surroundings.

Bus — A **dream about a bus** is an indication of slow progress along the path to the dreamer's goals. A **crowded bus** in which the dreamer is standing indicates a lot of competition. **Traveling on the wrong bus** means that the dreamer has chosen the wrong path in life and should reevaluate his aims.

Butcher — **Seeing a butcher slaughtering cattle** in a dream, with a lot of blood, means protracted and serious illness in the dreamer's family. If a **butcher is slicing meat**, it means that the dreamer's character is being scrutinized to his detriment. He should refrain from writing letters or documents.

Butter — Dreaming about butter means that the dreamer is not focused, and instead of concentrating his efforts in one field, he is spreading himself thinly over too many areas and not succeeding in any.

Butterfly — This indicates that the dreamer is involved in a passionate love affair.

Buttermilk — If the **dreamer drinks buttermilk**, a worldly enjoyment will be followed by sorrow, and an unwise action will harm his health. It is a very bad sign to **feed buttermilk to pigs**.

Buttons — **Wooden buttons** predict success following considerable effort. **Pearl buttons** foretell a trip in the near future. **Fabric buttons** indicate that the dreamer's health is deteriorating and he must take care of himself. **Losing buttons** in a dream signifies family problems as a result of financial losses. **Finding a button** in a dream signifies a promotion at work and prosperity in business. **Sewing bright shiny buttons on to a uniform** mean a successful military career for a young man, and a good marriage to a handsome, wealthy man for a young woman.

Buzzard — A **buzzard sitting on the railroad tracks** signifies an imminent accident or loss. If a **buzzard flies away** with the approach of the dreamer, it means that a scandal concerning either the dreamer or his friends will subside. **Buzzards in dreams** are a sign of malicious gossip or scandal involving the dreamer.

Cab — **Seeing a cab** indicates an enjoyable career and reasonable prosperity. **Riding in a cab** with others at night means that the dreamer has a secret. **Dreaming about driving a public cab** means that the dreamer is involved in manual labor and has little chance of advancing.

Cabbage — This attests to the dreamer's lazy nature, a characteristic which significantly influences the achievements in his life.

Cabin — This is not good, as it indicates an unsuccessful lawsuit.

Cable [cablegram] — **Seeing a cable** predicts that the dreamer will undertake something extremely dangerous that, if it is successfully completed, will bring honor and wealth. **Dreaming about receiving a cable** means that important news is about to arrive and cause unpleasant comments.

Cackling — This represents the shock caused by a sudden death in the dreamer's surroundings. It also means illness.

Cage — If a **single woman dreams about a cage**, it is a sign that she will soon receive a proposal of marriage. If a **man** dreams about a cage, it means that he will get married prematurely. **Two birds in a cage** indicate a wonderful and happy married life. **No birds in a cage** indicate the loss of a family member. **Seeing wild animals caged** means that the dreamer will defeat his enemies. If the **dreamer is in the cage with the wild animals**, it predicts ghastly accidents while traveling.

Cake — **Dreaming about a cake**, particularly a festively

decorated one, indicates good health and happiness. If a **young woman dreams about her wedding cake**, it is a sign of bad luck. **Baking wedding cakes**, however, is worse than **seeing or eating wedding cakes**.

Calendar — This warns the dreamer that he underestimates important issues and disparages other people, and this may very likely have a boomerang effect.

Calling by name — When the dreamer is called by name or calls another by name, it is a sign that he will soon have a good period regarding romance and marriage.

Calm — If the **dreamer feels calm** and happy, it means that his life is long and worthwhile. A **calm sea** means that success follows something that was very unsure. A **calm ocean** bodes well.

Calumny — Dreaming about calumny is a warning that malicious gossip is going to harm the dreamer.

Calves — This is a sign of festivities and enjoyment, as well as of increasing prosperity.

Camcorder — Using a camcorder indicates the something significant and exciting is about to happen in the dreamer's life.

Camel — This portends a good future. The dreamer will overcome obstacles with the help of good friends.

Cameo Brooch — This portends a sad event.

Camera — **Seeing a camera** dream signifies that the dreamer will find himself in unpleasant places. A **woman who dreams about taking photographs with a camera** is in for disappointments from a friend, as well as unpleasant things in her future.

Campaign — A **dream about a political campaign** shows that the dreamer wants to make changes in accepted business procedures, much to the dismay of his enemies. He will succeed. A **religious campaign** against sin means that the dreamer will be called upon to contribute money.

Camping — **Dreaming about sleeping outdoors** warns against routine and signifies the need for a vacation. **Dreaming about going to an army camp** predicts marriage in the near future.

Canal — **Dreaming about a canal of murky water** is an indication of problems and worries. **Clear water in a canal** signifies that problems will be solved quickly. **Weeds growing in a canal** warn of financial entanglement. **Falling into a canal** indicates a drop in status. **Jumping over a canal** means the dreamer will maintain his self-respect.

Canary — This is a sign of unexpected pleasures, such as the happy culmination of love, or success in the world of literature.

Cancer — **Curing cancer** in a dream signifies a sudden and drastic improvement in the dreamer's worldly position. To **dream about cancer** is a sign of illness in someone close to the dreamer, and disputes with loved ones. Business may suffer after this dream. **Dreaming about cancer** is a negative dream, indicating loss of love and futile business deals.

Candles — **Steady-burning candles** in a dream indicate stability in those surrounding the dreamer, and a solid fortune. A **girl lighting a candle** in a dream is meeting her lover in secret, against her parents' wishes. A **candle burning down in a draft** means that the dreamer's enemies are spreading vicious slander. **Dreaming of extinguishing a candle** portends the distress or death of friends.

Candlesticks — A candlestick with a whole candle in it is a good sign: changes for the better in one's life, health, happiness, love; participation in happy occasions and financial success.

Candy / Sweets — A **box full of candy** predicts that the dreamer's economic situation is about to improve. If a woman dreams about **receiving a box of sweets**, it is a sign that she has a secret admirer. If the **dreamer sends a box of candy** to another person, it predicts a disappointment.

Cane — **Growing cane** is a sign of advancement and prosperity, whereas **cut cane** indicates disaster.

Canker — **Canker on anything** is a sign of evil, predicting death and unreliable companions for young people, and death and sorrow for the elderly. If the **canker grows in the flesh**, it is a sign of future honor.

Cannibal — This is an indication of pressure, anxiety, or fears plaguing the dreamer. It is also possible that the dreamer is not physically healthy.

Cannibalism — This indicates a tendency toward self-destruction and loss of self-control.

Cannon — This predicts war, conflict or quarrels.

Cannonball — **Seeing a cannonball** is a sign that the dreamer has secret enemies conspiring against him. For a **young girl**, it means that she will fall in love with a soldier. For a **youth**, it means that he will have to fight for his country.

Canoe — Paddling a canoe on a calm stream means that the dreamer is perfectly capable of conducting his business successfully. If the **water is muddy**, however, there will be disappointments in business. If the dreamer's **loved one is in the canoe**, a solid marriage is indicated. If the **water is rough**, the dreamer will have to tame his sweetheart.

Canopy — If the dreamer sees a canopy or is under one, it means that dubious friends are trying to influence him negatively. He should look after those dear to him.

Cap — For a **woman to see a cap**, it is a sign of being invited to a party. **A prisoner's cap** means that the dreamer's courage is failing.

Cape — If the **dreamer is wearing a cape**, it is a sign that he inspires a feeling of confidence in his friends. If **another person is wearing a cape**, it is a sign that the dreamer deems him highly trustworthy.

Captain — Dreaming about a captain (of a boat or airplane) attests to the dreamer's ambitious nature and his desire to rule and lead others.

Captive — If the **dreamer is taken captive**, he may have to deal with treachery. Failing that, he will have misfortune and injury. A **dream about taking someone else captive** means that the dreamer is allying himself with people and things of a lower station. For a **woman to dream about being taken captive**, it indicates a jealous husband.

Car — Any kind of dream about a car means good things: problems will be solved, complications will sort themselves out and life will flow smoothly.

Caravan — This indicates that the dreamer will embark on a journey in the near future, and that he must beware of physical harm.

Cardinal — **Seeing a cardinal** is a bad dream, as it portends ruin to the point of having to move to another country. The **appearance of a cardinal** could signify the moral downfall of a woman. **Meeting a priest** in a dream could be a warning against imminent evil.

Cards — **Winning a card game** is a prediction of marriage in the near future. **Losing a card game** signifies that the dreamer will soon be forced to take risks.

Carnival — **Seeing a carnival** is a sign of forthcoming pleasures. **Masks at a carnival** indicate domestic strife and business problems.

Carousel — **Riding on a carousel** indicates a period of stagnation in the dreamer's life. If **others ride on a carousel**, it is a reference to the dreamer's unfulfilled wishes and hopes. A **carousel in the middle of nowhere** predicts doom and gloom.

Carpenter — The dreamer will increase his fortune by doing honest labor and foregoing superficial pleasures.

Carpenter's Plane — **Seeing a carpenter's plane** is a sign of pleasantness and success. The dreamer is not misled by false love. **Seeing carpenters using this tool** is an indication of the smooth execution of plans.

Carpentry — This signifies that the dreamer is bored with his profession or occupation and needs variety.

Carpet — **Walking on a carpet** indicates a love of

luxury. **Cleaning a carpet** means personal problems in one's family or romantic life.

Carriage — **Riding in a carriage** signifies a disease from which the dreamer will soon recover. **Seeking to buy a carriage** means that the dreamer has to work hard, but will become competent at his job.

Carrot — This signifies that the dreamer is not coping with his problems and chooses to ignore them.

Cart — **Seeing a cart** means bad news from family or friends. **Dreaming about driving a cart** means that the dreamer will be successful in business and other spheres. If a **couple of lovers ride in a cart**, they will be faithful to each other no matter what their enemies try to contrive.

Cartridge — **Seeing a cartridge** predicts disputes and rows. There are threats on the horizons. **Empty cartridges** indicate a lack of consistency in the dreamer's relationships.

Carving — **Carving poultry** means that the dreamer will not be well off, and will be irritated by other people. **Carving meat** is a sign of bad investments which can be avoided by a change in direction.

Cash — To dream about having plenty of cash, but it is borrowed, means that the dreamer gives the impression of being a straightforward man, but will be revealed for the cold, money-grabber that he is.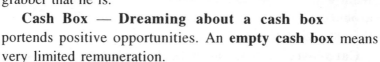

Cash Box — **Dreaming about a cash box** portends positive opportunities. An **empty cash box** means very limited remuneration.

Cashier — This means that other people are going to lay claim to the dreamer's possessions.

Cask — A **full cask** means prosperity and festivity. An **empty cask** indicates a joyless life, devoid of consolation.

Caster Oil — The dreamer is liable to bring about the downfall of a friend who has secretly been trying to implement his advancement.

Castle — A **dream about a castle** is an indication that the dreamer will acquire great wealth and will travel extensively. If the **castle is old and covered with creepers**, the dreamer is liable to become romantic, and should take care not to make mistakes when choosing a spouse. A **dream about leaving a castle** indicates that the dreamer is about to be robbed of possessions, or deprived of his love by death.

Cat — **Dreaming about a cat** is an indication of cunning, subversion, lack of trust and treachery. The dream urges the dreamer to examine his friends and confidants carefully. If the **dreamer sees a cat and does not manage to kill it**, it will bring bad luck. If the **cat attacks**, the dreamer is in danger of enemies who will slander and ruin him. If **he gets rid of the cat**, he will overcome all obstacles and rise in fame and wealth. A **thin, mean cat** foretells bad news from far away. **Hearing the mewing or howling of a cat** means that the dreamer is being harmed by a false friend. If a **cat scratches the dreamer**, he will lose all the fruits of his toil to an enemy. **Dreaming about a clean white cat** means becoming embroiled in seemingly harmless things which will eventually cause grief and financial loss.

Catechism — This foretells the offer of a well-paid position, but the dreamer will hesitate to take it because of the strings attached.

Caterpillar — **Dreaming about a caterpillar** is an indication of embarrassing situations and of hypocritical and unworthy people in the vicinity of the dreamer. **Seeing a caterpillar** portends losses in love and business.

Catfish — The dreamer will suffer embarrassment at the hands of his enemies, but will overcome it as a result of his presence of mind.

Cathedral — **Seeing a cathedral** is an indication of the dreamer's envious and covetous nature — of both material and spiritual things. If the **dreamer enters the cathedral**, his status in life will improve.

Cattle — **Seeing cattle** indicates financial success in the near future. It attests to the dreamer's conservative nature and tendency to calculate every step. **Long-horned, black cattle** means enemies.

Cauliflower — The dreamer can expect quiet times and a calm period in his life after a period of loss.

Cavalry — This is a sign of distinction and advancement.

Cave — If the dreamer is hiding in a cave, it is a sign that a certain person is spreading vicious rumors about him, and wishes to cause him harm.

Cedars — **Green, growing cedars** indicate success in a project. **Dead, dry cedars** are an indication of despair.

Celebration / Party — A **dream about a celebration or party** enjoyed by the dreamer is a sign of good things to come. A **dream about a formal party** — without dancing or warmth — is a sign that the dreamer has made a number of mistakes for which he must now pay the price.

Celery — This means that only good things will come the way of the dreamer, bringing abundance, happiness and joy into his life.

Celestial Signs — The dreamer will undertake unexpected journeys as a result of unhappy events. Love may evaporate, there may be problems in business, and domestic quarrels may occur.

Cellar — **Seeing a cellar** indicates doubts and loss of self-confidence on the part of the dreamer. There is also the possibility of a loss of property. **Dreaming about a wine cellar** represents a warning to a young woman against marrying a gambler. **Seeing a cellar filled with wine** means that the dreamer will be offered a share in profits originating from an unsavory deal.

Cellular Telephone — This means that the dreamer will soon find a solution to a problem that is bothering him. He will have more control over his professional life.

Cement — Any form of cement in a dream means a change for the better or an improvement in the dreamer's financial status.

Cemetery — **Seeing a cemetery** indicates that good news is on the way, or that a sick friend is recovering. A **dream about the death of a family member** predicts a period of stress and problems.

Cereal / Porridge — This warns of dangerous enemies that may embroil the dreamer.

Chaff — This foretells a futile undertaking and anxiety about illness.

Chain — A good sign. **Wearing a gold or silver chain**

predicts that the dreamer will receive a gift from an admirer or lover. **Dreaming about the clasp of a chain** indicates that the dreamer's problems will soon be solved.

Chair — If **someone is sitting on the chair**, it heralds the arrival of another person bringing money. An **empty chair** signifies that the dreamer is about to receive news from a friend abroad.

Chair Maker — The dreamer will have to face anxiety from something he enjoys doing.

Chairman — When a **chairman of some public body** appears, it means that the dreamer will seek and receive a higher position with a higher salary. It is not good to see a **bad-tempered chairman**. If the **dreamer sees himself as a chairman**, his fair-handedness and kindness will be renowned.

Chalice — The **appearance of a chalice in a dream** means that the pleasure experienced by the dreamer will be begrudged him by others. A **broken chalice** indicates that the dreamer will not be able to dominate a friend.

Chalk — **Using chalk on a blackboard** is a sign of bad luck. If the **dreamer holds a handful of chalk**, it indicates disappointment.

Challenge — Accepting any challenge indicates that the dreamer is prepared to suffer in order to cover for others.

Chamber — If the **dreamer is in a richly furnished chamber**, it means that he is about to come into a sudden fortune — either through inheritance or speculation. For a **woman**, it means that she is about to receive an offer of marriage from a wealthy man. If the **chamber is modest**, she will live a very ordinary life.

Chambermaid — Seeing a chambermaid is a sign of bad luck and necessary changes. If a **man makes love to a chambermaid** in a dream, it means that he is going to be the object of mockery as a result of his indiscreet behavior.

Chameleon — This is a symbol of deceit, capriciousness and advancement at the expense of others.

Champion / Championship — This indicates that the dreamer is ambitious and competitive, and will do anything to achieve his goal.

Chandelier — **Dreaming about a chandelier** indicates unexpected and undreamed of wealth and luxury. However, **if it is broken**, it is a sign of financial loss. If the dreamer sees **the lights in the chandelier go out**, it means that his previously rosy future will be plagued by illness and distress.

Chapel — **Seeing a chapel** indicates dissent in social circles and incomplete business, as well as disappointment. **Young people dreaming about chapels** may end up making mistakes in love.

Charcoal — **Unlit charcoal** is a sign of misery and unhappiness. **Glowing charcoal** portends great increases of fortune and a lot of joy.

Chariot — **Seeing a chariot** means that the dreamer is about to be offered good and profitable opportunities. If he sees **himself or others fall from a chariot**, it means a demotion from a high position.

Charity — **Receiving charity** is a sign that the dreamer's financial status will deteriorate slightly, but not significantly. **Giving charity** in a dream is a sign of improvement in his financial status.

Cheated — Dreaming about being cheated in business means that jealous people will try to bring the dreamer down.

Checkers — A dream about checkers means that the dreamer will become embroiled in difficulties, and ill-meaning people will come into his life.

Checks — If the **dreamer attempts to pay false checks** to his friends, it means that he will resort to any kind of cheating and deception in order to carry out his plans. If he **receives checks**, it means that he will be able to pay his debts; he will also inherit money. A **dream about paying out checks** means financial loss.

Cheese (hard, yellow) — This indicates that the dreamer has a difficult character and an uncompromising stubbornness that alienates his friends.

Chemise — If a woman dreams about a chemise, it means that she will hear malicious gossip about herself.

Cherries — **Seeing cherries** means good-naturedness and loyalty and predict good things. **Eating cherries** is a sign that your wishes are about to come true.

Cherubs — **Seeing cherubs** is a good dream which portends joy that will fill the dreamer's life. However, if the **cherubs look sad**, misfortune will strike the dreamer.

Chess — If the **dreamer is playing chess**, he can expect to have a serious quarrel with a friend or relative, with bitter results. A **chess board** means that the dreamer will meet new people as a result of a crisis which he has undergone.

Chest (box) — See **Box**.

Chest (body) — Whether it is a man's or a woman's chest, it is a symbol of an intimate relationship with a person who is close.

Chestnuts — Although financial losses are predicted by **dreaming about chestnuts**, the dreamer's love life will be good. A **dream about eating chestnuts** indicates temporary sorrow but ultimate happiness.

Chickens — **For those involved in agriculture** and breeding chickens, this dream predicts damage. **For others**, it indicates that they count their chickens before they're hatched, and should be more realistic. A **dream about eating chickens** means that the dreamer's good name is spoilt by selfishness. Matters of business and love will be uncertain.

Childbirth — A **dream about giving birth** foretells a safe delivery and a beautiful, healthy infant. However, if an **unmarried woman dreams about childbirth**, it means that she will lose her honor.

Children — A **dream about many beautiful children** signifies great prosperity and happiness. If a **woman dreams about children**, it means that she is satisfied with her family life. If **she dreams about a sick child**, she can expect her child to be healthy. If, however, she sees the **child dangerously ill or dead**, this predicts that she has a lot to fear, as her child's welfare is at stake. If a **man dreams about children**, it means that he can expect a period of quiet with regard to his domestic life.

Chiming of a Clock — This image always heralds good things: the louder the chiming, the happier life will be.

Chimney — A **dream about a chimney** predicts success. A **smoking chimney** heralds good tidings coming the way of the dreamer. A **broken chimney** is a foreboding of worries and problems.

China — If a woman dreams about arranging her china, it means she will be the thrifty matron of a prosperous household.

China Store — If a china merchant dreams that his store looks empty, it means that business will go sour and he will suffer losses.

Chocolate — A **dream about chocolate** signifies that the dreamer provides well for his dependants. It means that he will have pleasant friends and work. **Drinking chocolate** means that a good period will follow a brief period of adversity.

Choir — **Seeing a choir** predicts that sadness and suffering will be replaced by joy and cheer. If a **young woman** dreams about singing in a choir, it means that she will suffer because of her lover's roving eye.

Choking — See **Suffocating**.

Cholera — **Dreaming about being sick with cholera** means that the dreamer will become ill. If the **dream concerns an epidemic** throughout the country, it means that a deadly disease will rage, and many disappointments will follow.

Christ — A **dream about the Christ child** being worshipped portends peace, joy and knowledge. If **he is seen in Gethsemane**, the dreamer will be filled with nostalgia and yearning for change. If **he is seen chasing the merchants out of the temple**, it means that evil will be conquered and honesty will triumph.

Christmas Tree — **Seeing a Christmans tree** is a good, auspicious dream. **Dreaming about dismantling it** presages a painful event which will come hard on the heels of the festivities.

Chrysanthemum — A **dream about chrysanthemums** often symbolizes love or deep affection. **Dreaming about white chrysanthemums** is a sign of loss and confusion, while **colored chrysanthemums** means the cancellation of pleasant events. Walking down an avenue of white **chrysanthemums interspersed with occasional yellow ones** predicts a sense of sadness. **Bouquets of chrysanthemums** mean that the dreamer will miss out on love because of a foolish ambition.

Church — **Seeing a church** predicts disappointment in long-anticipated things. If the **dreamer enters a church in darkness**, it means he will soon be attending a funeral. There is not much hope for a better future.

Churchyard — If the **dream is about walking in a churchyard in winter**, it means that the dreamer will have a protracted struggle with poverty. He will live far away from his home and loved ones. In **springtime**, however, the dreamer will have pleasant company. If the dream is about **lovers in a churchyard**, it means that the lovers will never marry each other.

Churning — A **dream about churning** indicates that the dreamer will have to perform difficult tasks. He will succeed and become prosperous. If a **farmer dreams about churning**, it predicts an abundant and profitable harvest.

Cider — If the **dreamer drinks cider**, it indicates that he will be able to amass a fortune if he can resist material diversions. **Seeing other people drinking cider** means that the dreamer is susceptible to the influence of disloyal friends.

Cigarettes — If **someone lights a cigarette for the dreamer**, it means that the latter will soon need assistance from another person. If a **cigarette butt** appears in an ashtray, it is an indication of the inability to fulfill hopes and desires.

Cipher — This shows that the dreamer is interested in literary and classical subjects, and by study will become well-versed in them.

Circle — **Seeing a circle** warns about being mistaken in the calculation of business profits. It also warns a **young woman** dreamer against an indiscreet liaison which cannot lead to marriage.

Cistern — In a **dream about a cistern**, there is a risk that the dreamer will jeopardize his friends' rights and pleasures. If the **dreamer draws water from a cistern**, it means that he will be taking up a pastime that is not acceptable to society. An **empty cistern** symbolizes a drastic change from joy to sorrow.

City — If the dreamer is in a strange city, it means that circumstances have dictated that he change his place of residence or lower his standard of living.

City Council — This portends friction with public bodies, and there will not be much hope of a good outcome for the dreamer.

City Hall — **Seeing a city hall** is a symbol of lawsuits and disputes. A **young woman's** licentious behavior will cause her to lose her lover.

Clairvoyance — If the **dreamer sees himself** in his own future, it signifies changes in his profession as well as disputes with ill-intentioned people. Dreaming of a **visit to a clairvoyant** means bad luck in business and love.

Clams — **Seeing clams** is a symbol of dealing with a stubborn but honest person. **Eating clams** in a dream signifies enjoying someone else's prosperity.

Claret — **Drinking claret** in a dream means that the dreamer will be influenced by worthy people. If there are **broken bottles of claret**, the dreamer will fall under the evil influence of immoral people.

Clarinet — **Seeing a clarinet** means that the dreamer will act frivolously, as opposed to his usual dignified manner. A **broken clarinet** indicates that the dreamer will displease a close friend.

Clay — Clay can be a symbol of bankruptcy. This dream is a bad sign in love, business and social situations. Unpleasant surprises result from it.

Cleanliness — A dream about the cleanliness of objects means that the dreamer will soon have to shoulder an unbearable burden and experience feelings of extreme oppression.

Clergyman — If the **dreamer has sent for a clergyman** to make a eulogy at a funeral, it means that he is fighting in vain against a disease and bad influences. A **young woman who dreams about marrying a clergyman** will suffer from psychological anguish and all kinds of hardships.

Climb — Any type of climb — up a mountain, a ladder, etc. — means that the dreamer will overcome all the obstacles that stand in the way of attaining his objectives.

Clock — A **dream about any sort of clock** attests to the dreamer's achievement-oriented character, or to his actual achievements; a **clock** also symbolizes wealth and abundance.

Cloister — If the **dreamer sees a cloister**, he will soon experience a desire to change his surroundings. For a **woman**, this dream means that the rough hand of sorrow has made her life less egocentric.

Clothing — A **closet full of clothing** means that in the near future the dreamer can expect problems in different areas. If the dreamer is partially dressed, he has the ability to achieve his objective. **Getting dressed** in a dream means progress. **Getting undressed** means regression. If the dreamer is **dressed eccentrically**, it indicates substantial success.

Clouds — **Dark, heavy clouds** in a dream predict hardship and mismanagement. If it is raining, trouble and illness will follow. **Seeing bright clouds** through which the sun is shining means that success will follow a struggle. **Clouds in combination with stars** mean small joys and rewards.

Cloven Foot — This is a warning that some exceptional bad luck threatens the dreamer, who should avoid the company of strangers.

Clover — Because of the shape of its leaves, clover symbolizes a fork in the dreamer's path.

Clown — **Seeing a clown** shows that the dreamer is living a dishonest and deceitful life.

Masks mean that the dreamer is two-faced.

Club — If a **dreamer is attacked** by a club-bearing assailant, it means that his enemies will attack him, but he will ultimately defeat them. This will be followed by exceptional happiness and prosperity. If the **dreamer attacks anyone with a club**, a difficult and futile journey is in store for him.

Coach — **Traveling in a coach** is a sign of financial losses. **Driving a coach** signifies a move or changes in the dreamer's business dealings.

Coals — **Bright coals** predict joy and positive changes. If the dreamer actually holds them, the joy is limitless. **Burnt-out coals** are an indication of hardship and disillusionment.

Coat — Almost any context in which a **coat appears** (worn, sold or bought) indicates that a certain investment will pay off and the dreamer will benefit from it. **Wearing a coat** that belongs to someone else means that the dreamer needs help from that person. **Losing a coat** in a dream indicates that the dreamer should be cautious when making any business decisions.

Coat-of-Arms — If a dreamer sees a coat-of-arms, it is a sign of bad luck, meaning further that he will never receive a title.

Cobra — This is a sign of serious sexual problems (particularly in the case of men).

Cock Crowing — **Dreaming about a cock crowing in the morning** is a sign of good luck. For a **single person**, it means marriage in the near future and a beautiful home. A **cock crowing at night** is a bad sign - of tears and despair.

Cocktail — **Dreaming about drinking a cocktail** means that the dreamer pretends to his friends that he is a serious person while all the while he prefers the company of superficial, fun-seeking people. For a **woman**, this dream signifies a promiscuous and licentious lifestyle.

Cocoa — This dream means that the dreamer deliberately befriends unsuitable people in order to get ahead.

Coconut — This is a warning dream, telling the dreamer that so-called friends are actually enemies who want to dash all his hopes and destroy his expectations. If the dreamer sees dead coconut trees, they foretell sorrow and bereavement.

Coffee — **Dreaming about coffee** means that the dreamer is under emotional pressure and suffers from tension in his daily life. **Drinking coffee** warns of domestic strife and financial losses for a married person, while it implies the disapproval of an unmarried person's friends of his marriage plans. **Dealing in coffee** symbolizes business setbacks. **Selling coffee** indicates losses, but **buying it** means steady finances. A **young woman who sees or handles coffee** should act discreetly, so as to avoid scandal. **Ground coffee** means that enemies and setbacks will be overcome. **Roasted coffee** warns the dreamer to beware of strangers. **Green coffee** means implacable enemies.

Coffee House — This predicts that the dreamer will fall into the clutches of so-called friends who are actually enemies scheming his downfall. Women may attempt to corrupt the dreamer's morality and steal his possessions.

Coffee Mill — Seeing a coffee mill is a warning to the dreamer of a fast-approaching danger that can be warded off only by great alertness and fortitude. **Hearing the grinding of a coffee mill** means that the dreamer will have no trouble dispelling the evil being perpetrated against him.

Coffin — Dreaming about a coffin is an unlucky dream: **Farmers** will lose their crops, **businessmen** will suffer losses, **young people** will experience the death of loved ones. If the **dreamer sees his own coffin**, it is a sign of domestic strife and sorrow and business losses. If he **sees his own body in the coffin**, it means that he will be defeated in his endeavors despite his brave struggle.

Coins — A **gold coin** indicates that the dreamer has gone out to enjoy nature. A **silver coin** is a sign of bad luck, as it predicts domestic strife. A **worn coin** predicts a dreary day. A **copper coin** indicates bearing a heavy burden and serious responsibility. A **shining coin** means success in romance.

Cold — Dreaming about cold is a warning of enemies out to destroy the dreamer. His health is also in jeopardy.

Collar — If the collar is tight around the dreamer's neck, it signifies that he is afraid of a strong person who intimidates him.

College — Dreaming about college means that the dreamer will soon receive a promotion he has sought for a long time. If **he dreams that he is back in college**, it means that he is about to be awarded a prize for some excellent achievement.

Colliery or Coal Mine — Seeing a coal mine predicts a

plot for the dreamer's downfall. If, however, the **dreamer has shares in the mine**, it means that his investment in a deal is secure.

Collision — **Seeing a collision** predicts a serious accident or a setback in business. For a **woman**, it means that she will be unable to choose between lovers, and will be at the focus of a dispute.

Colonel — **Dreaming of either seeing or being a colonel** means that the dreamer's aspirations to reach social or professional distinction will not be realized. If a **colonel dreams this**, it means that he is attempting to pull rank on those around him.

Colors — **All the colors** of the spectrum, except black, are a good sign. **Bright colors** symbolize security and tranquillity. **White** means innocence and purity. **Blue** signifies overcoming problems with the help of one's friends. **Yellow** symbolizes high expectations. **Orange** or **gray** indicates that one must have patience. **Red** predicts social events. **Green** means envy. **Brown** heralds good news. **Pink** predicts a surprise. **Black** signifies bad moods and depression.

Comb — If the dreamer dreams about combing his hair, it means that a sick friend needs his help.

Combat — If a **dreamer dreams that he is in combat with someone else**, it means that he is trying to steal another person's love; his business reputation will be jeopardized. A **dream about combat** symbolizes the battle to maintain an even keel.

Comedy — **Attending a comedy** is a symbol of the

frivolous and superficial pleasures that the dreamer will participate in. **Dreaming about a comedy** symbolizes pleasures and agreeable tasks.

Comet — **Dreaming about comets** means that the dreamer will experience unexpected troubles, but he will overcome them and become famous. In the **dream of a young person**, comets are a prediction of death of a loved one and sorrow.

Comic Songs — **Hearing comic songs** means that the dreamer will forego an opportunity to promote his business matters in favor of the pursuit of pleasure. **Singing these songs** portends a long period of pleasure followed by troubles.

Command — If a **dreamer is commanded**, it means that he will be humiliated for having behaved in an insubordinate manner toward his superiors. **Giving a command** foretells some kind of honor for the dreamer — unless he does it in a tyrannical way, in which case difficulties are foreseen. If **he receives commands**, it means that he will succumb to the negative influence of people stronger-willed than he is.

Commandment — Reading or hearing the Ten Commandments in a dream means that the dreamer will make mistakes which even the wisest advisors will not be able to rectify.

Commerce — A **dream about commercial dealings** means that the dreamer exploits opportunities wisely. **Dreaming about negative aspects and results of commerce** presages serious trouble and financial loss. If **commerce improves in the dream**, it means that the dreamer will overcome his problems.

Committee — This indicates that the dreamer will be trapped into performing an unpleasant task, or that others will decide to give him a futile job to do.

Compact Disk — A dream about a CD indicates that the dreamer will soon become involved in a new romantic relationship which will go very well.

Companion — **Dreaming about one's spouse** portends minor worries and possible illness. **Dreaming about social companions** means that frivolous and superficial pastimes are distracting the dreamer from more important issues. **Dreaming about one's spouse as loving** is a sign of a warm, happy home with lovely children.

Compass — This symbolizes loyalty: the dreamer has loyal friends who will come to his aid in times of trouble.

Competition — See **Contest**.

Completion — Dreaming of completing a task means that the dreamer will soon become so competent in his work that he will be able to choose how to spend his time.

Complexion — **Dreaming about having a beautiful complexion** is a good dream, bringing happy events. **A bad and blemished complexion** is a sign of disappointment and illness.

Computer — **Dreaming about working on a computer** means that the dreamer will be given increased responsibility at work. If the **dreamer does not know how to use a computer**, it means that he will soon be given a task which he considers overwhelming.

Concert — **Dreaming about a highbrow concert** is a sign of lofty pleasures to come. For a **businessman**, it signifies financial gain. To the

young, it is a sign of perfect love. A **more popular concert** is a symbol of the wrong kind of companions, and losses in business.

Concubine — If a **man dreams about having a concubine**, it means that he is trying to conceal his true nature and the nature of his business from the world, and he risks public disgrace. Dreaming that **his mistress is unfaithful** means that he will have a confrontation with his former enemies, causing difficulties. If a **woman dreams about being a concubine**, it means that her own immoral conduct will bring about her downfall.

Confectionery — Stale confectionery is a sign that one of the dreamer's enemies, pretending to be his friend, will disclose the dreamer's secrets to his rivals.

Conference (business) — This means that the dreamer's financial situation will improve.

Confetti — If the dreamer can hardly see the wedding festivities because of all the confetti in the air, it means that he wastes too much time on trivia rather than concentrating on important issues.

Conflagration — If there is no loss of life, this symbolizes beneficial changes in the dreamer's life, bringing him prosperity and happiness.

Confusion — Chaos and disorder in a dream warn of accidents and obstacles. The dreamer should be more alert.

Conjurer — The dreamer will encounter troubles on his path to happiness and prosperity.

Conscience — If the **dreamer's conscience bothers him** in a dream, it is a sign that he will be tempted to do something bad, and will have to guard himself against it. If he dreams about **having a clear conscience**, it means that he has a good reputation.

Conspiracy — Dreaming about being the victim of a conspiracy signifies that the dreamer is going to make a mistake in the running of his affairs.

Consumption — Dreaming about having this disease means that the dreamer is placing himself in danger, and should stick with his friends.

Contempt — A dream of being in contempt of court means that the dreamer is guilty of unnecessarily committing a social or business *faux pas*.

Contest / Competition — This means that the dreamer must resist strong temptation.

Convent — **Entering a convent** is a sign that the dreamer will have no more worries and foes. However, if **he meets a priest**, this indicates that he will constantly be searching for a cure to worldly worries and stress. If a **young girl dreams about a convent**, her moral conduct is questionable.

Convention — **Being at a convention** indicates positive progress in business and love. An **unsatisfactory convention** foretells disappointment for the dreamer.

Conversation — A conversation between the dreamer and another person indicates difficulties that may arise at work or in business, such as theft, damage, etc.

Convicts — **Seeing convicts** in a dream is a forecast of bad news and catastrophe. **Dreaming about being a convict** means that the dreamer is worrying about a matter which will soon be clarified. If a **woman sees her lover dressed as a convict**, she will soon have doubts about his love.

Cook — See **Baker**.

Cookie — See **Biscuit**.

Cooking — **Dreams about cooking** are usually connected with sexuality. The **different stages of cooking** — before, during and after — are parallel to the past, present and future in the dreamer's life. **Dreaming about cooking** also warns of health problems.

Cooking Stove — This means that the dreamer will be able to avert a lot of unpleasantness.

Copper — This is a sign that the dreamer's superiors will tyrannize him.

Copperplate Writing — This is a warning against conflicting views at home, which are liable to lead to domestic strife and unrest.

Coppersmith — This is a symbol of a pleasant but badly-paid job.

Copy Machine — This dream warns against people stealing property or ideas from the dreamer. It is up to the dreamer to be more careful.

Copying — This is a sign that plans will fail.

Coral — **Seeing coral** warns against taking a particular step in any area of life. **Dreaming about colored coral** is a sign of lasting friendship that is always there in time of need. **White coral** predicts infidelity and problems in love.

Cork — A **dream about extracting corks** at a banquet means that the dreamer will soon enjoy prosperity that will allow him to raise his standard of living and improve his quality of life. A **young woman who dreams about champagne corks** will have a good-looking, dashing lover who indulges her. She should heed her parents' advice after this dream.

Corkscrew — This is a warning to the dreamer to control his urge to satisfy his desires, as they lead him down a dangerous path.

Corn and Cornfields — A **lush green cornfield** signifies a good harvest and prosperity for the farmer, as well as harmony and happiness for the dreamer. **Trampled ears of corn** portend bereavement and disappointment. If the **dreamer is husking corn**, he will enjoy success and a pleasurable life. Watching **others husk corn** means that the dreamer will rejoice in their prosperity. **Dreams about young corn** are all good, implying success, fame, wealth and fulfilled wishes. **Eating green corn** is a sign of harmony.

Corner — If the **dreamer hides in a corner** because he is afraid, this is a bad dream. If **he sees people congregated in a corner,** it means that his enemies are conspiring to ruin him. A close person may prove to be disloyal.

Cornmeal — The **appearance of cornmeal** in a dream means that the dreamer's most fervent desires will be realized. If **he eats cornmeal** baked in a loaf, he is unintentionally placing obstacles in his own path.

Corns — If the **dreamer has painful corns**, it means that enemies are conspiring to harm him, thus causing him anguish. If **he can get rid of the corns**, he will come into a large inheritance. A **woman with corns** will not have an easy time, especially with other women.

Coronation — This dream is a sign of the dreamer's close association with celebrities and VIPs.

Corpse — **Seeing a corpse** indicates that the dreamer is dealing with death, the occult or infinity. If a **businessman dreams about a corpse**, it means that his reputation will be ruined, he will fail in business or go bankrupt. If a **young man dreams about a corpse**, it suggests unrequited love.

Corpulence — If the dreamer dreams about being corpulent, it means that he will be wealthy and live well.

Corridor — If an unknown corridor appears in a dream, it is a sign that the dreamer must make an important decision which is not influenced by external factors.

Corset — This signifies that the dreamer is unsure about what is motivating people to pay attention to him.

Cot — **Seeing a cot** is a forecast of mishaps, illnesses and accidents. A **row of cots** indicates that the dreamer will not be alone in his troubles.

Cotton — This is a good dream: Both when the **cotton is growing** and when **it is ready for picking**, it signifies wealth and prosperity, as well as abundant crops for farmers.

Cotton Candy — This is a forecast of a nice trip in the near future.

Couch — Sitting relaxed on a couch means that the dreamer's hopes are unrealistic. If he does not pay careful attention to every nuance of his business, his hopes will not come to fruition.

Cough — If the **dreamer is suffering from a constant cough**, it is an indication of poor health that can improve with the right care. If **someone else has a cough**, it means that the dreamer will suddenly find himself in an unpleasant situation from which he will eventually extricate himself.

Counselor — Dreaming about a counselor means that the dreamer has a certain degree of this ability; he prefers his own opinion to that of others. He should take care when acting upon his instincts of "right."

Countenance — A **lovely and innocent countenance** portends some future pleasure, while an **ugly, scowling one** promises only bad things.

Counter — **Dreaming about counters** means that the dreamer's varied interests and activities prevent him from succumbing to harmful desires. **Empty and dirty counters** are a forecast of some bad meeting which will deprive the dreamer of peace of mind.

Counterfeit Money — This dream foretells problems with some worthless and difficult person. It is always bodes ill, whether the dreamer is the payer or recipient of the counterfeit money.

Counterpane — A **clean counterpane** is a very good sign, meaning satisfying professions for women. A **soiled counterpane** forecasts troubling situations and illness.

Counting — If the **dreamer counts his happy and sweet children**, it means that they will not cause him any trouble, and they will do well. If **he counts money**, it means that he will always be able to cover his debts. If **h e counts it for someone else**, it is a sign of loss and bad luck.

Country — Dreaming about a **lush, fertile, well-watered country** means that the dreamer could not hope for better times than this. He will acquire endless wealth, and will be able to live wherever he chooses. An **arid, barren country** is a forecast of hardships, famine and illness.

Courtship — It is very bad for a **woman to dream about being courted,** as this will invariably end in disappointment after brief pleasures and hopes. A **man who dreams about courting** does not deserve to find a companion.

Cousin — **Seeing a cousin** foretells sadness, sorrow and disappointment. If there is a **warm relationship between cousins,** it is the sign of an irreparable rift in the family.

Cows — **Seeing a herd of cows at milking time** is a sign of wealth that has been accumulated through hard work. If the **dreamer milks a cow with full udders,** it is a sign of good luck. If, however, a **calf has already drunk the milk,** it means that the dreamer is about to lose his lover because of indifference, or his property because of neglect of his business.

Cowslips — **Gathering cowslips** foretells the miserable termination of a close friendship. **Cowslips in full bloom** indicate a crisis in the dreamer's life — even to the point of destroying a harmonious home.

Crabs — A **dream about crabs** means that the dreamer will have to deal with many complex matters over which he will have to exercise the greatest judgment. For **lovers,** it foretells a long and rocky courtship.

Cradle/Crib — A **cradle with a beautiful baby in it** signifies prosperity and the love of darling children. An **empty cradle** speaks of a lack of confidence or health problems. **Rocking a baby in a cradle** indicates marital problems and illness in the family.

Crane — **Cranes flying northward** presage bad things in the realm of business, disappointment for a woman. **Cranes flying southward** indicate a happy reunion of friends and the continued faithful union of lovers. If the **cranes land**, it means that unusual occurrences are in the offing.

Crawfish — When the crawfish appears in the dream, it means tribulations in love.

Crawling — If the dreamer **hurts his hand while crawling** on the ground, it means that he will be given menial and demeaning tasks to do. To **crawl over rough ground** indicates that he has not taken proper advantages of the opportunities offered him. To **crawl in the mud** means that the dreamer's credibility in business is in jeopardy.

Cream — **Seeing cream** is a good sign, meaning prosperity for anyone but a farmer, for whom it indicates a good harvest and a harmonious family life. If the **dreamer drinks cream**, he will enjoy good fortune immediately.

Credit Card — This is an indication of a significant change for the better in the dreamer's fortune, either through new channels of income or via an inheritance.

Creek — **Seeing a creek** is a symbol of short trips and new experiences. An **overflowing creek** means brief but surmountable troubles. A **dry creek** symbolizes disappointment when the dreamer sees something that he wanted being given to another person.

Cremation — Seeing bodies cremated means that the dreamer's influence in the business realm will be reduced by enemies. The **dreamer's own cremation** signifies total failure in business if he allows any judgment but his own to influence him.

Crew — If the **dreamer sees a ship's crew** on the verge of sailing off, it means he will unexpectedly cancel a journey, to his detriment. A **crew battling to save a ship** during a storm is a sign of disaster.

Cricket — Hearing a cricket in a dream predicts unhappy news, possibly of a distant friend's death. **Seeing a cricket** signifies an ongoing struggle against poverty.

Cries — A **dreamer who hears cries of distress** will have serious problems, but will extricate himself from them and even benefit from them as a result of his alertness. A **cry of surprise** means that the dreamer will receive help from unexpected people. If **he hears a cry for help**, it means that friends or relatives are in distress or ill. **Hearing the cries of wild animals** signifies a serious accident.

Crime — An **encounter with a criminal** in a dream warns of questionable individuals. If the **dreamer himself appears as a criminal**, it is a sign that he is not sufficiently aware of the hardships of others.

Criminal — A dreamed association with a criminal is a sign that the dreamer will be assailed by immoral and scheming people trying to exploit him for their own benefit. If he **sees a fleeing criminal**, he is in danger of becoming privy to other people's sensitive secrets, which will cause him to be hunted down to prevent him from divulging them.

Cripple — See **Disabled Person**.

Crochet Work — This warns of embroilment in some ridiculous matter resulting from the dreamer's curiosity about other people's business. It is a warning not to confide too much in other people.

Crockery — Plenty of **clean, tidy crockery** is an indication of a good homemaker. If the dreamer is a business and finds himself in a **crockery store** in his dream, he will profit. A **messy store** indicates financial loss.

Crocodile — A dream about a crocodile signifies that someone close to the dreamer is behaving in an exceptionally friendly manner; however, beneath this hearty exterior, he is plotting to harm him.

Cross — **Seeing a cross** indicates trouble lying in wait for the dreamer, who should act accordingly. **Seeing a person bearing a cross** means that the dreamer will be called upon to give to charity.

Crossbones — This is a warning that other people will cause the dreamer trouble, and hinder prosperity.

Crossroads — If the dreamer is unable to choose which way to go, he will be aggravated by trivial matters. This dream may be followed by a significant decision in the realm of love or business.

Croup — Although a dream about a child having croup may be indicative of a mild illness, generally speaking it means harmony and good health for the family.

Crow — **Dreaming about a crow** is a symbol of sorrow and bad luck. **Hearing the cawing of a crow** means that others will influence you to give your property away in an illogical way. A **young man dreaming about a crow** will be seduced by women's wiles.

Crowd — **Dreaming about a crowd** is usually a good sign, if most people are wearing brightly colored clothes. A dreamer who sees a **well-dressed crowd of people at some entertainment event** will have good friendships, but **should anything happen to mar** the pleasant atmosphere, his friendships will be jeopardized and instead of friendly and beneficial relations, there will be distress and unhappiness. **Seeing a crowd** is also an indication of family dispute and discontent with the ruling government.

Crown — **Seeing a crown** is an indication of a change in the dreamer's way of life. It portends long journeys and new relationships. It foretells serious illness. If the **dreamer wears a crown**, he will suffer losses of personal possessions. If **he crowns another person**, his own good character is shown.

Crucifix — **Dreaming about a crucifix** is a warning of approaching trouble for both the dreamer and others. If the **dreamer kisses a crucifix**, it means that he is resigned to his troubles. A **young woman who carries a crucifix** is known to be modest and kind, winning the love of others and thus her personal gain.

Crucifixion — This dream will deprive the dreamer of his hopes and expectations, leaving him with nothing but frustration.

Cruelty — If **someone is cruel to the dreamer**, it means that he will have disappointment and trouble in some matter.

If the **cruelty is directed at someone else**, the dreamer will be given an unpleasant task which will lead to losses for him.

Crust — This is a sign of incompetence, as well as a possibility of terrible consequences because of duties not properly acquitted.

Crutches — If the **dreamer walks with crutches**, it means that he relies on others for help and progress. If he **sees others on crutches**, it means that the results of hard work are not good.

Crying — **Crying in a dream** generally heralds good tidings and indicates that there will be reasons for rejoicing and celebrating. However, at times, **crying** may be seen as a signal of distress from a friend.

Crystal — This is not a good dream, as it portends a deterioration in either business matters or in personal relationships. This dream often precedes violent electrical storms.

Cubs — See **Animal Young**.

Cuckoo — **Seeing a cuckoo** means that the sudden fall from grace of a friend will curtail the dreamer's happiness in life. **Hearing a cuckoo** is really bad, as it forecasts the serious illness or death of a faraway friend, or an accident in the dreamer's family.

Cucumber — **Seeing cucumbers** is a dream of health and wealth. A **sick person serving cucumbers** will recover soon.

Cunning — A **dream about cunning** indicates that the dreamer will put on a cheerful face in order to be liked by rich, merry people. If the **dreamer's associates are cunning**, it means that they are taking advantage of him in order to ensure their own profit.

Cup — A **cup full of liquid** is a sign of good luck. An **empty cup** signifies shortage. A **dark-colored cup** indicates problems at work or in business. A **light-colored cup** symbolizes a bright future. A **cup out of which liquid has spilled** predicts fighting and tension in the family.

Cupboard — A **full, clean cupboard** signifies comfort and enjoyment, while an **empty, dirty one** means poverty and misery.

Curb — **Stepping on a curb** means a rapid rise in the world of business, and high esteem for the dreamer. However, **slipping or falling off a curb** means all kinds of trouble.

Currants (red) — **Seeing currents** means that the dreamer is avoiding someone whom he is not able to confront. **Picking currents** is an indication of the dreamer's optimistic personality: the ability always to look on the bright side.

Currying a Horse — **Dreaming about currying a horse** indicates that the dreamer will have to work very hard, both mentally and physically, in order to realize his ambitions. If **he curries the horse well**, he will attain whatever he desires.

Cursing — If the **dreamer curses**, it suggests that one's goals and objectives will be attained after a particularly big effort. A dream in which **he is cursed by another** means that there are enemies conspiring behind his back.

Curtain — **Closing a curtain** in a dream means that people who are close to the dreamer are plotting against him and deceiving him. It is a symbol of unwanted guests who will cause nothing but trouble and anxiety. **Dirty or torn curtains** are a sign of shameful disputes and blame.

Cushion — Lying on **silk cushions** means that the dreamer will enjoy a life of ease through others. If the **dreamer sees cushions**, he will do well both in love and in business.

Custard — If the **dreamer is a married woman who dreams of making or eating custard**, it means that she will have to provide hospitality to an unexpected guest. If the **custard tastes revolting**, any happiness anticipated by the dreamer will be replaced by grief.

Customs House — **Seeing a customs house** is a symbol of competition in the dreamer's profession. If **he enters a customs house**, it means that he will compete for, or be offered, a long-coveted position. **Leaving a customs house** is a sign of financial loss, loss of status, or failure.

Cut — A cut is a sign of illness or frustration caused by the disloyalty of a friend.

Cutting — **Dreaming about cutting** indicates an unhealthy connection with someone close to the dreamer. **Cutting oneself** indicates family problems.

Cyclamen — **For men**, a dream about this flower symbolizes impotence. **For women**, it signifies the inability to forge healthy relationships with men.

Cymbal — If the dreamer hears the clash of cymbals in a dream, it means that a very old acquaintance of his is about to die.

Daffodil — This indicates that the dreamer suffers from problems relating to his sexual identity.

Dagger — A **dagger seen in a dream** is a sign of menacing enemies. If the **dreamer succeeds in wresting the dagger out of someone else's hand,** he will overcome his enemies and trouble.

Dahlia — Fresh, brightly colored dahlias are a sign of good luck.

Daisy — This predicts good times accompanied by happiness and inner security.

Damask Rose — A **bush of damask roses in full bloom** signals that a wedding will soon take place in the dreamer's family, and that hopes will materialize. If a **woman receives a bouquet of damask roses in spring,** her lover will be faithful, but not so **in winter.**

Damson — If the **dreamer sees the trees laden with purple fruit,** it is an excellent sign of prosperity. However, **eating the fruit** is a forecast of sorrow.

Dance — This is a sign of vitality, love of the good life, sexiness and health.

Dance Master — Dreaming about a dance master means that the dreamer favors trivial pursuits to matters of importance.

Dandelion — Fresh dandelions are a sign of happy love and prosperity.

Danger — This signifies success: the greater the danger in the dream, the greater the success in reality.

Dark-skinned Person — **Dreaming about a dark-skinned person** suggests that the dreamer does not have tension and excitement in his life. **Seeing a dark-skinned person** may also indicate that he has difficulties resulting from sexual tension.

Darkness — The appearance of darkness, or walking in the dark indicates that the dreamer is distressed, confused and restless.

Dates (fruit) — These predict the marriage of the dreamer or of one of his close friends in the near future.

Daughter — If the **dreamer sees his daughter**, many hassles will disappear, to be replaced by happiness and serenity. If **his daughter is disobedient**, the dreamer will experience anger and dissatisfaction.

Daughter-in-Law — This is an indication of an unusual event — good if the person is pleasant, and bad if she is not.

Day — A **nice day** foretells an improvement in life and good relationships, whereas a **gloomy day** is a sign of loss and failure.

Daybreak — Watching the daybreak signifies success in projects, as long as the scene is not blurred or strange, which would imply disappointment instead of success in love or business.

Dead — A **dream about the dead** is usually a warning. If the **dreamer talks to his dead father**, he is about to make a bad deal. He must take care. If **he sees his dead mother**, he must try to show more compassion and love toward his fellow man. If **he sees his dead brother, relative or friend**, he will be asked for charity.

Deafness — A symbol: What we do not know cannot hurt us!

Death — Contrary to what one might expect, **dreaming about death** heralds a long and good life. A dream about the death of person who is actually ill means that he will recover soon.

Debt — **Dreaming about a debt** forecasts trouble in love and business, but if the **dreamer can pay his debts**, everything will improve.

December — This is a sign of the acquisition of wealth, but the loss of friendship. Strangers will take the place of the dreamer in the hearts of his friends.

Deck — **Being on the deck of a ship in a storm** is a sign of catastrophe for the dreamer. If the **sea is calm**, he will be successful.

Decorate (a room) — If the dreamer decorates a room with flowers, it is a sign that business will improve.

Decorate (for action) — If the dreamer is decorating others or seeing others decorated for an heroic action, it means that he will be a person of distinction, but not well known.

Deed (to property) — **Seeing a deed** symbolizes a lawsuit. The dreamer should choose his attorney with care if he is to have any chance of winning. If the **dreamer signs anything**, it is a bad omen.

Deer — This symbolizes the father figure or the desire to resemble someone who is close to the dreamer and who constitutes an authority figure.

Defeat — **Defeat in a fight** indicates that the dreamer will lose his right to property. **Defeat in battle** mean that the dreamer's prospects will be ruined by the unsuccessful transactions made by others.

Delay — A delay in a dream means deliberate plotting by enemies against the dreamer's advancement.

Delight — **Feeling delight about any event** is a positive sign in all matters. When the **dreamer looks at an exquisite landscape and feels delight**, he will be very successful socially and in business.

Demand — The dreamer will be put out by **a demand for charity**, but eventually his good name will be restored. If **the demand is unreasonable**, the dreamer will become a leading member of his profession.

Dentist — If a dentist is working on the dreamer's teeth, it is a sign that someone with whom the dreamer is in contact has given him reason to doubt his sincerity and intentions.

Depression — Dreaming about depression indicates the opposite: the dreamer will have a golden opportunity to extricate himself from his present situation and improve his life unrecognizably.

Derrick — This represents obstacles and difficulties on the dreamer's path to success.

Desert — If the **dreamer is walking in the desert**, it predicts a journey. If a **storm breaks** out during the dream, it means that the journey will not be satisfying. If the **dreamer is in the desert and is suffering from hunger and thirst**, it means he needs to invigorate his life.

Desk — **Sitting at a desk** will bring the dreamer unexpected bad luck. If **he sees money on his desk**, he will get out of difficulties.

Despair — If the **dreamer experiences despair** in his dream, it means that he will have a lot of trials and tribulations in his profession. If **others are in despair**, it is a sign that someone close to him is in distress.

Detective — If the **dreamer is being tailed by a detective**, and he is innocent, it means that fame and fortune are approaching rapidly. If the **dreamer is not innocent**, his good name will be ruined, and his friends will abandon him.

Devil — This sometimes foretells an easier and better future, though in most cases, the devil is a symbol of temptation and seduction, and as such is negative.

Devotion — A **devout farmer** will grow abundant crops and will have peace with his neighbors. To **business people**, it is a warning against deception.

Dew — If **dew falls on the dreamer**, it is a sign of fever and illness. If **he sees the dew sparkling on the grass**, he will be given honor and wealth. He may make a very good marriage soon.

Diadem — The dreamer will soon be offered some great honor.

Diamond — A **dream about possessing diamonds** is a good dream, leading to honor and esteem from the highest authorities. **Losing diamonds** signifies disgrace, domestic quarrels, confusion and disorder in the dreamer's family life.

Diary — This symbolizes excessive acquisitiveness or a pathological jealousy of someone close to the dreamer.

Dice — **Dice** symbolize gambling. If the **dreamer's financial situation is actually good**, it means that he will profit substantially from gambling, and vice versa.

Dictionary — If the dreamer refers to a dictionary, it

means that he relies too much upon the opinions and advice of others in the running of his own affairs, something he could do perfectly competently himself.

Difficulty — **Dreaming about difficulties** is a symbol of passing embarrassment for all business people, but if **they manage to get themselves out of their difficulties,** they will experience prosperity.

Digestion — Dreaming about the digestive system, one of its components or the sensations connected to it, indicates health problems. (See **Digestive System**).

Digestive System — Any dream concerning the digestive system (including vomiting and diarrhea) is a sign of health or nutritional problems.

Digging — **Digging** indicates a battle for survival. If the **dreamer digs a hole and find something shiny there,** his luck will improve. If **nothing but mist is found,** his life will be dogged with bad luck and misery. If the **hole fills with water,** it means that nothing goes the way the dreamer wants it to, despite all his efforts.

Dinner — **Dreaming about eating dinner alone** means that the dreamer has reason to dwell on life's necessities. If the **dreamer is a guest at a dinner-party,** it means that he will soon be invited to partake of the pleasurable hospitality of people who can afford it.

Dirt — **Dreaming about dirt,** particularly if it appears on clothing, means that certain health problems must be attended to. **Dreaming about falling into dirt or garbage** predicts that the dreamer will move house in the near future. (See **Stains.**)

Disabled Person / Cripple — Any dream about a disabled person (the nature or level of disability is irrelevant) attests to the fact that the dreamer's conscience is urging him to help others less fortunate than himself.

Disaster — This is an indication of enemies plotting against the dreamer, particularly in the workplace, and warns him that he must seek protection from them.

Discotheque — This is a sign that the dreamer will soon be in a state of confusion, obsession and distraction about a new relationship.

Disease — If the dreamer has a disease in a dream, this may be a sign of mild and temporary illness or of some disagreement with a relative.

Disgrace — If the **dreamer worries about the conduct of relatives or children**, it means that he will be plagued by anxiety. If **he himself is in disgrace**, it means that he has lowered his moral standards and is about to lose his good name. In addition, he is being tracked by enemies.

Dishes — **Handling dishes** in a dream is a good sign. However, **breaking them** is the opposite. **Shelves of clean dishes** indicates a successful marriage, whereas **dirty dishes** are a sign of discontent and lack of hope.

Dishwasher — This means that a dispute in the dreamer's personal life is about to be resolved.

Disinherited — **Being disinherited** is a warning for the dreamer to examine his personal and business conduct. If a **young man dreams about being disinherited** because of insubordination, he can rectify the situation by marrying well. A **woman** should take this dream as a warning about misfortune resulting from inappropriate behavior.

Dispute — If the **dispute is about something trivial**, the dream is an indication of illness and unfair judgements. If the **dreamer disputes with knowledgeable people**, it means that he has the potential, but has not exploited it to the full.

Distance — This usually means long journeys and travel. **Dreaming about being far from home** means that the dreamer will soon go on a journey in which strangers will ruin his life. **Seeing friends at a distance** is a sign of disappointment.

Distress — If the dreamer dreams that he is in distress, it is a sign that his financial situation will improve substantially.

Ditch — **Falling into a ditch** is an indication of personal loss and humiliation. However, if the **dreamer jumps over the ditch**, he will overcome any allegations of guilt concerning him.

Ditch-Digging Machine — This indicates that a deep dark secret is soon to be revealed. The dreamer must brace himself to face it.

Dividends — A **dream about dividends** portends increased profits or harvests. If the **dreamer failed to obtain the coveted dividends**, it means mismanagement and failure in love.

Diving — **Diving into clear water** means that some embarrassing situation has come to an end. **Diving into muddy water** foretells worries about the dreamer's affairs. **Seeing other people diving** means congenial company.

Divining Rods — This is a foreboding of bad luck.

Divorce — Some claim that **dreaming about divorce indicates sexual problems**. If the **dreamer is married**, it means that he is happily married. If a **single person who has a partner dreams about divorce**, it means that he feels insecure about the relationship.

Docks — The **presence of the dreamer at the docks** is an indication of an unfortunate journey, threatened by accidents. If the **dreamer wanders around the docks in the dark,** he will be in danger from enemies, but **in the sunlight** he will be safe.

Doctor — **Meeting with a doctor in a clinic** indicates an urgent need for help. If the **dreamer meets the doctor at a social gathering**, it is a sign of good health and prosperity, as he will not have to pay the doctor.

Dog — **Seeing a dog** signifies that the dreamer has a desperate need for security in his relationships with others, and indicates his willingness to enjoy the protection provided by another person. **Owning a pedigree dog** is a sign of wealth. **Dreaming about a dog show** means all kinds of good luck. **Dogs biting the dreamer** mean domestic and business strife. **Dirty, scrawny dogs** are a sign of business losses and sick children. **Vicious dogs** mean bad luck and enemies. **Snarling, growling dogs** mean that the dreamer will be the victim of other people's plots, and a bad domestic atmosphere. **Fighting dogs** mean that the dreamer will fall victim to his enemies. A **mad dog** is a terrible sign of failure and impending disease. If the **dreamer is bitten by a mad dog**, it predicts insanity and catastrophe in his family. If a **dog shows affection**, it is an indication of prosperity and good friends. If the **dreamer walks along followed by a dog**, his friends will be faithful and he will succeed. **Small dogs** show that the dreamer's enjoyments and preoccupations are trivial. **Barking dogs** predict bad news. **Bleak, howling dogs** symbolize death or separation. If **coddled, groomed lapdogs appear**, it is an indication of the dreamer's egoism and narrow-mindedness. A **sudden fight between a dog and a cat** means failure in love and business, unless the dreamer manages to calm them down. If the **dreamer sees a dog killing a cat**, the dreamer will do good business and enjoy himself. If the **dreamer sees a dog killing a snake**, it is a sign of good luck. A **congenial white dog** is a good sign for love and business — even for marriage. **Swimming dogs** indicate happiness and prosperity.

Dolphin — In a **dream about dolphins**, the dreamer is seeking solutions to problems in the realm of magic and mysticism. **Seeing dolphins** also suggests that the dreamer is removed from reality.

Dome — **Dreaming about viewing an unfamiliar vista from a dome** means that the dreamer is about to undergo a positive change. He will enjoy the esteem of strangers. **Seeing a dome from a distance** means that the dreamer will never realize his ambitions, and his love will not be returned.

Dominoes — **Winning a game of dominoes** indicates that the dreamer enjoys being appreciated by people of unsavory reputation and receiving compliments from them, which will please him, but cause anguish to his relatives. **Losing a game of dominoes** means that the dreamer's problems also trouble others.

Donkey — The **braying of a donkey** means that the dreamer is in a process of overcoming a painful family connection. **Leading a donkey by a rope** attests to the strength of the dreamer's will power and ability to influence people, especially women. If the **dreamer is a child**, it means he needs friends. **Seeing donkeys carrying loads** means that the dreamer will succeed in his travels or in love, after a long battle. If the **dreamer rides on a donkey**, he will travel to exotic and inaccessible places. **Driving a donkey** signifies that the dreamer requires all his wits to defeat a desperate enemy. If the **dreamer is kicked by a donkey**, it means that he is involved in illicit relationships, and is terrified of being discovered. **Falling off a donkey** means bad luck in business and love. **Dreaming about a white donkey** means a secure and enduring fortune for the dreamer to spend on whatever he likes. For a **woman to see a white donkey**, it means that she will at last enter the social circle she has yearned for. If the **dreamer sees a strange donkey among his livestock**, he will come into an inheritance.

Doomsday — If the **dreamer has hopes of living until doomsday**, he would be well advised to keep an eye on all his possessions and concerns, as cunning friends are all too ready to abscond with them and leave him destitute. A **young woman** who has this dream should discard flashy but unsuitable men and marry the honest, loving man near her.

Door — A **closed door** warns of wastefulness and extravagance. An **open door**, through which people can enter and leave, suggests that the dreamer will soon experience economic difficulties due to poor business management. A **revolving door** indicates surprises and new experiences.

Doorbell — This portends unexpected news or a summons to visit a sick relative.

Doorman (in a hotel or luxury building) — This signifies the dreamer's fierce longing to go on trips to other countries; alternatively, it shows the desire to make far-reaching changes in one's life.

Dough — This is a symbol of wealth, money and possessions.

Dove — **Seeing a dove** attests to a happy family life and great economic success. A **flock of doves** portends a journey or long trip. A **flock of white doves** is a sign of innocent, peaceful enjoyments and a happy future. **Hearing the lonely mournful voice of a dove** is a prediction of sadness and disappointment because of the death of someone who was supposed to help the dreamer. **Seeing a dead dove** means the separation of a couple because of infidelity or death. The sight of white doves presages abundant crops and totally loyal friends.

Dragon — **Seeing a dragon** symbolizes that in times of distress, the dreamer turns to a higher power for help, and does not make any effort on his own part to improve his situation. If the **dreamer is young**, a dragon is a sign of an upcoming wedding.

Drama — **Seeing a drama staged** signifies joyful reunions with faraway friends. If the **dreamer finds himself bored while watching a drama**, it means that he will be landed with a tiresome companion at some event. If **he writes**

one, it signifies that he will suddenly experience trouble and debt, but will amazingly emerge unscathed.

Dressing — **Difficulties in dressing** indicate that the dreamer is being bothered by bad people. If **he is unable to dress in time to catch a train**, it means that he will suffer from the incompetence of others. He should depend on himself alone.

Drinking — **Drinking alcoholic beverages** indicates financial loss. If the **dreamer sees himself drunk on wine**, he can expect great success. **Drinking water**, however, predicts being let down by someone close.

Driving — If the **dreamer is the driver**, it means that he feels the need to act independently in life. If **another person is driving**, it is a sign that the dreamer trusts him. A **dream about speeding** intimates that the dreamer suffers from emotional problems.

Dromedary [camel] — The dreamer is about to receive a generous amount of wealth and honor, which he will bear in a dignified manner. He will be magnanimous and charitable.

Drought — This is a very bad dream, predicting war and bloodshed between nations, as well as disasters at sea and on land, feuding families, and illness. The dreamer's business affairs will also founder.

Drowning — If the **dreamer sees himself drowning**, it is a sign that cooperation with a professional colleague will be profitable. If the **dreamer sees other people drowning**, it foretells bad things in the future.

Drum — The **indistinct beat of a drum** calls on the dreamer to assist a faraway friend who is in distress. **Seeing a**

drum testifies to a congenial nature and a loathing of dissent and disputes. **Dreaming about a drum** is a positive sign for tradesmen, farmers and sailors.

Drunkenness — This is basically a negative dream, as **being drunk on alcohol** indicates a dissipated nature. The dreamer will face disgrace when he resorts to stealing. However, **wine-induced drunkenness** foretells luck in business and love, as well as lofty literary and esthetic experiences. If the **dreamer sees others drunk**, it predicts unhappiness.

Duck — A **wild duck** symbolizes happiness and good luck, especially in travel. **White ducks** predict a bountiful harvest. If **ducks are shot**, it is a warning of the interference of enemies in the dreamer's business. **Flying ducks** are a symbol of a happy future, marriage and children.

Duet — A **duet in a dream** is a symbol of peaceful, harmonious coexistence between lovers. It is a sign of desultory competition between **business people**. However, **musicians** see this as blatant rivalry and a clawing for the top position. A **singing duet** predicts the advent of unpleasant news, but it will soon be eclipsed by nice things.

Dumb — **Dreaming about being dumb** means that the dreamer is unable to convince others to adopt his opinions by means of his silver tongue. If the **dreamer is dumb**, it is a sign of insincere friends.

Dun — If a dreamer receives a dun, it is a warning that he must see to his affairs — both business and love — and avoid neglecting them.

Dungeon — **Seeing a dungeon** means that the dreamer's wisdom will enable him to emerge victorious from the vicissitudes of life. A **woman who dreams about a dungeon** will bring about her own ostracism by her indiscretions.

Dunghill — **Dreaming about a dunghill** signals prosperity stemming from very unexpected places. **For a farmer**, it is a sign of good fortune, of abundant harvest and livestock. For a **young woman**, it indicates a marriage to a wealthy man (unbeknown to her).

Dusk — This is a sad dream, as it foretells premature aging and unfulfilled hopes. After this dream, trade and business seem to be at a standstill for a long time.

Dust — **Dust covering the dreamer** means that the lack of success of others will have repercussions on him, too. If the **dreamer uses his brains,** he will shake off this setback and continue on his path to success.

Dwarf — **Seeing a dwarf** is an indication of good tidings. A **sick or wounded dwarf** suggests that the dreamer has hidden enemies.

Dye — The **dyeing of cloth** in a dream portends good or bad luck depending on the color: **Blue, red** and **gold** indicate prosperity, while **white** and **black** are signs of every kind of sorrow.

Dying — If the **dreamer sees himself dying** in a dream, it indicates a bad conscience or guilt feelings. If **another person is dying**, it means that the dreamer is trying to rid himself of feelings of responsibility for that person.

Dynamite — **Seeing dynamite** is a sign that change is approaching, that the dreamer is about to increase his affairs.

If **he is afraid**, it means that an unknown enemy is undermining him, and if **he is not cautious**, that enemy will ambush him at a vulnerable moment.

Dynamo — **Seeing a dynamo** means that if the dreamer is meticulous in his business practices, he will succeed. A **broken-down dynamo** indicates that he is drawing close to enemies whose aim is to embroil him.

Eagle — If an **eagle appears in a dream**, it is not to be taken lightly. It is quite significant and indicates an extraordinary desire on the part of the dreamer to realize his potential. **Seeing an eagle flying high above** means high ambitions which, after a struggle, the dreamer will realize. **Seeing an eagle perched far away** means that the dreamer will be blessed with fame, wealth, and the highest possible status in his country. **Young eagles in their nest** means that the dreamer will benefit from his association with people in high positions, and will receive a rich legacy. **Killing an eagle** means that no obstacle will stand in the dreamer's way to realizing his ambitions. His enemies will be defeated, and he will be extremely wealthy. **Eating an eagle** is the sign of a powerful, single-minded will, and immediate wealth. A **dead eagle** means that the dreamer's high position and fortune will be taken from him mercilessly. **Riding on an eagle's back** mean long, exploratory journeys into unknown countries, gaining knowledge and wealth.

Earrings — **Seeing earrings** means that the dreamer can expect good news and interesting work. **Broken earrings** indicate malicious gossip about the dreamer.

Ears — A dream in which the dreamer sees ears means that his conversations are being bugged by an enemy.

Earth — **Earth** symbolizes abundance and all good things awaiting the dreamer. **Arid land** indicates disrespect of others and the need for soul-searching.

Earthquake — This is an indication of financial failure as well as of internecine warfare and all the attendant misery.

Eating — **Eating alone** is a sign of loss and depression. **Eating together with other people** signifies enduring friendship, personal gain, merry surroundings and prosperity.

Eavesdropping — If **others are eavesdropping** on the dreamer, it warns of trouble. If the **dreamer is eavesdropping** on others, he can expect happy surprises!

Ebony — Any dream concerning an item made of ebony portends strife and dissent in the dreamer's house.

Echo — **Hearing an echo** means that bad times are lying heavily upon the dreamer. If **he is ill,** he may lose his job, and his friends will not be there for him.

Eclipse — A **dream about an eclipse** means temporary set-backs in business, as well as domestic unrest. An **eclipse of the sun** is a portent of a turbulent and perilous period, but these will ultimately end. An **eclipse of the moon** signifies contagious illnesses and death.

Ecstasy — Dreaming about ecstasy indicates that the dreamer can look forward to a visit from a dear and distant friend.

Edifice — The meaning of the dream lies in the height of the edifice. **Average height** indicates changes in the near future. A **higher-than-average** edifice portends brilliant success in the near future.

Eel — This is a good dream if the dreamer manages to hold on to it. If **it wriggles out of his grasp,** his luck will not last. **Seeing a dead eel** means that the dreamer will defeat his most vicious enemy. **For lovers,** the eel signifies marriage.

Egg — The **appearance of an egg or the eating of an**

egg indicates that the dreamer will soon increase his wealth and become more established in life. A **broken or rotten egg** portends failure or loss.

Egg Yolk — Good times are on the way. If a person who gambles dreams of the yolk of an egg, it means that he will be successful at gambling.

Eggs — **Dreaming about a number of eggs** means improvement in the dreamer's financial situation. **Two eggs** in a nest attests to the support of a loving family. **Three eggs** in a nest indicate an addition to the family!

Elbow — This indicates that the dreamer is involved in activities that do not do justice to his abilities.

Elderberries — Leafy and fruity elderberry bushes signify a happy home in the country, and sufficient money for pleasurable activities such as traveling.

Election — If the dreamer is at an election, it means that he will get involved in some controversial matter which will do him no good financially or socially.

Electric Blanket — This dream predicts that the dreamer will soon be in need of support and comfort.

Electric Mixer — This is an indication of an increased social life.

Electricity — **Dreaming about electricity** indicates unexpected changes in the dreamer — not particularly to his benefit. If the **dreamer reacts badly to it**, he is in grave peril. A **live wire** means that enemies will undermine the dreamer's painstakingly developed plans.

Elephant — This predicts that the dreamer will meet people who will become his friends.

Elevator — If the **elevator is ascending**, it means that the dreamer is hankering after positive changes in his life. A **descending elevator** indicates the absence of financial success and a lack of initiative.

Elixir of Life — This is a positive dream indicating new joys and new opportunities.

Elopement — If the **dreamer elopes**, he will be considered unworthy of his position by the married establishment, and he risks his good name. To the **unmarried population**, elopement is an indication of disappointments in love and the infidelity of men.

Eloquent — If the dreamer appears eloquent in a dream, he can expect good news concerning somebody for whom he is working.

Embalming — If the **dreamer sees the process of embalming**, it indicates that he is going to experience a reversal of fortune. If the **dreamer himself is being embalmed**, it means that he will keep company with the wrong people.

Embankment — **Dreaming about driving along an embankment** predicts problems and heartache for the dreamer. If **he manages to continue driving without anything happening**, it means that he will be able to use the prediction for his own benefit.

Embracing — If the **dreamer embraces his/her spouse indifferently**, it is a sign of possible illness and domestic disputes and rows. If the **dreamer embraces relatives**, they will become ill and unhappy. **For lovers**, it is a sign of fights following infidelity. **Embracing a stranger** presages unwanted guests.

Embroidery — Dreaming about embroidery is a good dream for a woman, as it means that she is resourceful, thrifty and tactful. **For a married man**, it signifies an addition to his household.

Emerald — Seeing an emerald signifies a trouble-fraught inheritance for the dreamer. If a **lover sees his beloved wearing an emerald**, it is a sign that he is about to be dumped. A **dream about purchasing an emerald** is a sign of a bad deal.

Emperor — If the dreamer meets a foreign emperor during his travels, it means that he will be going on a long, futile and unenjoyable trip.

Employee — If the **dreamer sees one of his employees being belligerent or offensive**, there will be trouble. If the **employee is pleasant**, everything will be fine.

Employment — Dreaming about employment is an unfortunate dream, indicating business failure, unemployment and illness. If the **dreamer himself is unemployed** at a given moment, he can rest assured that he will find a job because of his diligence. If the **dreamer employs others**, he will suffer loss.

Empress — Dreaming about an empress indicates that the dreamer will receive high honors, but will not be popular because of arrogance. A **dream about an empress and an emperor** has no particular significance.

Emptiness — An empty container or a feeling of emptiness warns of a bitter disappointment that the dreamer will have to cope with and that will weaken him severely, both physically and mentally.

Enchantment — **Being enchanted** is a warning to the dreamer not to be seduced by evil in the guise of something pleasurable. If the **dreamer withstands enchantment**, it means that people will seek his advice and enjoy his generosity. If the **dreamer tries to enchant others**, he will sink into evil.

Encyclopedia — If the dreamer sees or uses an encyclopedia, it means he will sacrifice life's comforts for literary prowess.

Enemy — **Defeating enemies** means overcoming business difficulties and enjoying prosperity. This is always good for the dreamer. If the **enemies overcome the dreamer**, it means trouble. If **enemies spread slander about the dreamer**, he will suffer setbacks and failure in his profession or business. If the **dreamer kisses an enemy**, it means that he is making up with a friend with whom he quarreled.

Engagement — This foretells temporary disagreements with one's partner that will be resolved.

Engine — **Seeing engines** means that with the help of good friends, the dreamer will be able to overcome the serious difficulties in his path. **Engines in a state of disrepair** symbolize bad luck and the death of relatives.

Engineer — Seeing an engineer in a dream signifies happy reunions after exhausting journeys.

English — A foreigner meeting English people will be subject to the egoistic intentions of others.

Entrails — **Dreaming about human entrails** symbolizes overwhelming, terrible despair, with no glimmer of hope. The **entrails of a wild animal** mean that the dreamer will defeat an enemy. If the **dreamer tears out another person's entrails**, it signifies that he is willing to resort to sadistic behavior in the name of his own interests. **Dreaming about his own child's entrails** foretells the downfall of one of the two.

Envelope — A **sealed envelope** indicates hardship, complexes, frustration and difficulties. An **open envelope** signifies that the dreamer will overcome obstacles that are not too formidable.

Envy / Jealousy — If the **dreamer is envious of another person**, it predicts possible disappointment. If **another person is envious of the dreamer**, it heralds success and good luck.

Epaulets — A **soldier who dreams about epaulets** will be in temporary disfavor, but will soon receive a promotion. If **a woman dreams about meeting a person with epaulets**, it means that scandal is about to follow.

Epidemic — This indicates mental deterioration and anxiety caused by unpleasant tasks. People close to the dreamer will be exposed to illness.

Ermine — If the **dreamer is wearing ermine**, it is a sign of wealth and high status, with immunity from poverty and misery. If **he sees someone else clothed in it**, he will associate with rich and cultured people. A **lover seeing his beloved in ermine** can be assured of fidelity; however, if the **ermine is tatty or soiled**, the opposite is true.

Errands — **Going on errands** is a sign of pleasant relationships at home and with friends. If a **young woman**

sends someone on an errand, she will lose the man she loves because of her indifferent behavior.

Escalator — A **dream about riding the up escalator** is a sign of professional progress. A **dream about the down escalator** is a sign of professional stagnation. If the **escalator is out of order** and the dreamer has to walk up it, he will not receive the promotion he expected.

Escape — **Dreaming about escape from injury or mishap** is generally negative. **Escaping from a place where the dreamer had been locked up** means that his diligence in business affairs will bring success. **Escape from illness** means health and wealth. A **failed escape attempt** means mistreatment and ruined reputation at the hands of enemies.

Estate — A **dream about inheriting an estate** indicates that the dreamer will indeed receive a bequest one day, but not what he expects. A **woman dreaming about an estate** foretells an extremely modest inheritance for her.

Eulogy — This is a sign of good news (usually marriage) brought by a close friend.

Europe — If the dreamer dreams about traveling in Europe, he will soon go on a trip during which he will become familiar with foreign ways. His profit will be both educational and financial.

Eve and the Apple — Dreaming about the story of Eve in the Garden of Eden usually symbolizes the dreamer's ability to withstand temptation.

Evening — A **dream about evening** is a sign of no hope and unlucky deals. If the **stars are shining brightly**, there will be trouble, but it will be followed by good fortune. **For lovers walking in the evening**, this dream means that one of them will soon die. **Dreaming about a pleasant evening** predicts that the dreamer will soon enjoy a period of tranquillity and calm.

Evergreen — A **dream about evergreens** is a wonderful dream for everyone as it foretells riches, joy and knowledge. **Icicles on evergreens** are an omen of a promising future being tainted.

Exchange — **Dreaming about an exchange** is a sign of good business dealings. A **young woman who dreams of exchanging boyfriends** with her friend should follow this through if she wants to ensure her future happiness.

Execution — **Seeing an execution** means that the dreamer will suffer because of the sloppiness of others. If **he is about to be executed**, but his execution is miraculously stayed, it means that he will defeat his enemies and become rich.

Exile — For a woman to dream of being exiles is a sign that she will be compelled to travel and miss out on an event she was looking forward to.

Explosion — **Dreaming about an explosion** is a very negative dream. **Seeing an explosion** means that one of the dreamer's friends is in danger, and that the dreamer will suffer the disapproval of those close to him, and this will cause him anger and loss.

Eye — **Seeing an eye** is a warning that the dreamer's enemies are spying on him, waiting to harm him. A **lover** should watch out that someone else does not steal his beloved away from him. **Blue eyes** mean a lack of resolve. **Brown eyes** mean lies and deception. **Gray eyes** mean that the dreamer loves being flattered. **Sore eyes**, or the loss of an eye means problems. Seeing a **one-eyed man** means serious trouble.

Eyebrows — This is an indication of frightening obstacles in the path of the dream.

Eye Doctor — This warns the dreamer to keep his eyes open and be aware of his situation, in order not to miss any opportunities that may come his way.

Eyeglasses / Binoculars — These indicate that the dreamer will experience a great improvement in his life, as things that were previously unclear to him will be clarified and understood.

Fables — **Reading or narrating fables** indicates passing the time pleasantly, as well as a literary bent. **Dreaming about religious fables** means that the dreamer will become very pious.

Face — **Seeing one's face in a mirror** indicates that in the near future the dreamer will be privy to secrets that will influence his life significantly. **Happy faces** in a dream are a good sign, while **ugly or scowling faces** are a bad one.

Factory — This is an indication of unprecedented business activity.

Failure — Contrary to what might be expected, for a lover, a **dream about failure** actually predicts success. However, a **businessman who dreams about failure** should be warned of loss and mismanagement, which, if he does not rectify, will bring him down.

Fainting — This dream portends illness in the family and bad news about faraway people.

Fair / Bazaar — Dreaming about being at a fair means that the dreamer must maintain a low profile in the near future and not be conspicuous.

Fairy — This dream bodes well for everybody, as it is the embodiment of beauty.

Faithless — Strangely enough, this is a positive dream. A **dream about faithless friends** means that they hold the dreamer in high esteem. If a **lover dreams that his beloved is faithless**, it is a sign of a happy marriage.

Falcon — This dream means that people will envy the dreamer's wealth. It indicates vicious gossip.

Fall — If the **dreamer falls and this frightens him**, it means that he will be successful after a long, uphill battle. If **he is injured in the fall**, he will lose his friends and meet with trouble.

Fame — A dream about fame, whether that of the dreamer or of somebody close to him, warns of events that will be a source of nervousness and restlessness.

Family — A **dream about a happy family** signifies health and comfort. However, a **dream about illness or strife in a family** foretells disappointment and unhappiness.

Famine — **Seeing famine** is a bad dream, predicting business failure and illness. If the **dreamer's enemies die of famine**, he will be successful.

Famish — If the **dreamer is famished**, it means that a project he was sure of succeeding in is on the road to failure. A **dream about others being famished** is a sign of bad luck both for the dreamer and for other people.

Fan — An **elaborate fan** signifies that the dreamer is arrogant and egocentric. A **new fan** predicts good news. An **old fan** indicates that there is reason to be concerned about serious incidents or unpleasant news.

Farewell — If the **dreamer dreams about bidding farewell**, it means that he will hear bad news about faraway friends. If **a young woman bids her beloved farewell**, it means that he no longer cares about her.

Farm / Ranch — A **dream about a walk around a farm** means success in business. If the **dreamer is in love**, a happy relationship can be expected.

Farmer — This suggests a life of prosperity and

abundance; success in all areas: economic, social, personal and health.

Fat — A **dream about becoming fat** foretells a change for the good in the dreamer's life. **Dreaming about others being fat** is a sign of prosperity.

Fates — A dream about the Fates foretells misery and disputes.

Father — When the **dreamer is addressed by his father**, joyful events will soon occur in his life. If the **father merely appears in the dream**, worries and problems can be expected.

Father-in-Law — A **dream about a father-in-law** is an indication of dissent with relatives or friends. If the **father-in-law is healthy and happy**, it is a sign of a harmonious domestic situation.

Fatigue — This warns against making incorrect decisions that the dreamer will regret all his life.

Faucet — A faucet with water flowing out of it indicates business growth and financial success.

Favor — **Asking favors** of someone is a sign of a comfortable lifestyle, wanting nothing. **Granting favors** means that the dreamer will suffer a loss.

Fawn (animal) — Seeing a fawn in a dream is an indication of true, faithful friends and fidelity in love.

Fawn (behavior) — If someone fawns on the dreamer, it is a sign that enemies pretending to be his friends are nearby.

Fax Machine — **Receiving a fax** in a dream is an indication that the dreamer is about to receive bad news pertaining to his profession or business. **Sending a fax**

means that the dreamer will suffer a let-down at the hands of one of his business associates.

Fear — **Feeling fear** in a dream signifies that future undertakings will fail. **For a woman to feel fear**, it means disappointment in love.

Feast — A **feast in a dream** is an indication of pleasant surprises being planned for the dreamer. A **chaotic, disorderly feast** means that there will be rows and unhappiness as a result of the illness of someone else. If the **dreamer arrives late at a feast**, it means that he will have worries.

Feather — **Seeing falling feathers** in a dream means that the dreamer's burdens will be light. **Eagle feathers** indicate the realization of aspirations. **Chicken feathers** mean trifling irritations. **Goose or duck feathers** symbolize prosperity and thrift. **Black feathers** indicate disappointment in love.

February — **Dreaming about February** is a sign of illness and sadness. **Dreaming about a bright day in February** means some unexpectedly good thing will happen.

Feeble — Dreaming about being feeble means that the dreamer is not in a beneficial occupation, and is beset with worries. He is advised to effect a change in his life.

Feet — **Dreaming about one's own feet** is a sign of despair and domination by others. **Dreaming about other people's feet** is a sign of the dreamer's assertiveness as far as his rights and status in life are concerned. **Dreaming about washing one's feet** is a sign of being taken advantage of. **Sore feet** indicate domestic strife.

Red, swollen feet are a sign of family crisis, such as separation, which will cause gossip.

Fence — **Destruction of a fence** in a dream is a sign that problems will be resolved in the near future. If a **young woman dreams about a fence**, it indicates that she is longing to be married and have children. A **green fence** signifies true love.

Fern — This indicates an unusually strong sexual appetite.

Ferry — **Waiting for a boat at a ferry** when the water is rough and muddy means frustration of the dreamer's wishes. A **ferry crossing on calm, clear water** is a sign of good luck and successful accomplishment of plans.

Festival — This indicates the discarding of conservative values in favor of new, superficial pleasures. Although the dreamer will never be short of anything, he will not be self-supporting.

Fever — A high fever warns against incorrect actions and deeds which bring negative results.

Fiddle — This is a positive dream, predicting domestic harmony and happy events.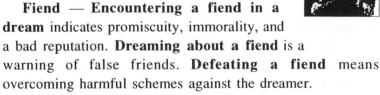

Fiend — **Encountering a fiend in a dream** indicates promiscuity, immorality, and a bad reputation. **Dreaming about a fiend** is a warning of false friends. **Defeating a fiend** means overcoming harmful schemes against the dreamer.

Fife — **Hearing a fife** means defending one's honor or that of a close acquaintance. **Playing a fife** means that one's reputation is good.

Fig — This is a prediction of good news.

Fight — **Involvement in a fight** represents disagreeable conflicts in business, as well as lawsuits. **Seeing a fight in a dream** is a sign of wastefulness — of money and time. It warns women against gossip. **Losing a fight** means loss of the dreamer's right to property. **Winning a fight** means that the dreamer will obtain wealth and esteem by courage and perseverance.

Figures — This is a negative dream meaning mental anguish and misdeeds. The dreamer will suffer great losses if he is not careful of what he says and does.

Filbert — In a **dream about filberts**, peace, domestic harmony and prosperity are indicated. **Eating filberts** is a sign of good friendships for young people.

File (office) — **Dreaming about files** is a sign of a very bad business transaction. **Seeing files and filing away documents** means serious discussions about important matters which will cause the dreamer anxiety. It does not bode well for the future.

Fillings (teeth) — This indicates that something of value that the dreamer had lost will be found, after causing him much anguish.

Finger — A **hurt finger** indicates a wounded self-image. The **hurt finger of another person** indicates incitement, vicious gossip or slander, all directed against the dreamer.

Fingernails — **Dirty fingernails** in a dream are a sign of imminent disgrace in the dreamer's family as a result of the bad behavior of the younger members. **Well-groomed nails** are an indication of cultural proclivities and achievements, as well as thrift.

Fingers — If the **dreamer's fingers are dirty, injured, and bloody**, it is a sign of future suffering and hardship. He will have no hope of advancement in life. **Well-groomed hands with white smooth fingers** are an indication of happy love and altruism. Dreaming about **amputated fingers** is a sign of financial loss due to the evil machinations of enemies.

Fire — **Dreaming about fire** warns of problems that might arise if the dreamer dreams of getting burnt. If the **dreamer's home is on fire**, it means domestic harmony. If a **businessman sees a store on fire**, he can expect a great wave of prosperity. **Fighting fire** in a dream means a lot of worry concerning business affairs. **Fire-destroyed stores** are a sign of bad luck which will be reversed by the dreamer.

Firebrand — This dream is favorable if the dreamer is neither burnt nor frightened by it.

Fire Drill — This is a sign of strife concerning a financial matter.

Fire Engine — **Seeing a fire engine** is a sign of worry which will be resolved agreeably. If a **fire engine breaks down** in a dream, it is a sign of loss or mishap.

Fireman — This is a symbol of loyal friends.

Fireplace — This is indicative of an upcoming period of prosperity, growth and economic stability for the dreamer.

Firewood — If the dreamer's business concerns firewood, it means that he will be successful after working hard.

Fireworks — This is a sign of good health and enjoyment.

Firmament — A **star-filled firmament** means that the path to fulfillment of the dreamer's ambitions will be very difficult, and that enemies will attempt to undermine him. If the **dreamer sees people he knows in the firmament**, it means that he will be involved in doing unfortunate deeds that will affect others adversely. This is a bad dream.

Fish — A **single fish** heralds success or means that the dreamer has a particularly successful and brilliant child. A **school of fish** means that the dreamer's friends care about him and are doing things for his benefit. **Fishing in a dream** signifies treachery on the part of a friend or friends. **Eating fish** predicts success following hard work and enduring relationships.

Fish Eggs — This is a sign of calm and comfort for the dreamer.

Fisherman — This signifies that the dreamer is approaching a period of unprecedented prosperity.

Fishhooks — This dream means that if the dreamer takes advantage of the opportunities available to him, he can achieve wealth and fame.

Fish Market — **Visiting a fish market** brings joy. However, if the **dreamer sees rotten fish**, he will experience distress that will not be recognizable as such at first.

Fishnet — A **fishnet in good repair** means a lot of minor pleasures and profits. A **torn one** means troubles and disappointments.

Fishpond — A **muddy fishpond** indicates illness. A **clear one filled with fish** means prosperity and an enjoyable life. If a **young woman falls into one**, she will be happy in love. An empty fishpond is an indication of the proximity of dangerous enemies.

Fits — If the dreamer has fits, it means that he will become ill and lose his job. If he sees others having fits, it means that there will be quarrels in his circle.

Flag — Seeing a flag means that the dreamer has a pleasant and tranquil character. Waving a flag in a contest means that the dreamer should take a break from the rat race and rest. A torn flag indicates disgrace.

Flame — A dream of fighting flames indicates that the dreamer will have to make great efforts if he is to succeed in becoming rich.

Flash Flood — Seeing a flash flood is an indication of danger on the horizon. Overcoming a flash flood or strong stream of water indicates overcoming obstacles and attaining success as a result of hard work.

Flax — This is a sign of prosperity.

Flax Spinning — This is a symbol of diligence and thrift.

Fleas — These mean that the dreamer's life is chaotic and extremely disorganized.

Fleeing/Flight — If the dreamer flees, it means bad news about faraway people. If anything flees from the dreamer, it means that he will be triumphant in any disagreement.

Fleet — If the dreamer sees a rapidly sailing fleet, it means that there will be a positive turnabout in sluggish business.

Flies — This is an indication of daily concerns, illness, contagion and enemies.

Floating — Dreaming about floating in the air is very

common. It usually indicates that the dreamer should focus his efforts on one objective. **Floating in water** means overcoming seemingly insurmountable obstacles. If the **water is muddy**, the dreamer's success will not give him joy.

Flood / Heavy Rain — Seeing a flood symbolizes hardship and the inability to reach an understanding with one's surroundings. **Dreaming about a destructive flood** covering the country with wreckage and mud is a sign of illness, business losses and conjugal misery.

Flour — Dreaming about flour is a symbol of a simple but contented life. **Trading in flour** is a sign of risky speculation.

Flowers — Dreaming about blooming flowers is a sign of profit and pleasure. **Picking flowers** in a dream signifies that the dreamer may count on his friends not to disappoint him. **Throwing flowers** in a dream is a prediction of a quarrel with someone close to him in the future. If the dream is about **arranging flowers**, a pleasant surprise can be expected. If **graves or coffins are bedecked with white flowers**, the dreamer should not indulge in pleasurable or worldly activities.

Flute — If the dreamer himself is playing the flute, it is an indication of hidden musical talent. **Listening to the flute being played by somebody else** means that the dreamer can rely on his friends.

Flux (diarrhea) **— Dreaming about having diarrhea or believing that one has it** is a sign that either the dreamer or one of his family will be struck by a fatal illness. If **others have it**, it means that the dreamer will experience failure in some matter because of the lack of cooperation of others.

Flying — A **dream in which the dreamer sees himself flying in the sky** indicates that he does not have both feet firmly planted on the ground. He is not aware of his serious financial situation and ought to save more money and reorganize his economic strategies. **Flying high** indicates conjugal troubles. **Flying with black wings** is a sign of keen disappointments. **Flying with white wings** over green vegetation means success in business and love. If a **woman flies from one place to another**, she will have to resist false declarations of love, and she will face the danger of illness and the death of someone close. If a **young woman is shot at while flying**, it means that her enemies are doing everything to prevent her ascent up the ladder of progress and promotion.

Flypaper — This means illness and breakup of friendships.

Flytrap — **Dreaming about a flytrap** is a sign of conspiracies against the dreamer. A **flytrap full of flies** means that minor embarrassments will save the dreamer major ones.

Foal — This indicates new enterprises in which the dreamer will be very successful.

Fog — If the **dreamer is in fog**, it is a sign that his plans will be fulfilled. If **fog is seen from afar**, it indicates disagreement between the dreamer and those close to him.

Folder/Binder — This means that the dreamer needs to consult with friends or receive their help.

Food — If the dreamer sees himself eating and enjoying

himself, it heralds good and happy times to come: His aspirations will be realized!

Foot — When a person's foot appears in a dream, it means that the dreamer suffers from physical ailments that stem from his mind.

Forehead — A **smooth forehead** means that the dreamer is well thought of for his good judgment and fairness. An **ugly forehead** means that the dreamer is unhappy with himself. If the dreamer **caresses the forehead of his child,** it means that the child will be praised because of his talent. A **young woman kissing her lover's forehead** means that he will be upset at her behavior.

Forest — **Entering a dense forest** suggests problems in the near future, particularly in the financial realm. A **forest** also indicates domestic strife.

Fork — The dreamer should be aware that his enemies are working to undermine him.

Form — Something **ill-formed** is an indication of disappointment. A **beautiful form** indicates good health and prosperous business.

Forsaking — If a young woman dreams about forsaking a friend or her home, it means that she will be disappointed in her lover, who will not live up to her expectations.

Fort — **Defending a fort** means that the dreamer's honor and possessions will be attacked, causing him great worry. **Attacking a fort** and conquering it means that the dreamer will defeat his biggest enemy and be successful.

Fortress — If the **dreamer is inside a fortress,** it means that he possesses a burning desire to become rich. If a

fortress is seen in the distance, it suggests frustration and a feeling of having missed out. If the **dreamer lives in the fortress**, it means that he will acquire much wealth.

Fortune — Squandering a fortune in a dream means that the dreamer will be plagued by domestic worries.

Fortune-telling — Dreaming about having one's fortune told means that the dreamer is worried by some bothersome affair and should be careful before agreeing to its solution.

Fountain — A **clear fountain** is an excellent dream, signifying wonderful pleasures, wealth and enjoyable trips. A **clouded fountain** means disappointments in love and in business associates. A **dry, non-functioning fountain** is a sign of death and an unhappy existence.

Fowl — A dream about fowls means a passing concern or illness.

Fox — **Seeing a fox** means that the dreamer is esteemed by those around him and enjoys a good reputation. If the **dreamer chases a fox**, it means that he is divorced from reality.

Fraud — If the **dreamer practices fraud**, it means that he will cheat his boss, live a dissipated life and lose his good reputation. If the **dreamer is defrauded**, it signifies that his enemies are trying in vain to destroy and discredit him. If **he accuses someone of fraud**, he will be offered a high position.

Freckles — If a **woman dreams that she has freckles on her face**, it means that her happiness will be eroded by many unpleasant incidents. If **she sees the freckles in a mirror**, it is a warning that she will lose her sweetheart to a rival.

Freezer — This means that a situation which has caused the dreamer anxiety will resolve itself.

Freight Train — A good dream which presages advancement for the dreamer.

Friend — If a **friend appears in a dream**, it means that he is in trouble or in danger. **Faithless friends** in dreams mean that they hold the dreamer in high esteem.

Frightened — This is a symbol of transient anxieties.

Frogs — **Frogs in the grass** symbolize a good life, happy and carefree, with good friends. **Catching frogs** means that the dreamer neglects his health and thus causes anxiety to his family.

Frost — **Frost on a dark morning** means exile to a distant country, but ultimate peace. **Frost sparkling in the sun** is a sign of enjoyable things that the dreamer will abandon later in life.

Fruit — This is usually a prediction of good and pleasant things for the dreamer in the future.

Fruit (dried) — A warning: The dreamer was not cautious when taking a certain stand, or he made a hasty decision.

Fruit Seller — This is a warning of financial loss and the inability to recoup one's losses.

Fuel / Gasoline — A warning: It indicates that the dreamer must distance himself from any situation which might lead to a confrontation with those close to him.

Funeral — **Seeing a funeral** symbolizes an unhappy marriage, unhealthy children, and domestic problems. **Seeing the funeral of a stranger** is a symbol of worries. If the **dreamer sees the funeral of his child**, it means good health for the family, but also a bitter disappointment from an unexpected source. **Wearing black to a funeral** means early widowhood.

Fur — Dry fur predicts wealth, good luck, and happiness. **Wet fur** heralds success only after an about-face in one's life. **Trading in fur** is a sign of prosperity and varied interests. **Being dressed in fur** means being far from destitute or poor. Seeing good fur symbolizes wealth and honor. If a **woman wears expensive furs**, she will marry a clever man.

Furnace — A **functioning furnace** is a sign of good luck. A **malfunctioning furnace** means problems with children or employees. **Falling into a furnace** foretells succumbing to an enemy in business.

Future — This is a symbol of thrift and avoidance of extravagance.

Gaiety — A dream about especially great merriment, laughter and joy actually warns of hard times ahead.

Gaining Weight — This predicts bad times for the dreamer in the near future.

Gaiters — This is a forecast of amiable rivalries and pleasures.

Gale — Being caught in a gale means business losses and problems for working people.

Galloping — Galloping on a horse confirms that the dreamer is on a direct path to success.

Gallows — If the **dreamer sees a friend about to be hanged on the gallows**, it means that he must deal with terrible emergencies with a cool head, or catastrophe will follow. If the **dreamer himself is on a gallows**, it means that he has false friends. **Rescuing someone from the gallows** will result in possessions. If the **dreamer hangs his enemy**, it means that he will be successful in everything.

Gambling — Actively gambling at a table in a dream symbolizes a future loss in business.

Game (hunting) — **Any dream about hunting game** means success, but with selfishness. If the **dreamer hunts and does not kill any game**, it means mismanagement and loss in business.

Games — If the **dreamer is participating in a competitive game**, it means that he will soon receive good, happy news. If the **dreamer is just watching a game**, it means that in reality, he is very jealous of one of his friends.

Gang — **Dreaming about a gang** reflects the dreamer's profound need for belonging and intimacy. A **violent**

meeting with members of a gang suggests a fear of intimacy and close relationships.

Gangrene — If the dreamer sees anyone with gangrene, it foretells the death of a parent or close relative.

Garbage — Piles of garbage indicate bad business and social scandal.

Garden — **A dream about a garden** means good tidings: a successful marriage, economic prosperity and material abundance. A **garden with blooming flowers** symbolizes an expanding business and inner peace. A **vegetable garden** indicates the need to take precautionary measures.

Gargoyle — **Dreaming about a gargoyle** indicates a falling out between the dreamer and a close friend. If a **gargoyle comes to life**, it means that sadness and mishaps are soon to follow.

Garlic — **Dreaming about garlic** is interpreted according to the dreamer's taste: If the **dreamer likes garlic**, it is a positive dream predicting success. If the **dreamer is revolted by garlic**, it portends bad times.

Garret — **Climbing up to a garret** means that the dreamer deals with theories and leaves others to struggle with the bitter realities of life. If a **poor person dreams this**, it means that his situation will improve.

Garter — If a **lover finds his sweetheart's garter**, he will soon lose out to a rival. If a **woman loses her garter in a dream**, it means that her lover is jealous. A **married man who dreams of a garter** will soon have his secret affairs exposed to his wife.

Gas — **Dreaming about gas** is a sign that the dreamer will misjudge others and will suffer pangs of conscience for it. **Asphyxiation by gas** means that the dreamer's extravagant behavior will lead to trouble. **Extinguishing gas** means destroying one's own happiness.

Gasoline — See **Fuel**.

Gate — A **closed gate** indicates social problems. A **broken gate** means problems on the ladder of promotion at work. If the **dreamer sees himself swinging on the gate**, it means that he prefers rest to work.

Gauze — **Gauze** is a symbol of uncertain luck. If a **lover sees his beloved dressed in semitransparent gauze**, it means that he can influence her positively.

Gavel — **Dreaming about a gavel** means that the dreamer will have to do some futile but not disagreeable task. If a **gavel is used**, it means that the dreamer's friends will be supercilious toward him.

Gazelle — This signifies that the dreamer is a loner.

Gems — This portends good luck in love and business.

Genealogical Tree — This symbolizes many worries in the realm of family. The dreamer will seek his pleasures elsewhere.

Genitals — A **dream of malformed or diseased genitals** (male or female) means that the dreamer will be tempted into an illicit and scandalous affair, which will be destructive. If **he exposes his genitals**, it means that he is about to lose his good reputation.

Geography — Dreaming about geography means that the dreamer will travel far and wide.

Germ — This is an indication of the dreamer's hypochondria and constant fear of illness.

Getting Lost — This attests to frustration, embarrassment, confusion and a general dissatisfaction with life, especially regarding a romantic relationship in which the dreamer is involved.

Ghost — The appearance of a ghost and a conversation with it indicate difficulties coping with someone's death and the desire to make contact with the world of the dead.

Giant — **Dreaming about a giant** is a sign of the dreamer's ability to cope with and overcome problems, despite the hardships involved. **Seeing a giant** may also be an indication of an emotional problem that manifests itself mainly in feelings of inferiority.

Gift — If the dreamer receives a gift from somebody, it means that the latter is plotting against him, attempting to deceive and undermine him.

Gig — Traveling in a gig means that the dreamer will have to give up on an enjoyable trip because of an unwelcome guest. Illness is also predicted.

Giraffe — This signifies serious sexual problems, particularly if the dreamer is a single man.

Girdle — A **tight girdle** means that people with hidden agendas will influence the dreamer. A **velvet or jewel-studded girdle** means that wealth is more important to the dreamer than honor. A **girdle** is a sign of honor for a woman.

Girl — A **bright, healthy girl** is a sign of good luck and

domestic happiness. A **thin, pale girl** is a sign of
a sick person in the family, as well as
unpleasantness.

Glass — **Looking through glass** portends
bitter disappointment. **Breaking glass dishes** is a
sign of bad luck in business. **Cut glass** is a
symbol of the dreamer's brain and talent. **Looking through
a clear glass window** means that the dreamer will find
employment with superiors, but **looking through clouded
glass** means a bad job.

Glass Blower — This means that the dreamer will effect a
cosmetic change in his business that will not help him.

Glass House — A **dream about a glass house** symbolizes
the damage that will occur as a result of flattery. A **young
woman dreaming about living in a glass house** is warned of
trouble and losing her good reputation.

Glasses (for drinking) — **Dreaming about glasses** means
that the dreamer's business will undergo changes caused by
strangers, and he will be taken for a ride. **Broken glasses**
signal disputes resulting from engaging in illegal pastimes.

Gleaning — **Seeing gleaners busy in a dream** is a sign
of prosperity to the dreamer, and of plentiful crops to the
farmer. If the **dreamer is involved in gleaning,** he will come
into an estate for which he will have to fight.

Gloom — This is a warning of imminent loss and bad
luck.

Glory — This is a sign that the dreamer has reached the
peak of his achievements and from here on, it is only
downhill.

Gloves — Losing gloves means a loss of control in

business or a monetary loss due to incorrect decision-making.

Glue — A **dream about glue** signifies confidence and a senior position in the work place. If the **dream is about fixing objects with glue**, it is a warning about financial problems.

Goat — This symbolizes virility. It sometimes foretells a substantial reward for hard work.

Goblet — **Drinking from a silver goblet** predicts bad business results. **Fancy goblets** mean that the dreamer will receive favors and good things from strangers.

God — A **dream about God** as an abstraction, as a concrete object (such as a religious sculpture) or as a deity image, or if **one dreams of any kind of ritual**, this reflects the dreamer's connection to religion. A **dream about God** heralds calmness, stability, and security. **Worshipping God** means that the dreamer will feel remorse for an error for which he alone is responsible.

Goggles — This is a warning to the dreamer not to be conned into lending money to dubious companions.

Gold — **Finding gold in a dream** means that the dreamer will attain high achievements and reach the goals which he has set for himself. **Losing gold** means that the dreamer underestimates  important issues. **Touching gold** means that the dreamer will find a new hobby or occupation. **Gold coins** are a sign of prosperity and enjoyable trips.

Goldfish — **Dreaming about goldfish** is a forecast of

great adventures and good marriages. However, **dead goldfish** are a sign of great disappointment and burdens.

Gold Leaf — This is a portent of a successful future.

Golf — A **dream about golf** is a sign of pleasant daydreaming and wishing. If **anything bad happens in golf**, the dreamer can expect to be humiliated by the thoughtlessness of another.

Gong — This is a false warning of illness, or a sign of an extremely annoying loss.

Goose — **Dead geese** warn that the dreamer's expectations will not be fulfilled and he can expect losses. If **he dreams about geese in the grass**, great success can be expected. **Swimming geese** shows an increase in wealth. If the **dreamer is disturbed by the honking of geese**, it is a prediction of a death in his family. **Plucking a goose** is a prediction of an inheritance. **Eating a goose** means that other people will lay claims to the dreamer's assets.

Gooseberries — **Picking gooseberries** is a sign that problems at home or in business will gradually be solved. The dreamer is warned not to eat **green gooseberries** which will bring bad things. **Seeing gooseberries** means that the dreamer will escape doing some awful task.

Gossip — If the **dreamer participates in low gossip**, he will suffer the embarrassing consequences of having confided too much in the wrong person. **Dreaming about being the object of gossip**, however, is a sign of unexpected good things.

Gout — A dream about suffering from gout means that the dreamer will be driven to distraction by the stupidity of some relative, and will also lose money because of the same person.

Grain — This is an excellent dream, predicting wealth and happiness.

Grandparents — Dreaming about a conversation with one's grandparents indicates almost insurmountable difficulties, but the dreamer will ultimately overcome them by taking good advice.

Grapefruit — This is an indication of health problems and a lack of energy and vitality.

Grapes — These symbolize hedonism and the pursuit of pleasure.

Grass — A **dream about grass** indicates that whatever the dreamer desires is within his reach. There is no need for him to wander far off, as it is within his grasp. **Green lawns** indicate that wishes and expectations will be fulfilled.

Grasshopper — A threat is hanging over the dreamer's head.

Grave — **Dreaming about a grave** symbolizes everything the dreamer is lacking: health for a sick person, money for someone of limited means, marriage for single people, etc. **Walking on a grave** is an indication of a bad marriage or premature death. An **empty grave** means disillusionment and losing friends. **Being buried alive** means that the dreamer is about to make a terrible mistake which will be exploited by his enemies. If **he is rescued**, the mistake will ultimately be rectified.

Gravel — **Dreaming about gravel** symbolizes futile

business ventures. **Gravel mixed with sand** means loss of property through bad speculation.

Gravy — Eating gravy means ill health and unprofitable business.

Grease — If the dreamer is covered in grease, it portends that he will be with well-groomed but unpleasant strangers.

Greek — A **dream about reading Greek** means that the dreamer's ideas will finally be heeded and adopted. **Failure to read it** means that he has technical problems.

Green — **Green clothing**: prosperity and happiness; **green fields**: prosperity and abundance for all; **green fruit**: failed efforts, hasty action; **green grass with dry patches**: illness or problems in business; **newly cut-down green trees**: pleasure marred by unhappiness.

Greyhound — **Dreaming about a greyhound** is a good dream. If the **dog is following a young girl**, the dreamer will receive an unexpected bequest. If the **dreamer owns a greyhound**, he will find friends where he expected to find enemies.

Grindstone — **Turning a grindstone** indicates an energetic life that brings prosperity. If the **dreamer is sharpening tools on the grindstone**, he will make a good marriage. **Dealing in grindstones** means a small but honest income.

Groans — **Hearing groans** warns the dreamer that he has to act quickly if he wants to prevent his enemies from harming him. If **he is groaning with fear**, he will be delighted at the upward trend of his business, and at pleasant encounters with friends.

Groceries — Fresh, hygienically wrapped groceries signify a pleasant life without hardship.

Grotto — This is a sign of unsatisfactory friendships. The dreamer's quality of life will deteriorate from relative comfort to insufferable poverty.

Grove — A **dream about a grove**, particularly a green grove, means that life will change for the better. A **dying grove** (as a result of fire or disease) means that the dreamer should make provision for his old age.

Guardian — Dreaming about a guardian means that the dreamer will be treated considerately by his friends.

Guitar — If the **dreamer has a guitar**, it is a sign of merrymaking and being deeply in love. **Playing a guitar** symbolizes domestic harmony.

Gulls — A **dream about gulls** prophesies dealing amiably with miserly people. **Dead gulls** mean estrangement from friends.

Gun / Pistol — Dreaming about a shot from a pistol suggests a lack of progress in business, as well as stagnation. The dreamer must change his ways in order to alter the trend.

Guidance / Instruction — This means that there is likely to be a meeting in the near future with a person who has a positive influence over the dreamer.

Gutter (of a roof) — The **gutter in all its forms** means that the dreamer can expect a long and worry-free life. **Climbing up a gutter** indicates that the dreamer wants to run away from solving his problems.

Gutter (of a street) — **Seeing a gutter in a dream** is a sign of dissipation. The dreamer will cause misfortune to others. If **he finds something valuable in a gutter**, his right to particular property will be queried.

Gymnast — This dream means bad luck in business ventures.

Gypsy — **Dreaming about a gypsy** warns the dreamer to watch out for a swindler who will make him suffer in the future. **If the dreamer himself appears as a gypsy**, it is a sign that in the future he will wander to another land to seek happiness. **Dreaming about visiting a gypsy camp** means that the dreamer will receive an important proposition. If a **woman has her fortune told by gypsies**, she will make a hasty and bad marriage. If **she is married**, she will be unjustifiably jealous of her husband. For a **man to talk to a gypsy** is a warning about losing of valuable assets. **Trading with a gypsy** predicts loss of money as a result of speculation.

Haggard — Seeing a haggard face means bad luck in love. If the **dreamer's own face is haggard and unhappy**, it means that women are making him unable to deal with his business affairs as he should.

Hail — **Dreaming about being caught in a hailstorm** means failure in any enterprise. If the **dreamer sees hail falling while the sun is shining**, he will be bothered by small worries which will soon disappear. **Hearing the pounding of hail** is a bad sign.

Hair — **Thick, healthy hair** means that the dreamer will soon be involved in successful projects. If a **man dreams about thinning hair**, it means that his over-generosity will lead to poverty. **Neatly combed hair** is a sign of good luck. A **dream about unusually colored hair** indicates anxiety, hesitation and suspicion. If **one's hair turns white overnight**, it portends a sudden tragedy.

Hairbrush — Seeing a hairbrush is a sign of mismanagement of the dreamer's affairs. An **old hairbrush** means illness.

Hairdresser — Dreaming about a hairdresser reflects the dreamer's dejection and depression. It is also a sign of a possible scandal, both for men and for women.

Hairy Hands — **Dreaming about hairy hands** signifies that the dreamer is conspiring against innocent people, and that he has enemies who aim to stop him. **Hands covered with hair** also mean that the dreamer will never be prominent among his associates.

Halter — **Putting a halter on a young horse** predicts success in business and love. **Leading a donkey by the**

halter means that the dreamer will be influential with both sexes.

Ham — A **dream about ham** is a warning against treachery. **Large slices of ham** mean that the dreamer will overcome all competition. If **he eats ham**, he will lose something of value. **Dealing in ham** is a sign of health and prosperity.

Hammer — The dreamer should consider his steps carefully and not waste money.

Hand — A **beautiful hand** is a sign of great esteem and professional success. An **ugly, misshapen hand** indicates poverty and disillusionment. **Washing hands** predicts the dreamer's participation in a happy event. A **dirty hand** means that the dreamer is facing a difficult period in his life. A **bound hand** indicates that his sadness will turn into happiness and joy. **Seeing blood on one's hands** is a sign of immediate bad luck.

Handbills — **Dreaming about distributing handbills** foretells lawsuits and disputes. **Printing handbills** is a sign of bad news.

Handcuffs — **Handcuffs** symbolize an impossible relationship or problems related to the judicial system. A **dream about being released from handcuffs** means that the dreamer is not an ordinary person.

Handicap — If the **dreamer dreams that he is handicapped**, he can expect an improvement in his status and in other areas of life. **Overcoming a handicap** means that the dreamer will overcome obstacles along his path; the **opposite** is true as well.

Handkerchief — **Searching for a handkerchief** in a dream is a sign of an imminent separation. If a **handkerchief is found easily**, it means that the dreamer will soon receive a gift. **Seeing silk handkerchiefs** means that the dreamer's warm and charismatic personality will bring joy to others, and therefore to himself. **Dreaming about dirty handkerchiefs** warns that the dreamer will be corrupted by unsuitable companions. **Torn handkerchiefs** are a sign of irreconcilable breakups between lovers. **Pure white handkerchiefs** signify that he will resist the flattery of immoral people and will succeed in love and marriage. **Colored handkerchiefs** mean that the dreamer's affairs are not exactly pristine, but he is so discreet and skilled in handling them that he cannot be censured.

Handsome — If the **dreamer sees himself as handsome**, it means that he is excellent at flattery. If **others are handsome**, the dreamer will hang out with dubious company.

Handwriting — Dreaming of identifying one's own handwriting means that enemies will use the dreamer's opinions to thwart his aspirations for a particular position.

Hanging — If the **dreamer sees himself being hanged**, it indicates a promising career. If **another person is being hanged**, it means that one of the dreamer's acquaintances will become famous.

Happiness — Contrary to what it seems, dreaming of happiness forecasts times of hardship and danger, particularly at the workplace.

Harbor — See **Port**.

Hare — If a **hare escapes from the dreamer**, he will lose something of value. If the **dreamer catches a hare**, he will win a competition. A **dead hare** signifies the death of a friend. A **hare being chased by dogs** means strife among the dreamer's friends. **Shooting a hare** means that the dreamer will have to resort to violence to defend his property.

Harem — If the **dreamer keeps a harem**, it means that he is wasting himself on base pleasures. A **woman who dreams about belonging to a harem** generally goes after married men.

Harlequin — A **dream about a harlequin** means trouble. If the **dreamer is dressed as a harlequin**, he will make serious mistakes that will cost him dearly, both in money and in moral conscience.

Harlot — **Being with a harlot** means trouble socially and financially. **Marrying a harlot** means placing one's life in jeopardy at the hands of an enemy.

Harness — A shiny new harness is an indication of a nice trip.

Harp — **Hearing the sound of a harp** attests to the dreamer's melancholy nature. A **broken harp** means that the dreamer has health problems. If the **dreamer himself is playing the harp**, it is a warning that he is the victim of some sort of deception concerning his love life.

Harvest — One of the best images one can dream. It predicts economic, family and social success.

Hash — **Eating hash** is a sign of trouble and unhappiness which will undermine the dreamer's health. **Cooking hash** indicates that a woman will be jealous of her husband.

Hassock — This dream indicates that the dreamer will forfeit his power and possessions to someone else.

Hat — If the **dreamer wears a hat**, it signifies imminent disappointment. If **he loses a hat**, it means he will soon receive a gift. **Finding a hat** in a dream is a sign that the dreamer will soon lose a small item. The **inability to remove one's hat** is a warning of disease.

Hatchet — As a result of profligacy, the dreamer will be the victim of the plots of people who are envious of him.

Hate — **Dreaming about hating someone** warns the dreamer that he is liable to cause that person an injury, and that he will suffer financial losses and worries. If the **dreamer is hated unjustifiably**, it means that his friends and associates are positive and faithful. Usually, this is a bad dream.

Hawk — **Seeing a hawk** is a sign that the dreamer will be cheated. **Shooting a hawk** means that he will finally overcome stubborn obstacles. It also means that the dreamer will probably win a competition with his enemies. A **dead hawk** means the defeat of enemies.

Hay — **Mowing hay** is a good sign, a sign of abundance for farmers. **Newly cut hay** indicates prosperity. **Carrying, storing, loading** hay indicates good fortune. **Feeding cattle with hay** means that the dreamer will help someone who will reciprocate by promoting the dreamer to a higher position.

Head — **Seeing a well-shaped head in a dream** means that the dreamer will meet powerful people who will help him in important undertakings. **Dreaming about his own head** is a warning of trouble in that part of the body. **Seeing a bloody severed head** is a sign of bitter disappointments and dashed hopes. **Dreaming about having an aching head** is a sign of worry. A **swollen head** means that the dreamer's life will basically be positive. **Dreaming about a child's head** is a sign of enjoyment and prosperity. **Seeing an animal's head** is a sign of base desires and solely material pleasures. If the **dreamer washes his head**, important people will seek his advice and judgment. If the **dreamer sees himself wounded in the head**, it is a sign that he has hidden enemies. **Having two or more heads** indicates a meteoric rise in life, but one that is not enduring.

Headache — This indicates that one of the dreamer's friends needs his help.

Headgear — **Rich headgear** is a sign of success and fame. **Old, worn headgear** means that the dreamer will have to relinquish his possessions to someone else.

Headlights — If the dreamer is blinded by the headlights of a car, it means that he should take steps quickly in order to prevent possible complications.

Hearing Aid — Using a hearing aid means that the dreamer did not pay enough attention to something that would be of great significance to him.

Hearing Voices — If the **voices are pleasant**, the dream signifies a reconciliation. If **they are strident**, trouble and disappointment will follow.

Hearse — **Seeing a hearse** is a sign of domestic strife and trouble in business. It also signifies the illness or death of someone close to the dreamer. If a **hearse crosses the path of the dreamer**, he will have to take on a sworn enemy.

Heart — An **aching heart** is a sign of trouble in the dreamer's business. If the **dreamer sees his own heart**, he will become weak and ill. An **animal's heart** means victory over enemies and winning other people's respect.

Heartache — If a young woman has a heartache, it means that she will suffer from the shabby treatment she receives at the hands of her lover.

Heaven — **Going up to heaven** means that the dreamer will not receive esteem, and happiness will become sadness. **Being in heaven and meeting Christ** means that the dreamer will suffer many losses. **Climbing up to heaven on a ladder** means an unprecedented rise in status without much joy.

Heaviness — A feeling of heaviness means that the dreamer is grappling with heavy and fateful issues.

Heavy Rain — See **Flood**.

Hedges — **Evergreen hedges** portend prosperity and happiness. **Bare hedges** portend unhappiness and mistakes in business. **Being caught in a thorny hedge** means that the dreamer will be held back in his work by partners or subordinates.

Heel — A broken heel means that the dreamer will have to confront problems and hardship in the near future.

Heir — Dreaming about being an heir to property means that the dreamer risks losing what he has. Sometimes good things follow this dream.

Helicopter — A **helicopter hovering over the dreamer** is a sign that a guest is about to arrive. If the **helicopter seems menacing**, the visitor will be dangerous. **Hearing the noise of a helicopter** is a sign of an imminent journey.

Hell — **Dreaming about hell** indicates that the dreamer is greedy and materialistic, and that the thing that preoccupies him most is money. A **dream about hell** does not bode well. Financial losses can be expected, and the dreamer's enemies will rejoice.

Helmet — This means that sadness and loss can be prevented if the dreamer acts wisely.

Hemp — This signifies success in all ventures.

Hemp Seed — This is an indication of deep, enduring friendship, as well as the opportunity to make money.

Hen / Rooster — A **hen with chicks** indicates the need to plan ahead with precision before acting. **Hearing a rooster in a dream** indicates exaggerated self-confidence.

Hen's Nest — This symbolizes domestic harmony and delightful children.

Herbs — After **dreaming about herbs**, the dreamer will experience some hassles, followed by enjoyment. **Poisonous herbs** indicate enemies. **Helpful herbs** mean good business and friendships.

Hermit — **Dreaming about a hermit** signifies distress and loneliness as a result of disloyal friends. If the **dreamer is a hermit**, he will take great interest in current affairs. If **he finds himself in a hermit's hut**, it is a sign of great unselfishness and magnanimity toward both friends and enemies.

Heron — Dreaming about a heron suggests a change occurring in the dreamer's life. **Seeing a heron** can be interpreted as a symbol of stagnation, lack of development and being stuck in a groove.

Herring — This indicates an embarrassingly tight financial situation from which the dreamer will finally extricate himself.

Hide (of an animal) — This is a sign of a secure job and prosperity.

Hiding-place — If the dreamer hides in a hiding-place, this is a sign that he will soon receive bad news.

Hieroglyphs — **Seeing hieroglyphics** portends that the dreamer's indecisiveness in an important matter will cause him trouble and financial loss. If the **dreamer can decipher hieroglyphs**, it means that he will overcome bad things.

High School — Dreaming of a high school means progress in love, social and business affairs.

High Tide — This is a sign of progress in the dreamer's ventures.

Hills — **Reaching the top of hills** is good, but if the dreamer does not get there, he will have to combat envy and setbacks. A **bald hill** is a sign of famine and suffering.

Hippopotamus — This warns of being overweight or refers to feelings of inferiority.

Hips — **Admiring curvy hips** means that the dreamer will be yelled at by his wife. If a **woman admires her own hips**, she will be disappointed in love. If she **dreams that her hips are narrow**, it predicts illness and disappointment.

Hissing — A **dream about hissing** signifies that the dreamer will be furious at the inconsiderate treatment he is subjected to by new acquaintances. If **they actually hiss at the dreamer**, he risks losing a friend.

History — Dreaming about reading history means passing time pleasantly.

Hives (on body) — If the **dreamer sees hives on his child**, it means that the child will be obedient and healthy. If **strange children have hives**, the dreamer will be worried about his own children.

Hoe — **Seeing a hoe** means that the dreamer will have to work hard to support others. **Using a hoe** means that the dreamer will avoid poverty by working hard. A **woman who dreams of hoeing** will be self-sufficient.

Hogs — **Fat, healthy hogs** mean positive changes in business. **Lean hogs** mean trouble with children and employees. **Hearing hogs squeal** is a sign of bad news from faraway friends, death, or losses in business. **Feeding hogs** signifies an increase in the dreamer's assets. If **hogs are eating fruit in an orchard**, the dreamer will lose property while trying to take something that does not belong to him. **Dealing in hogs** means that the dreamer will make a lot of money, but will have to work very hard for it.

Holiday — This is a sign that interesting strangers will enjoy the dreamer's hospitality.

Holy Communion — **Taking communion** warns that the dreamer will give up his principles in order to pursue some superficial pleasure. If the **dreamer feels worthy of taking**

communion, but is denied it, it means that he will receive a position that he never dreamt possible. If **he feels unworthy**, he will have trouble.

Home — **Visiting one's old home** portends good news. If **the old home is dilapidated**, it warns of the death or illness of a relative. **Returning to a bright and pleasant home** means domestic harmony and prosperity in business.

Homesick — This means that the dreamer will miss out on the chance to take pleasant trips.

Homicide — This foretells great humiliation at the hands of others, and the dreamer's despair will distress others.

Hominy — This is an indication of love which is a wonderful diversion from study and business preoccupations.

Honey — This symbolizes happiness and joy. The dreamer will attain his objectives and enjoy the fruits of his labor and efforts.

Honeysuckle — This signifies prosperity and domestic bliss.

Honor — This is a sign that the dreamer must take precautions in money matters and adopt more economical patterns of behavior.

Hood — A young woman who wears a hood in a dream will soon try to seduce a decent man.

Hook — This is a sign of heavy, unpleasant burdens for the dreamer.

Hoop — **Dreaming about a hoop** is an indication that the dreamer will befriend important people. His advice will be sought. **Dreaming about anyone jumping through hoops** indicates problems that will ultimately be solved.

Hops — This is a sign of energy, thrift and the ability to make the most of any business venture.

Horn (animal) — Dreaming about an animal's horn signifies sexual problems. The interpretation of the dream depends on the context in which the horn appears.

Horn (brass) — **Hearing notes from a horn** foretells excellent news. A **broken horn** is a sign of death or mishap. **Seeing children playing horns** signifies domestic harmony. A **woman blowing a horn** means that she wants marriage more than her lover does.

Hornet — **Seeing a hornet** signifies broken friendships and financial loss. If a **woman is stung by one**, it means that her rivals want to humiliate her in front of her admirers.

Horoscope — **Dreaming about having a horoscope drawn up** indicates a long journey and changes in business matters. If the **stars are pointed out to the dreamer while being read,** he can expect disappointment instead of luck.

Horse — **Dreaming about a horse** symbolizes passion or lust. **Riding a white horse** indicates business and social success. **Riding a black horse** signifies failure. A **runaway horse** is a sign of financial losses. **Falling off a horse** indicates a hasty, rushed marriage. **Riding a wild horse** reflects strong sexual passion. **Racing horses** means a predilection for a wild life. **Riding bareback** is a sign of faithful associates and success. If the **dreamer rides bareback with women,** he will have lewd desires, and these will prevent him from being really successful. A **dead horse** means disappointment. **Killing a horse** means hurting friends as a result of egoism. **Seeing piebald horses** is a sign of lucrative deals. If the **horse fords a stream**, it is a sign of good luck and great enjoyment. A **muddy stream** will mean that the pleasures are diminished. **Swimming on a horse's back through a limpid stream,** the dreamer's fantasies of ecstasy will come true. This is a good dream for **a businessman. Having a horse shod** is a sign of good luck — and for a woman, of a faithful husband. If the **dreamer shoes a horse,** he will probably succeed in a spurious deal.

Horse Race — If the **dreamer is a woman**, it indicates she will soon have marital problems. If the **dreamer is a man**, it warns of danger from an unexpected source. The dreamer must take care and beware. (See also **Horse.**)

Horseradish — **Dreaming about horseradish** foretells amicable friendships with pleasant and intelligent people. It is also a sign of prosperity. **Eating horseradish** in a dream means that others will tease the dreamer gently.

Horseshoe — This means the dreamer will set out for a sea voyage in the near future.

Horse Trader — A **dream about a horse trader** means that risky ventures will be extremely profitable. If the **dreamer is cheated by a horse trader**, it means that he will have bad luck in love or business. If the **horse received in the trade is better than the dreamer's previous one**, it is a sign of increased wealth.

Hospital — If a **healthy person dreams about a hospital,** it means that he fears disease and death. **Dreaming about**

being treated in a hospital by a medical staff indicates fear of the future.

Hot Pepper — This reflects feelings of pride resulting from the success of someone close to the dreamer.

Hotel — **Dreaming about a hotel** means that the dreamer needs changes in his life and warns against making hasty decisions in life. **Dreaming about living in a hotel** is a sign of comfort and prosperity. **Visiting women in a hotel** is a sign of a decadent life. **Seeing a fine hotel** means travel and wealth. **Being the proprietor of a hotel** means that the dreamer will accumulate all the money he is ever meant to earn. **Working in a hotel** hints that the dreamer could find a more lucrative job. **Searching for a hotel** means that the dreamer will be foiled in his search for riches and happiness.

Hounds — A **dream about hunting hounds** portends positive changes and pleasures. If a **woman dreams about hounds**, she will love a man of a lower social class. If **she is being followed by hounds**, she will have many admirers who feel very little for her.

House — **Dreaming about building a house** means that the dreamer will make good changes in his business affairs. **Owning a nice house** means that the dreamer will soon move to an even better one. **Old, shabby houses** are an indication of bad luck in every venture.

Housekeeper — **Dreaming about being a housekeeper** means that the dreamer is happy with his/her tasks and occupations. **Employing one** means that the dreamer will be comfortably off.

Hug — Hugging, particularly a family member or a

person close to the dreamer, reflects his need to give of himself to others.

Humidity — This is a sign of a fierce struggle against enemies, which the dreamer will lose totally. It also indicates that the dreamer will be cursed and will not be able to view the future with any optimism.

Hunchback — This indicates great success in the near future.

Hunger — **Dreaming about hunger** is a bad sign, as it indicates a lack of domestic harmony. For **lovers**, it is a sign of a bad marriage.

Hunting — The dreamer struggles for impossible things. If **he hunts animals successfully**, he will achieve his objectives despite the obstacles along the way. **Hunting deer** signifies failure in business or agriculture.

Hurricane — **Seeing a hurricane rampaging** means that the dreamer will experience terrible tension as he attempts to save his business from disaster. If the **dreamer is trying to rescue someone from the ruins of a house**, it means that he will move house and make changes, but not achieve happiness. If **he sees hurricane casualties**, it means that he will be upset about other people's troubles.

Hurt — If the **dreamer hurts someone in a dream**, he will hurt other people cruelly. If **he is hurt**, he will be defeated by enemies.

Husband — If a **woman dreams that her husband is leaving her for no reason**, a bitter period will be followed by reconciliation. If **she dreams about her husband's death**, she will have grief and disillusionment.

Hut — **Dreaming about sleeping in a hut** predicts illness and discontent. A **hut in a green pasture** means prosperity, but not constant happiness.

Hyacinth — This portends a heart-rending separation from a friend, which, however, will ultimately turn out for the better.

Hydrophobia (rabies) — If the **dreamer has hydrophobia**, it is an indication of enemies and changes in the dreamer's business. If **he sees others with the disease**, death will interrupt his work. If a **rabid animal bites him**, it means that he will be betrayed by his closest friend, amidst flurries of scandal.

Hyena — A **dream about a hyena** is a sign of misfortune and trouble, as well as of unpleasantness with acquaintances. An **attack by a hyena** portends an attempt to ruin the dreamer's reputation.

Hymns — This is a sign of domestic happiness and reasonable prosperity.

Hypnotist — If the **dreamer is in a hypnotic state**, it means that his enemies have him in their power. If **he is the one who has others in his power**, it means that he will rule his environment.

Hypocrite — If **anyone has acted hypocritically toward the dreamer**, it means that he has been betrayed to his enemies by disloyal friends. If **h e himself is a hypocrite**, he will act falsely with his friends.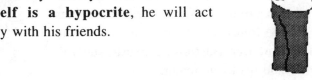

Ice — **Seeing ice** is a sign of trouble, as evil people will try to sabotage the dreamer's work. **Ice floating in a clear stream** means that the dreamer's contentment will be disrupted by the malice of envious friends. **Walking on ice** means risking solid benefits for fleeting pleasures. **Eating ice** is a sign of illness, as is drinking ice water.

Ice-skating — A **dream about ice-skating** warns of flattery, or of a shaky relationship with the person who is most loved by the dreamer. If the **dreamer sees himself ice-skating**, it warns him that he may lose his job.

Ice-cream — A **dream about ice-cream** indicates success in ventures undertaken by the dreamer. If **children eat ice-cream in a dream**, it indicates joy and prosperity. **Ice-cream that has gone off** means that the dreamer's joy will be marred. **Melted ice-cream** means that his pleasures will not reach consummation.

Icicles — **Icicles falling off trees** means the disappearance of worries. If **they are on the eaves of houses**, it is an indication of poverty, lack, and illness. If **they are seen on the fence, on trees or on evergreens**, it is a prediction of bad things and an unhappy future.

Ideal — A **dream about the ideal man** means that a woman will have uninterrupted enjoyment and happiness. A **dream about the ideal woman (by a bachelor)** means that he will soon experience a positive change in his affairs.

Idiot — An **idiot in a dream** predicts losses and disputes. If the **dreamer is the idiot**, he will experience humiliation and sadness about failed plans. If **children are idiots**, nothing good is in store for the dreamer.

Idle — **Dreaming about being idle** means a failure to attain one's objectives. **Idle friends** mean that they will have a problem.

Idols — A **dream about idol-worship** means that the dreamer will not advance as he allows little things to get to him. **Iconoclasm** means that the dreamer will succeed, whatever the obstacles. **Others worshipping idols** means that the dreamer will fall out with his friends.

Illness — If a woman dreams about having an illness, it means that she will be furious about missing some entertainment event she had been looking forward to due to unforeseen circumstances.

Illumination — **Strange illuminations in a dream** mean failure on every count. **Illuminated heavens** with distorted heavenly bodies means grief and sorrow in the extreme. If the dreamer sees **illuminated snakes or other crawling creatures**, it means that his enemies will go to any length to defeat him.

Images — The **sight of images** presages failure in love and business. **Ugly images** mean domestic strife.

Imitation — A dream about imitation means that the dreamer will be deceived.

Immortality — If the dreamer discusses the immortality of the soul, it means that he is on the path to greater knowledge and the opportunity to discuss things with cultured people.

Implements — A **dream about implements** means that the dreamer cannot carry out his plans. **Broken implements** mean illness, death, or business failure.

Imps — Dreaming about imps is a forecast of trouble resulting from casual enjoyment. If the **dreamer is an imp**, his own stupidity will lead to poverty.

Inauguration — Dreaming about an inauguration intimates that the dreamer will reach the highest position he has ever had.

Incantation — **Using incantations in a dream** indicates disputes between spouses or lovers. If **others repeat the incantation**, it signifies that your friends are not being genuine in their behavior.

Incense — A dream in which the dreamer burns or smells incense is an indication of dear friends and a promising future.

Incest — Dreaming about incestuous actions means that the dreamer will fall in disgrace from a high position, as well as suffering financial losses.

Incoherence — This is usually a manifestation of a state of great agitation because of a rapid sequence of events.

Income — **Dreaming about receiving one's income** means that the dreamer might cheat someone or cause his family anguish. If **someone in his family comes into an income**, it means success. If the **dreamer's income is not enough**, this means that there will be trouble for people close to him.

Increase — Dreaming about an increase in one's family means that the dreamer may face failure in some plans, and success in others.

Independence — If the **dreamer dreams about being very independent**, it is a warning of a rival who seeks to do him harm. If he **dreams about becoming independently wealthy**, it means that his future looks rosy.

Indifference — This dream indicates brief, amiable friendships.

Indigestion — This is an indication of an unhealthy, depressing environment.

Indigo — **Seeing indigo** means that the dreamer will con friendly and innocent people out of their possessions. **Indigo water** is an indication of a sordid love affair.

Indistinctness — If the dreamer sees things indistinctly, it is a sign of disloyalty in friendships and unsuccessful business ventures.

Indulgence — If a woman dreams about indulgence, it means that her behavior will be censured.

Industry — A dream about being industrious means that the dreamer will spend a lot of time and effort devising plans and ideas for advancement, and these will pay off.

Infants — **Seeing a newborn infant in a dream** predicts good things for the dreamer. If the **infant swims**, it means that the dreamer will extricate himself from some embroilment.

Infirmary — Dreaming about leaving an infirmary symbolizes escaping from enemies who cause the dreamer a lot of concern.

Infirmity — An **infirmity** is a negative sign, meaning bad luck in business, health and love. Enemies should not be underestimated. If **other people have infirmities**, it means that the dreamer will be unsuccessful and disappointed in business.

Influence — If the **dreamer hopes to advance by means**

of the influence and intervention of people in high places, he will be disappointed. If, however, **he is highly placed**, his prospects are excellent. If **he sees highly placed friends**, he will be free from anxieties.

Inheritance — **Dreaming about receiving an inheritance** means that the dreamer will attain all his wishes and objectives. **Inheriting jewelry** signifies unexpected, but not altogether positive, prosperity.

Injury — If someone does the dreamer an injury, it signifies that he will soon be aggravated by some mishap.

Ink — If **ink is spilt on the dreamer's clothing**, he will be subjected to many little nasty digs. If **he has ink on his fingers**, his jealousy will cause him to hurt someone else, unless he controls himself. **Red ink** is a sign of serious trouble. **Making ink** is indicative of a lowly occupation, and **bottles of ink** mean enemies and failure in business.

Inkstand — **Full inkstands** are a sign of vicious slander spread by enemies. **Empty ones** mean a narrow escape from public censure for some alleged injustice.

Inn — A **well-appointed, comfortable inn** signifies prosperity and an enjoyable life. A **wretched, miserable inn** is a sign of failure, undesirable jobs and unwanted journeys.

Inquest — This indicates bad luck in friendships.

Inquisition — A **dream about the inquisition** means nothing but trouble and distress. If the **dreamer is brought before an inquisition**, he will be powerless in the face of vicious slander.

Insanity — **Being insane** is a terrible forecast if it occurs at the beginning of a project. It could involve the dreamer's ill health. If **others are insane in the dream**, it means that the dreamer will have unpleasant contact with poor, distressed people. He should exercise great caution after this dream.

Inscription — **Seeing an inscription** indicates the approach of bad news. If the **dreamer is reading inscriptions on tombs**, he will become seriously ill. If he writes one, he will lose a dear friend.

Insect (crawling) — Despite unpleasant connotations, a significant, positive change can be expected in the dreamer's life.

Insect — This symbolizes difficulties and disappointments in the business or domestic life of the dreamer.

Insult — This indicates that the dreamer has a strong desire for change in his life (in his job or place of residence).

Intemperance — Being intemperate in love or other emotions presages illness, financial loss or a drop in esteem.

Intercede — If the dreamer intercedes on the part of someone else, he will receive assistance in time of need.

Interpreter — Dreaming about an interpreter means that the dreamer will become involved in unprofitable matters.

Intersection — This signifies exactly that: The dreamer has come to a crossroads in his life and must make decisions that will affect his destiny.

Interview — An interview suggests that there will be a promotion in the near future and good news from a close acquaintance.

Intestines — The **appearance of intestines in a dream** is extremely negative, predicting a catastrophe that will cause the death of the dreamer's friend. If **he sees his own intestines**, it means that he will fall ill with a disease that will cut him off from his surroundings.

Intoxication — This is an indication that the dreamer is harboring secret immoral desires.

Inundation — **Seeing cities or countries underwater** predicts catastrophes and massive loss of life. If **people are swept away in an inundation**, it is a sign of death and despair. If an **extensive area is under clear water**, it signifies prosperity after what seemed a hopeless battle.

Invalid — A **dream about invalids** means that the dreamer is in disagreeable company who want to harm his interests. If **he is an invalid**, it warns of negative conditions.

Invective — **Dreaming about invective** is a warning against outbursts of anger with close friends. If **others spew invective**, it means that the dreamer is being trapped by enemies.

Inventor — **Dreaming about an inventor** means that the dreamer will soon be renowned for some special project. If the **dreamer is inventing something**, he will be successful in his plans and in financial matters.

Invite — A **dream about inviting people to one's home** means that some disturbing event is imminent. **Receiving an invitation** means that the dreamer will hear bad news.

Iron (metal) — **Dreaming about iron** is a very bad sign. An **iron weight** in a dream means worries and financial loss. **Old rusty iron** is a symbol of poverty and disillusionment. A

red-hot iron means lack of success due to misguided enthusiasm.

Ironing — This is a sign of a good period during which the dreamer will cooperate successfully with those around him.

Island — **Being on an island in a clear-water stream** means good trips and luck in business. **For a woman**, it also means a happy marriage. A **barren island** means exactly the opposite, due to the dreamer's extreme behavior. **Seeing an island** is a positive sign for the dreamer's future after many struggles.

Itch — A **dream about itching** means disagreeable jobs. If the **dreamer itches**, he will be viciously accused, and will defend yourself by accusing others.

Ivory — **Seeing ivory** is a lucky dream. **Seeing large pieces of ivory** means unadulterated enjoyment and financial gain.

Ivy — **Dreaming about ivy** indicates that the dreamer is sensitive and dedicated to the traditions he grew up with and to the people close to him. **Ivy growing on trees** is a forecast of joy, excellent health and good fortune. **Withered ivy** is a symbol of misery and broken relationships.

Jackdaw — A **dream about a jackdaw** is a bad sign, forecasting disease and disputes. If the **dreamer catches a jackdaw**, he will overcome his enemies. **Killing a jackdaw** means receiving controversial property.

Jail — Seeing others in jail means that the dreamer will be compelled to give undeserving people privileges.

Jailer — A **jailer in a dream** means that the dreamer's interests will be threatened by treachery. He will be fascinated by bad women. If **he sees a jail being overrun by a rowdy mob**, he will be in extreme danger of having money extorted from him.

Jam — **Dreaming about eating jam** is a sign of nice surprises and trips. **Making jam** indicates a happy home and good friends.

Janitor — This dream signifies mismanagement, undisciplined children, and uncooperative employees.

January — The dreamer will be landed with unwanted companions or children.

Jar — **Empty jars** are a sign of poverty and trouble. Full jars are a sign of success. **Broken jars** warn the dreamer of illness and profound disappointment.

Jasmine — This indicates that the dreamer is not exploiting even a fraction of his talents and abilities.

Jasper — This is a good sign, meaning love and success.

Jaundice — **Dreaming about jaundice** is a sign of prosperity after a setback. If the **dreamer sees others with jaundice**, he will be plagued by business worries and disagreeable companions.

Javelin — If the **dreamer has to defend himself with a javelin**, it means that his most private affairs have become public in order to prove him guilty of perjury; only after a lot of arguing will he establish his innocence. If a **javelin wounds him**, his enemies will defeat him. **Seeing others carrying javelins** is a threat to the dreamer's interests.

Jaws — **Ugly, distorted jaws** symbolize disputes and bad feelings between friends. **Dreaming about being in the jaws of a wild animal** means that the dreamer's business and domestic harmony are being threatened by enemies.

Jaybird — A **dream about a jaybird** is a forecast of agreeable visits with friends and pleasant conversation. A **dead jaybird** means domestic strife and trouble.

Jealousy — **Being jealous of one's wife** shows that the dreamer has fallen under the influence of his enemies and mean-minded people. A **woman jealous of her husband** will get many shocks which will shake her out of her complacency. If **people are jealous about ordinary things**, they will be plagued by many anxieties in daily business.

Jelly — **Dreaming about eating jelly** is indicative of many nice interruptions. A **woman making jelly** will have happy reunions with friends.

Jester — This implies a neglect of important things for the pursuit of trivial things.

Jewelry — **Dreaming about jewelry** is a sign that that the dreamer is lucky. **Broken jewelry** portends disappointment. **Receiving jewelry as a gift** signifies a happy marriage. **Losing jewelry in a dream** suggests troubles brought about by gambling.

Jewels — **Dreaming about jewels** is usually a dream of happiness and wealth. **Wearing them** — either the dreamer or others — is a sign of rank and fulfilled ambitions. **Jeweled clothing** is amazing good luck for the dreamer. For a **woman to receive jewels** means happiness and a good marriage. **Losing jewels** means that she will be taken in by flattery and conned. **Buying jewels** means that the dreamer will be extremely successful in love.

Jew's Harp — **Dreaming about a jew's harp** indicates a slight improvement in the dreamer's affairs. If **he plays one**, he will fall in love with a stranger.

Jig — **Dancing a jig** is a sign of happy, lighthearted and joyful pastimes. If the **dreamer's sweetheart dances**, it is a sign of a cheerful disposition.

Jockey — **Dreaming about a jockey** means that the dreamer will be glad to receive a gift from an unexpected quarter. If a **jockey is thrown from his horse**, the dreamer will be asked to provide assistance to strangers.

Jolly — **Being jolly in company** means that the dreamer will be blessed with well-behaved children and success in business. If the **jollity is marred at all**, he will have worries.

Journey — A **good, pleasant journey** signifies positive things, while a **bad, uncomfortable journey** means the opposite. If a **long journey is cut short**, it means that the dreamer finished a long project in a short time, but was paid the same, so it was profitable.

Journeyman — **Dreaming about a journeyman** indicates money wasted on futile trips. For a **woman**, the trips are unexpected but nice.

Joy — If the dreamer feels joy about some event, harmony will reign among his friends.

Jubilee — This dream means that the dreamer will be involved in many happy events.

Judge — **Dreaming about a judge** clearly indicates that the dreamer must not be quick to judge other people or determine their guilt or innocence. **Coming before a judge** means that a dispute will only be settled in court.

Judgment Day — If the **dreamer is optimistic about being unpunished on Judgment Day**, he will accomplish some complicated work. If **he is not optimistic,** he will fail.

Jug — **Dreaming about a jug** is a symbol of good luck. If the **jug is full**, this is a sign of extremely good luck, as well as of true friends who want to promote the dreamer's welfare. A **broken jug** is an indication of illness and employment setbacks. **Drinking wine from a jug** signifies excellent health, optimism and *joie de vivre*. If the **dreamer drinks an unpleasant-tasting drink from a jug**, it means that the anticipation of happy events will turn into disappointment and revulsion.

July — This is a dreary dream, but a sudden change will occur and the dreamer will have unprecedented happiness.

Jumping — **Jumping in a dream** is not a good sign: it means the dreamer can expect hardships, disappointment or frustration. **Jumping rope** is a sign that the dreamer's associates will be dazzled by a daredevil display. If **he jumps rope with children**, it means that he is overbearing and bossy, and his children do not treat him with respect. If **cattle jump over a fence** into the dreamer's property, he will receive unforeseen help. If **they jump out of his property**, he can expect losses.

June — A **dream about June** portends great success. If a **woman dreams that the country is drought-stricken**, this means that she will experience grief and bereavement.

Juniper Trees — **Dreaming about juniper trees** is a symbol of happiness and wealth emerging from misery and poverty. It bodes well for a person recovering from an illness. However, **eating or picking juniper berries** portends problems and disease.

Jury — A **dream about a jury** is a sign of the dreamer's discontent with his job, and he will look for a new one. If the **dreamer is acquitted by the jury**, his business will be successful. If **he is convicted**, he will be roundly defeated by his enemies.

Justice — If the **dreamer demands justice from somebody**, it means that he has been falsely accused by people who are out for his blood. If **someone demands justice of him**, it means that his good name and conduct are being questioned, and it is almost sure that he will not be able to defend them adequately.

Kaleidoscope — This is a symbol of quick changes that will not be of great value.

Kangaroo — A **dream about a kangaroo** means the dreamer is not satisfied with one partner. **Seeing a kangaroo** indicates that the dreamer will outwit a cunning enemy. A **kangaroo hide** is a symbol of success. If a **kangaroo attacks the dreamer,** his good name is in danger.

Katydids — These large green grasshopper-like insects do not bode well, as they are a sign of bad luck and dependence of the dreamer on others.

Keg — A **dream about a keg** symbolizes the dreamer's struggle to free himself from a situation of tyranny. If **the keg is broken,** it is a sign of separation from loved ones.

Kennel/Doghouse — This indicates emotional stress and a lack of calmness, and warns of health problems and physical weakness.

Kettle — **Seeing kettles in a dream** means that there is a lot of work ahead of the dreamer. If the **kettle has not boiled,** it warns against loss of assets. If the **water has boiled,** it predicts changes, success and good luck.

Key — **Any situation involving a key** (except the loss of a key or a broken key) is good news: success in one's personal, social, financial and family life. **Loss of a key** is a warning of things to come. **Broken keys** portend loss through bereavement or envy.

Keyhole — If the **dreamer spies on others through a keyhole,** it means that he will cause mischief by divulging someone else's secrets. If **others spy on him through a keyhole,** it signifies that others are prying into his affairs for their own benefit. **Inability to find a keyhole** means unwitting damage to a friend.

Kidney — **Dreaming about kidneys** is a warning of a serious illness or marital problems for the dreamer. A dream of **overactive kidneys** indicate that the dreamer will be involved in a juicy affair. **Underactive kidneys** mean that a scandal will erupt, not to the dreamer's advantage.

Kid — This dream indicates that the dreamer lacks scruples when it comes to pleasure-seeking. He will break hearts.

Killing — If the **dreamer kills an unarmed man**, it forebodes trouble and sorrow. If the **killing occurs in self-defense**, it means victory and advancement.

King — If a king appears or speaks to the dreamer, it means good things or a change for the better in the dreamer's life.

Kiss — If the **dreamer dreams that he is kissing a stranger**, it is a sign that he is not completely aware of what is occurring in his surroundings, and this could do him great harm. **Kissing his mother** means success and esteem. **Kissing a sibling** means getting on well with him/her. **Kissing his sweetheart in the dark** means illicit behavior, while **in the light** means honorable intentions. **Kissing a strange woman** means promiscuity. **Illicit kissing** means immoral behavior that will bring sorrow into a home. A **rival kissing the dreamer's sweetheart** means that he will go down in her estimation. **Married people kissing** means a happy home. **Kissing on the neck** means succumbing to base passions. **Kissing a bride** means friends making up after a quarrel. If a **bride kisses the dreamer**, it foretells health and prosperity.

Kitchen — A **dream about a kitchen** signifies that the dreamer will have to cope with an unexpected and depressing emergency. In a **woman's dream**, it attests to satisfaction with family life and loyal friends.

Kite — Flying a kite in a dream indicates that the dreamer enjoys sharing his feelings with others and that he will attain all of his objectives in life.

Kittens — **Dreaming about kittens** symbolizes endless hassles and irritations, and the only way to end them is to kill the kittens. A **plump white kitten** means that a woman will be in danger of being deceived, but her common sense prevents it.

Knapsack — A dream about a knapsack indicates happiness that does not come from the company of friends.

Knee — A **smooth, unblemished knee** signifies success and happiness. A **hurt knee** suggests the need to deal with difficulties that will put the dreamer's patience to the test. A **painful knee** means disaster. Knees that are **too big** means imminent bad luck.

Knife — **Dreaming about a knife** is usually a warning. **Any type of knife** can only mean bad times: business losses, family quarrels, lack of understanding, violent outbursts and fears. A **rusty knife** means domestic strife, lovers' spats. A **sharp knife** indicates worries and enemies. **Broken knives** are a symbol of failure at everything. A **knife wound** means trouble with children.

If the **dreamer stabs someone else with a knife**, it means that he is not particularly admirable, and should try and improve himself.

Knife Grinder — People will treat the dreamer's possessions with a total lack of respect.

Knight — Dreaming about a knight indicates that the dreamer is bothered by issues of status and hierarchy, and the relationship between the ruler and the ruled.

Knitting — A **woman dreaming** about knitting is a sign of a good life and a harmonious home. If the **knitting needle or the ball of wool falls**, it is a warning of enemies.

Knocker — This means that the dreamer will be compelled to seek the advice and assistance of others.

Knocking — A **dream about knocking** is a sign of serious news in the offing. If the **dreamer is woken up by knocking**, the news will be extremely serious.

Knot — A **knot in a dream** is a sign of economic problems and financial losses. **Tying a knot** is a sign of independence and assertiveness.

Label — If a label or sticker indicating a name or an item appears, it heralds a future full of surprises.

Labor — Seeing **animals laboring** under heavy loads means prosperity for the dreamer, but he will mistreat his subordinates. Seeing **men laboring** means profits and health. If the **dreamer labors**, it indicates future success in any venture.

Laboratory — This is indicative of time wasted on useless things when it could be put to better use.

Labyrinth — A **dream about a labyrinth** is a sign of business embroilments as well as domestic strife and lovers' quarrels. A **dark labyrinth** symbolizes temporary but serious trouble and illness. A **labyrinth of green vines** means success after sure failure. A **labyrinth of railroads** indicates long, boring and futile trips.

Lace — Seeing lace is a sign of fidelity in love and a rise in status. A **woman dreaming about lace** will realize all her ambitions and desires. **Buying lace** denotes wealth. **Selling lace** means living beyond one's means. **Making lace** is a sign of finding a good-looking, rich husband. **Embellishing wedding clothes with lace** means that a woman will have many admirers, but her wedding will remain in the far distant future.

Ladder — If the **dreamer climbs a ladder successfully**, it is a sign that his ambitions are about to be realized and that he will be prosperous. **Fear of ascending a ladder**, or an unsuccessful climb (such as falling off the ladder) is a dire prediction. A **ladder leaning against a wall** means that one of the dreamer's relatives is not loyal to him. A **broken ladder** is an indication of total failure.

Ladle — **Seeing a ladle** means luck with a companion and with children. A **dirty or broken ladle** is a forecast of a terrible loss.

Ladybug — If this red insect with the black spots appears, it is a sign that the dreamer will soon chance upon a golden opportunity which will allow him to realize his greatest dreams.

Lagoon — Misuse of the dreamer's intellectual resources will drag him into confusion and uncertainty.

Lake — If the **dreamer is sailing on a smooth, clear lake**, he will soon make good friends and enjoy the fruit of his labors. Positive developments in his life can be expected. A **young woman alone on a lake** will have to face great difficulties as a result of her past conduct. A **muddy lake** means business and love will come to a bitter end. A **muddy lake surrounded by greenery** means that the dreamer will subdue his passionate nature. If the **lake is clear but has barren banks**, the dreamer's passionate nature will win. A **reflection of the dreamer in a clear lake** is a sign of happiness. A **reflection of trees**  means that the dreamer will have his fill of passion and joy. **Slimy disgusting creatures** in a lake foretell failure and illness due to the dreamer's pursuit of immoral pleasures.

Lamb — **Frisky lambs** are a sign of friendship and happiness. They mean prosperity for the **farmer**. A **dead lamb** symbolizes sorrow and death. The **bleating of lambs** will inspire the dreamer's generous side. **Slaughtering lambs** means wealth at the expense of peace of mind. **Eating lamb chops** means worry about children. **Wolves or dogs tearing**

lambs apart means guiltless people suffering because of unscrupulous thieves. **Owning lambs** is a sign of prosperity and comfort. **Shearing lambs** is a sign of a dispassionate, money-loving nature. **Carrying lambs** means that the dreamer will bear the burdens of his loved ones happily. **Seeing lambskins** means that other people's joy and comfort have been taken away from them.

Lame — If a woman sees someone lame in a dream, it presages disappointment and bitterness.

Lament — **Lamenting the loss of possessions or friends** signifies that joy and prosperity are imminent. **Lamenting the loss of relatives** means illness that cements friendships.

Lamp / Flashlight — A **bright lamp** means that the dreamer is a honest person and seeks justice. A **dim lamp** indicates a feeling of embarrassment, jealousy and confusion. A **broken lamp** symbolizes bereavement. **Carrying a lamp** is a sign of independence and leadership. **Lighting a lamp** means making changes in business which will be profitable.

Lamppost — The **dreamer who sees a lamppost** will be helped by a stranger in time of need. If the **dreamer bumps into a lamppost**, he is in danger of being conned by enemies. **Seeing a lamppost in his path** means that he will have many hassles in his life.

Lance — **Dreaming about a lance** is a sign of powerful enemies. If the dreamer suffers **an injury from a lance**, it means that he will be irritated by an error of judgment. If he **breaks a lance**, he will overcome previously insurmountable obstacles and achieve success.

Land — **Fertile land** is a good sign, but **barren land** is a sign of failure and despair. **Seeing land while sailing on the ocean** foretells great wealth and joy.

Landing (from flight) — This predicts hardships for the dreamer in the near future. However, he will overcome them.

Lantern — **Seeing a lit lantern in the dark** is a sign of sudden wealth. If **it suddenly disappears**, financial affairs will go sour. **Carrying a lit lantern** is a sign of altruism. **Breaking it** means that while helping others, the dreamer will harm himself. **Losing a lantern** means business losses.

Lap — **Sitting on someone's lap** is a sign of being protected from hassles. A **woman with someone on her lap** can expect to be criticized. If **she holds a cat on her lap**, she is in danger of being seduced by a cunning enemy.

Lapdog — A **dream about a lapdog** is a sign that friends will help the dreamer out of a predicament. If the **dog is skinny and sickly**, the dreamer's business will suffer a setback.

Lard — A **dream about lard** is a sign of increased prosperity. A **lard-covered hand** means disappointment.

Lark — **Larks flying or singing** are a sign of joyous events, prosperity and a perfect marriage for the dreamer. If **larks fall and sing**, all the joy will be destroyed by despair. If the **dreamer sees larks caught in a trap**, it means that he will have no problem feeling love and respect. An **injured or dead lark** signifies grief or bereavement. **Killing a lark** means causing damage to innocent victims. **Seeing larks eat** is a sign of abundant crops.

Laser — The dreamer is warned not to waste his time and thoughts on trivialities when he should concentrate on important matters.

Latch — **Dreaming about a latch** means that the dreamer will turn a deaf ear to an appeal for assistance. A **broken latch** means falling out with friends, as well as illness.

Lateness — If one is late in a dream, despite attempts to arrive on time, it attests to the fact that people value the dreamer's opinion and are waiting to hear what he has to say.

Latin — Studying Latin is a sign that dreamer's opinion on important matters of state has prevailed.

Laudanum — **Taking laudanum** in a dream is a sign of the dreamer's weak character and liability to be influenced by others. **Preventing others from taking laudanum** means that the dreamer will be the bringer of excellent news. **Giving laudanum** means that a member of the dreamer's household will become mildly ill.

Laughter — The **dreamer's laughter** is actually an indication of sad things that he is liable to experience. If **others are laughing**, it is a sign that the dreamer's life will be happy and full of joy. **Children's happy laughter** in a dream is an indication of the dreamer's joy and health. **Laughing at other people's embarrassment** means that the dreamer will hurt his friends in order to gratify his own wishes. **Hearing mocking laughter** is a sign of disappointment and ill health.

Laundromat — Doing one's laundry in a laundromat means that an unsuccessful relationship will end, and will be replaced by a good one.

Laundry — **Dreaming about laundry** is a warning of failure and family problems, but with a good ending. If the **clothes are well laundered**, the dreamer will be happy. If **they are badly washed**, he will not.

Laurels — **Dreaming about laurels** is a rare dream symbolizing forthcoming honor, glory, fame, love and wealth in the dreamer's life. If a **young woman places a laurel wreath on her lover's head**, she will find a faithful, famous man.

Law — **All the elements relating to the law** (including courts, police, lawyers, etc.) warn the dreamer: Think carefully before making a decision concerning financial issues.

Lawnmower — This is a symbol of a boring social duty the dreamer will have to perform.

Lawns — **Walking on manicured lawns** symbolizes wealth and happiness. A **party on a lawn** indicates business appointments and light-hearted entertainment. A **woman** who dreams about **waiting for a friend or lover on a green lawn** means that her wishes concerning marriage will come true. If the **lawn is muddy or dry**, she can expect a break-up.

Lawsuit — A **dream about a lawsuit** means that the dreamer has a conservative nature: He lives a full and peaceful life, but is not spontaneous and does not break his routine easily. **Dreaming about getting involved in a lawsuit** means that the dreamer has dangerous enemies who are slandering him. A **young man who dreams about studying law** will succeed in any profession. For a **woman to dream**

about a lawsuit means that she will be the subject of slander by so-called friends.

Lawyer — **Dreaming about a lawyer** means that the dreamer is in need of assistance, advice and guidance. If a **young woman dreams about any kind of connection with a lawyer,** it means that her behavior will spark gossip and censure.

Lazy — **Acting or feeling lazy** in a dream means that the dreamer will make a mistake in a business venture, leading to disappointment. If a **woman dreams that her lover is lazy,** she will not have luck finding the right man.

Lead — **Lead** is a sign of failure. **Lead ore** foretells accidents and business failure. **Melting lead** means that the dreamer will cause failure through his impatience. A **lead mine** means that the dreamer's friends will regard his income with suspicion. **White lead** means that the dreamer's children are in jeopardy because of his carelessness.

Leaking — A **leak in anything** symbolizes losses and worries. A **leaking tank** is a sign of financial losses. A **leaking thatched roof** means danger, but the dreamer's quick action can avert it. A **leaking umbrella** means that the dreamer will not feel good about his lover or friends.

Leaping — If a young woman dreams about leaping over an obstacle, it means that her wishes will come true after a lot of hassles.

Learning — **Dreaming about learning** means that the dreamer will enjoy acquiring knowledge. Going into **places of learning** means fame and fortune for the dreamer. **Dreaming about learned people** is a sign that the dreamer's friends will be well-known and interesting. If a **woman dreams of associating with learned people**, she will realize her ambitions of status and fame.

Leather — **Leather** is a sign of business success and success with women. If the **dreamer is dressed in leather**, he will have luck in a particular venture. **Leather ornaments** denote fidelity. **Piles of leather** are a sign of wealth and joy. **Dreaming about being a leather merchant** means that changes in one's business dealings must be made if the dreamer is to be successful.

Leaves — A **dream about leaves** is a sign that one's love life and business will improve. **Withered leaves** mean that the dreamer is frustrated with a bad decision he made, and loss and disappointment will follow. **Fresh green leaves** are the sign of an excellent marriage for a woman — whereas **dry leaves** mean a lonely life, and sometimes death.

Lecture — If the dreamer is giving a lecture in front of an audience, it indicates that he will enjoy great professional success.

Ledger — **Keeping a ledger** in a dream is a sign of difficulties and disappointments. **Making mistakes in a ledger** foretells quarrels and minor losses. A **lost ledger** implies losses through carelessness. A **ledger that is destroyed by fire** means misfortune to the dreamer because of his friends. If a **woman is keeping the dreamer's ledger**, he will suffer financial loss because of mixing business and pleasure.

Leeches — **Dreaming about leeches** means attacks by the dreamer's enemies. If **leeches bite the dreamer**, it warns of danger from surprising quarters.

Leeward — **Sailing leeward for a sailor** is a sign of a happy voyage. For **other people**, it means a pleasant trip.

Leg — If the **dreamer's legs are emphasized,** it means that he is rational, self-aware, and has a lot of self-confidence and good friends. A **dream about admiring lovely women's legs** means that the dreamer will make a fool of himself over a woman. **Misshapen legs** are a sign of bad company and foolish deals. An **injured leg** signifies losses and disease. A **wooden leg** means false behavior toward friends. **Inability to use one's legs** is a sign of poverty. **Having three or more legs** means a lot of dreamed-of business ventures that will never be realized. If a **woman dreams about admiring her own legs**, she is vain, and finds her lover revolting. If **her legs are hairy,** she will dominate her husband.

Legerdemain — If the **dreamer practices legerdemain,** or **sees others doing** so, he will become embroiled in a difficult situation which he will have a hard time getting out of.

Legislature — Dreaming about belonging to the legislature means that the dreamer will boast of his wealth and will mistreat his family. He will not get a promotion.

Legume — This is a symbol of economic success and prosperity in business.

Lemon — **Lemons on trees** mean groundless jealousy. **Eating lemons** signifies despair resulting from a great love for and disappointment in one's spouse. **Green lemons** are a sign of illness. **Dried-up lemons** signify the break-up of couples.

Lemonade — Drinking lemonade in a dream means that the dreamer is allowing others to take advantage of him to finance some amusement they want.

Lending — **Lending money** in a dream is an indication of inability to pay debts. **Lending other things means** that over-generosity will lead to poverty. A **refusal to lend things** is a sign of the dreamer's assertiveness. If **others offer to lend the dreamer objects or money**, it is a sign of good friendship and wealth.

Lentils — A **dream about lentils** is a sign of disputes and a bad environment. A **young woman** will be compelled by her parents to choose a man she does not love.

Leopard — A **caged leopard** warns of an enemy who is attempting to harm the dreamer, but will not succeed. **Killing a leopard** means success. A **leopard attacking the dreamer** means difficulties along the path to success. **Leopards in the wild** escaping from the dreamer mean problems in business and love, but they will be overcome. **Leopard skin** means that the dreamer will suffer at the hands of a false friend.

Leprosy — If the **dreamer has leprosy**, it is a prediction of sickness, financial loss and abandonment by others. **Other people with leprosy** means disappointment in love and business.

Letter — **Dreaming about a registered letter** means a quarrel over money with someone close. For a **young woman to receive a letter** is a sign of other people's dishonorable intentions toward her. For **a lover**, it means that his sweetheart is looking elsewhere. Receiving **an anonymous letter** means an unexpected blow. **Writing a letter** means rivalry; it also means that the dreamer judges someone too quickly, and this leads to regrets. **Receiving letters containing bad news** is a sign of trouble and illness. If the **news is good**, the dreamer will experience good things. **Failing to read a letter** means business or social losses. **Hiding a letter** from a woman close to the dreamer means that he is up to no good. A **black-bordered letter** is a sign of death. A **recurrent dream of receiving a letter from a friend** means that he will soon show up. A **torn letter** means that the dreamer's mistakes will ruin his good name.

Lettuce — **Eating lettuce** is an indication of problems relating to sexuality and a person's love life in general. **Seeing lettuce growing** means success after some hassles. **Planting lettuce** seeds means untimely death. **Picking lettuce** is a sign of over-sensitivity and jealousy that cause the dreamer pain. **Buying lettuce** means that the dreamer will be responsible for his own failure.

Liar — **Dreaming about other people as liars** means that the dreamer will no longer support the plan that he himself proposed. To be **accused of being a liar** means that the dreamer will have worries caused by dishonest people. If a **woman** thinks **her lover is a liar,** she will lose a good friend.

Library — A **dream about being in a library** means that the dreamer will become bored with his occupation and will seek knowledge. If the dreamer is **in a library but not for purposes of knowledge,** he is trying to deceive his friends.

Lice — **Dreaming about lice** signifies that the dreamer suffers from feelings of social alienation or inferiority, as well as from worries about ill health. **Lice on cattle** means famine and ruin. **Body lice** signify that the dreamer will behave badly with people around him. **Becoming infected with lice** is a prediction of illness and fear of death.

License — A **license** is a sign of quarrels and losses. If a **woman dreams about a marriage license**, she will soon become involved in a bad relationship.

Lie — If the dreamer or another person lies in a dream, it is a warning to beware of a shady deal or fraud.

Lie Detector — If the dreamer is forced to take a lie detector test, he will soon be the focus of some scandal.

Life Insurance Salesman — **Seeing a life insurance salesman** in a dream signifies that the dreamer will soon meet someone who will be beneficial to his business. If the **man is somehow distorted**, the dream is not good.

Lifeboat — **Being on a lifeboat** means an escape from something bad. A **sinking lifeboat** means that the dreamer's friends will have a hand in his troubles. Being **lost in a lifeboat** means that the dreamer will be overwhelmed with vicissitudes. If **he is saved**, he will be spared disaster.

Light — The meaning of the dream changes according to the intensity of the light. A **bright, shining light** indicates success, wealth and happiness; a **dull light** — disappointment and depression; a **green light** — the dreamer's jealousy; a **light that goes out** — a failed venture; a **dim light** — partial success; a **brilliantly lit street** — transient pleasure.

Lighthouse — If the **dreamer sees a lighthouse in a storm**, he will experience trouble and sadness which will then be replaced by joy and prosperity. If he sees the **lighthouse from a calm sea**, life will be pleasant and calm for the dreamer.

Lightning — **Lightning** heralds particularly good tidings, especially concerning agriculture and farming the land. If **lightning strikes near the dreamer**, he will be hurt by a friend's good luck. **Lightning overhead** is a symbol of happiness and prosperity. **Lightning coming from dark clouds** is a bad omen, foretelling loss, in both business and family.

Lightning Rod — **Seeing a lightning rod** means the threatened destruction of the dreamer's pet project. If **lightning strikes a lightning rod**, it foretells an accident or bad news. If the **dreamer is having a lightning rod installed**, he should be warned of how to begin a new venture so that it will not end in disappointment. **Dismantling a lightning rod** means a good change in plans. **Seeing lots of lightning rods** means all kinds of trouble.

Lily — The lily is considered to be a symbol of holiness amongst Christians and is connected to holy sites and people. **Dreaming about a lily** means suffering from disease and death. **Growing lilies** means early marriage and early death. Seeing **children among lilies** means that they will not be robust. **Inhaling the scent of lilies** means that the dreamer will move to a higher plane as a result of suffering.

Lime (fruit) — Eating limes in a dream signifies bad luck and illness.

Lime — This predicts temporary disaster followed by unprecedented good fortune.

Limekiln — This tells the dreamer that nothing good lies in the immediate future, neither in business nor in love.

Limousine — This is a prediction of sudden and unexpected good luck.

Limping — If the **dreamer is limping**, it is a sign that he will always have friends around him. If **another person is limping**, it is a sign that the dreamer is about to be bitterly disappointed.

Line — If the dreamer sees himself standing on line, this indicates that a relationship with an old friend, severed due to an argument, will be soon renewed.

Linen — **Dreaming about linen** is a sign of happiness and prosperity. If the dreamer sees **someone dressed in linen clothes**, it means that he will soon hear good news about an inheritance. If the **dreamer is wearing good, clean linen**, he will have a wonderful life. If the **linen is dirty**, there will be the occasional bout of sorrow and bad luck.

Lion — A **dream about a lion** is a sign that one of the dreamer's friends will be very successful, and that in the future, the dreamer will benefit highly from this success, as well as receive help from the friend. If a **lion overpowers the dreamer**, he will be vulnerable to the attacks of enemies. **Controlling a lion** signifies success in business, great intelligence, and attention from women. **Young lions** mean new, possibly successful ventures. For a **woman, young lions** mean interesting new lovers. **Hearing a lion's roar** means a sudden promotion and success with women. **Overpowering a lion** means victory in any of the dreamer's endeavors. A **lion's hide** means prosperity and joy. **Riding a lion** means the ability to overcome obstacles.

Lips — Fleshy, red lips signify happiness and prosperity for the dreamer. **Thin, pale lips** are an indication of cerebral abilities. **Swollen, tender lips** signify unhealthy urges and deprivation.

Liquor — **Dreaming about buying liquor** means that the dreamer has designs upon property which does not belong to him. **Selling liquor** is a sign of impending criticism. **Drinking liquor** means that the dreamer will come into money in a slightly suspicious way, but friends and women will try to get him to spend it on them. **Liquor in bottles** is a sign of very good fortune. A **woman drinking liquor** means an easy-going, superficial character and lifestyle, with no jealousy or hard feelings.

Liver — **Dreaming about any liver disorders** means that the dreamer's mate will be bad-tempered, and disharmony will reign in his home. **Dreaming about eating liver** means that the dreamer's beloved has been seduced by another.

Lizard — **Dreaming about lizards** is a warning that an enemy is conspiring against the dreamer, and he should be careful. **Killing a lizard** means recouping one's ruined reputation or finances. If **it escapes**, there will be nothing but trouble in business and love. If a **woman dreams about a lizard crawling up her leg or scratching her**, it is a sign of trouble and grief — she will be left a poor widow.

Loan — If **someone requests a loan from the dreamer**, it means that the latter will soon suffer considerable financial losses. If the **dreamer is unsuccessful in his attempt to pay back a loan**, it is a good sign, foretelling an improvement in his economic situation.

Loaves — **Loaves of bread** in a dream indicate thrift. **Loaves of cake** signify good luck in love and business. **Broken loaves** foretell lovers' quarrels.

Lobster — **Seeing lobsters** is a sign of great prosperity. **Eating them** signifies falling into frivolous company. **Lobsters in a salad** mean that the dreamer will take full advantage of all pleasures. If he **orders a lobster**, it means that he will have a high position, with many people under his command.

Lock — A **dream about a lock** is a sign of confusion. If the **dreamer can work the lock**, it means that someone wants to harm him. **In love,** it means that the dreamer will neutralize a rival. **Seeing a lock** also symbolizes a successful journey. **An unyielding lock** means a lack of success in love and dangerous, futile journeys. If the **dreamer places a lock around his beloved's neck**, it means he doubts her fidelity.

Locket — A **young woman dreaming about her lover placing a locket around her neck** will soon be married and have beautiful children. If **she loses the locket**, her life will be marred with grief from bereavement. If a lover dreams that **his sweetheart returns his locket**, he can expect disappointment. She will not behave in the way he likes toward him. **Breaking a locket** means that a women will have an erratic husband, who is totally inconsistent in his relationship with her and in business.

Lockjaw — Trouble as the result of someone else's betrayal awaits the **person who dreams about having lockjaw**. If a **woman sees somebody else with lockjaw**, her happiness will be diminished by friends giving her unpleasant things to do. If **cattle get lockjaw**, the dreamer will lose a friend.

Locomotive — A **speeding locomotive** is a sign of greatly improved fortune and travel to distant places. A **stationary locomotive** means trouble and stagnation in business, and canceled trips. A **smashed locomotive** is a sign of anguish and financial loss. **Hearing a locomotive** means news from far away, and beneficial changes in business strategies. **Hearing its whistle** portends the arrival of a long-lost friend, or the offer of a good job.

Locusts — **Dreaming about locusts** is a sign of business irregularities that will cause the dreamer anxiety. A **woman who dreams about locusts** will squander her affection on undeserving people.

Lodger — If a **woman dreams of having lodgers**, it means that she will be unwillingly privy to bad secrets. A **lodger who leaves without paying** means that she can expect trouble with men. If **the lodger pays**, it is a good sign, meaning financial gain.

Looking Glass — If a woman dreams about a looking glass, it means that she will soon come face to face with appalling treachery which can lead to terrible quarrels or break-ups.

Loom — Seeing a **loom operated by a stranger** indicates trouble — but with some joyous anticipation. If a **pretty woman is operating the loom**, it is a good sign for lovers, as it signifies compatibility and many common interests. If a **woman is weaving at an old-fashioned loom**, it means that she has a good husband and lovely children. If the **loom is idle**, the dreamer will have to deal with a petulant, time-consuming person.

Lord's Prayer — If **the dreamer recites the Lord's Prayer**, it means that secret enemies are endangering him, and he will need all the help he can get from his friends. If **someone else says the prayer**, it means that the dreamer's friend is in danger.

Loss — Losses, wounds or injuries are interpreted as warning signs. Be alert to and aware of changes in life or to any situation fraught with potential danger.

Lottery — If the **dreamer is involved in the draw**, it means that he is wasting his time, and will have to go on a futile journey. If his **number comes up**, his winning will cause him anxiety. If **others win in a lottery**, it means lots of fun, laughter and socializing. Any kind of **lottery in a young woman's dream** means that she is not entirely responsible, and will marry someone unreliable. **Dreaming about a lottery** indicates bad business connections and temporary love relationships.

Love — **Loving anything** in a dream means satisfaction with life. If an **unmarried person dreams about love**, it indicates marriage in the near future. If the **dreamer is married**, it predicts a domestic quarrel. A **dream which deals in general**

with a couple's relationship — one that is based on pure intentions — hints at happiness, joy and success. If the **dream relationship is based on exploitation**, it symbolizes disappointment in reality.

Loveliness — Lovely things in a dream mean that everyone close to the dreamer will benefit. If a **lover dreams about the loveliness of his sweetheart**, he will soon marry and enjoy much happiness. If the **dreamer sees her own loveliness**, she will have a lot of joy in life.

Lozenges — Lozenges are an indication of minor successes. If a **woman eats or discards them**, her joy in life will be diminished by the barbs of jealous people.

Lucky — **Dreaming about being lucky** is just that — a lucky dream. Wishes will come true, and the dreamer will enjoy the things he has to do. If **the dreamer is in despair**, this dream provides hope for new happiness and prosperity.

Luggage — **Dreaming about luggage** indicates unwanted troubles. The dreamer will have unpleasant people hanging round his neck. If **he carries his own luggage**, he will be so involved in his own anguish that he will be impervious to that of others. **Losing luggage** indicates domestic disputes. If an **unmarried person dreams about losing luggage**, it is a sign of broken romances or engagements.

Lumber — **Dreaming about lumber** indicates numerous difficult, unpleasant and badly paid tasks. **Piles of burning lumber** foretell an unexpected windfall. **Sawing lumber** means bad business deals and general bad luck.

Lute — **Playing on a lute** is a sign of good news from faraway friends. **Hearing lute music** portends pleasant things.

Luxury — **Dreaming about wallowing in luxury** means that the dreamer's wealth is rapidly diminishing due to corrupt and hedonistic living. If a **poor woman dreams about luxury**, it means that her circumstances are going to change.

Lying — If the **dreamer lies in order to escape punishment**, it means that he will behave despicably toward an undeserving person. If the **dreamer lies in order to cover for a friend**, it means that unjustified criticism will be leveled at him, but he will overcome it and become well-known. If the **dreamer hears others lying**, it means that they are trying to bring him down.

Lynx — **Seeing a lynx** means enemies who are trying to ruin the dreamer's business and undermine his home. If a **woman dreams about a lynx**, it means that there is a rival for her lover. If **she kills the lynx**, she will have beaten her rival.

Lyre — **Listening to lyre music** indicates innocent pleasures, pleasant company and smooth business dealings. If a **young woman plays a lyre**, an excellent man will love her exclusively.

Macaroni — **Eating macaroni** is a sign of minor losses. **Seeing large amounts of macaroni** means that the dreamer will save money by being very economical. If a **young woman sees macaroni**, it means that a stranger will come into her life.

Mace (tear gas) — If the dreamer uses mace to defend himself against attackers, he is being warned about a danger that he can avert if he is ready for it.

Machinery — **Dreaming about machinery** indicates a difficult project that will finally be successful. **Seeing old machinery** means that enemies are plotting against the dreamer. If the **dreamer gets caught in machinery**, he will suffer financial losses and trouble.

Machines — Machines used for production or other sophisticated machinery indicate complex problems in all areas of life.

Mad Dog/s — **Dreaming about a mad dog** means that despite the dreamer's efforts, he will fail in his endeavors, and may be very ill. If the **mad dog bites him**, it signifies impending insanity or catastrophe for him or someone close to him. **Seeing a mad dog** is a sign of enemy attacks on the dreamer and his friends. If **he manages to kill the dog**, he will succeed in life.

Madness — A **dream about madness of any kind** is a bad sign, predicting sickness and unhappiness. **Seeing other people's madness** means unreliable friends and dashed hopes. If a **young woman dreams about madness**, she will not realize her expectations in marriage or financial status.

Magic — If the **dreamer does magic**, it predicts changes for the better in his life, especially in finance and health. If **others do magic**, the dreamer will profit from it. **Seeing a magician** means interesting travel for the academic.

Magistrate — Dreaming about a magistrate is a warning of impending lawsuits and financial losses.

Magnet — **Dreaming about a magnet** means that the dreamer will be influenced by bad forces — possibly seduced by a woman. If the **dreamer is a woman**, it means that she will gain wealth and patronage.

Magnifying Glass — **Looking through a magnifying glass** in a dream means failing to implement projects successfully. For a **woman to have one** means that she seeks relationships with people who will dump her.

Magpie — This is a sign of disputes and unhappiness. It is a warning to the dreamer.

Mailman — If a **mailman delivers letters to the dreamer**, it means that news about some unsavory person is about to arrive. If the **mailman does not bring letters**, it predicts sadness and disappointment. If the **dreamer gives letters to the mailman**, suffering as a result of jealousy will occur. **Talking to a mailman** is an indication of future scandal.

Malice — If the **dreamer feels malice toward someone**, it means that his friends will dislike him for his bad nature. If **others act maliciously toward the dreamer**, he is being undermined by an enemy pretending to be a friend.

Mallet — Dreaming about a mallet means that the dreamer will be mistreated by friends because he is ill. There will be disharmony in his home.

Malt — **Dreaming about malt** is an indication of a good, wealthy life. **Drinking malted drinks** is a sign of dangerous undertakings that will work out very profitably.

Man — **Dreaming about a handsome man** indicates good things for the dreamer. A **deformed man** means worries and disappointments. If a **woman dreams about a handsome man**, she will be honored. If **she dreams about an ugly man**, one of her friends will cause her anxiety.

Manager / Boss — Any dream about a manager or boss, whether the dreamer himself is the manager or another person is the boss, indicates a promotion at work, as well as improvement in one's economic and social status.

Man-of-War — **Dreaming about this ship** means long journeys and separations. There is a danger of political unrest. If the **ship is sailing on rough seas**, strife with other powers may influence the dreamer's personal business.

Manners — Seeing **bad-mannered people** in dreams means failure in projects due to the unpleasantness of one of the associates. **Well-mannered people** signify changes for the better.

Mansion — If the **dreamer sees himself entering a mansion**, he can expect good news and wealth. If he dreams about **leaving a mansion in a hurry**, or about a **haunted room in a mansion**, it foretells difficult problems that await him. **Seeing a mansion from a distance** means promotion.

Manslaughter — If a woman dreams about being linked in any way to manslaughter, it means that she is afraid of being named in some scandal.

Mantilla — This indicates a bad undertaking which will cause the dreamer damage.

Manure — Seeing manure is a very good sign, predicting good things — especially for farmers.

Manuscript — An **unfinished** or a **lost manuscript** signifies disappointment. A **completed manuscript** means that expectations will be realized. **Working on a manuscript** means that the dreamer is anxious about something; if **he keeps working single-mindedly**, he will be successful. If a **manuscript is rejected**, the dreamer will be distraught, but his dreams will eventually come true. A **burning manuscript** is a sign of success and profit.

Map — **Dreaming about a map** is a sign that the dreamer can expect some kind of change in his life — sometimes disappointing, sometimes good. **Looking for a map** means that the dreamer will change his direction in life because of a sudden realization that he is not happy with his present state.

Marble — **Dreaming about a marble quarry** signifies financial success but social failure. **Polishing marble** indicates an inheritance. If **marble breaks**, the dreamer will incur the displeasure of his colleagues because of immoral behavior.

March — This is an indication of business disappointments.

March (music) — Marching to music means that the dreamer wants to become a soldier or public official. It warns the dreamer to consider all the aspects.

Marching — **Marching along an uneven road** suggests

misunderstandings and a lack of communication with the dreamer's surroundings. If **women dream about men marching**, it means that they have set their sights on important men.

Mare — **Mares grazing in pastures** mean prosperity in business and pleasant company. A **dry pasture** means good friends but poverty. If a **young woman dreams about a mare**, it means a good marriage and lovely children.

Marigold — This tells the dreamer to make do with a simple life.

Mariner — **Dreaming about being a mariner** is a sign of a long, agreeable journey to faraway places. If the **dreamer sees his ship sailing off without him**, rivals will cause him trouble.

Market — **Dreaming of being in a market** is an indication of being economical and busy. An **empty market** is a sign of depression and sadness. For a **woman**, a market indicates good changes.

Marmalade — Dreaming about eating marmalade is a sign of illness and unhappiness.

Marmot — **Seeing a marmot** is a warning of enemies in the guise of pretty women. For a **woman**, it is a sign of temptation in her path.

Marriage / Nuptials — If a woman dreams about **marriage to an old and ugly man**, it is a sign of great trouble and illness for her. Seeing a marriage with **brightly dressed guests** means joy. **Somber dress** means bereavement and sorrow. Seeing **anything bad connected to marriage** in a dream is a prediction of catastrophe in the dreamer's family. If the **dreamer is present at a marriage**, he will have joy and prosperity.

Mars — **Dreaming about Mars** is a bad sign: Friends will treat the dreamer cruelly, enemies will try to bring him down. If the **dreamer rises up toward Mars**, he will acquire an excellent sense of judgment which will place him light-years ahead of his friends.

Marsh — Walking through a marsh means ill health as a result of overwork. The dreamer will bear the brunt of a relative's bad behavior.

Martyr — **Dreaming about martyrs** is a sign of hypocritical friends, domestic strife, and business losses. If the **dreamer himself is a martyr**, he will lose his friends and be badmouthed by enemies.

Mask — **Wearing a mask** signifies that the dreamer is two-faced. **Seeing masks** warns the dreamer of betrayal by a person close to him who is acting behind his back in an attempt to undermine him. If **others wear masks**, the dreamer will overcome the envy of others. If a **young woman wears a mask**, she will impose on other people. If **she takes it off**, others will not admire her in the way she wanted.

Mason (trade) — Dreaming about a mason is good news for the dreamer — financially and socially.

Mason (secret order) — Seeing members of the Masonic Order in their full dress means that the dreamer will have others to worry about and provide for besides himself.

Masquerade — **Participating in a masquerade** means that the dreamer is wasting time on trivial things and neglecting important matters. For a **woman**, it means that she will be deceived.

Mast — **Seeing a ship's masts** means a long, pleasant voyage, new friends and assets. **Seeing the masts of wrecked vessels** means changes for the worse and sacrifices in the dreamer's life. If a **sailor dreams about a mast**, he will soon embark on an eventful voyage.

Master — Dreaming about **having a master** means that the dreamer is not competent enough to be a leader, and requires the direction of someone stronger. **Being a master** of many subordinates signifies the dreamer's fine judgment, high status and great wealth.

Mastiff — **Feeling frightened of a big mastiff** means difficulty in rising above mediocrity. If a **woman dreams of a mastiff**, she will marry a kind, clever man.

Mat — This is a sign of grief and worry.

Match — **Dreaming about matches** predicts change and wealth. **Striking a match in the dark** portends sudden news and change in fortune.

Matting — **Matting** is a sign of good prospects and news from faraway loved ones. **Old or torn matting** mean worries.

Mattress — **Dreaming about a mattress** is a sign of new obligations in the near future. **Sleeping on a new mattress** means satisfaction with one's life. **Dreaming about a mattress factory** signifies shrewd business partners and wealth.

Mausoleum — **Dreaming about a mausoleum** means the illness, death or misfortune of the well-known friend of the dreamer. If the **dreamer is in a mausoleum**, it means that he is ill.

May — **Dreaming about May** is a sign of enjoyment and prosperity. If there are **extreme weather changes**, the good times will be spoiled by sorrow and cares.

May Bugs — The dreamer will have a sour-tempered partner instead of a pleasant one.

Meadow — This is a prediction of joyful reunions and the expectation of prosperity.

Meals — The dreamer neglects important matters for trivial ones.

Measles — **Dreaming about having measles** is an indication of business worries and anxieties. If **others have measles**, the dreamer will be anxious about their state of health.

Meat — If the **dreamer cooks meat**, it means good tidings. If the **dreamer eats meat prepared by someone else**, he can expect bad times. A **dream about raw meat** means that the dreamer will not be encouraged in his aims. **Cooked meat** means that others will accomplish his objective. **Roast meat** is a sign of domestic unhappiness and conspiracy. **Salting meat** is a sign of bothersome debts.

Mechanic — Dreaming about a mechanic means that the dreamer will move house and experience an improvement in his business and income.

Medal — **Dreaming about medals** indicates rewards resulting from hard work. **Losing medals** is a sign of bad luck brought about by other people's treachery.

Medicine — **Any kind of medicine** in a dream signifies that in the near future, the dreamer's life will be temporarily upset by worries and hardships. **Revolting medicine** predicts a serious illness or tragedy for the dreamer. **Giving others medicine** means that the dreamer is hurting people who trust him.

Medium (clairvoyant) — If one dreams about an individual who acts as an intermediary between the world of the living and the world of the dead, it predicts that the dreamer will undergo a serious crisis in the near future.

Melancholy — If the **dreamer feels melancholy**, he will be disappointed in what he thought would be successful. If **others are melancholy**, his business will be badly disrupted. For **lovers**, it is an omen of a break-up.

Melon — **Seeing melons growing** means that the dreamer can expect changes for the better in his life, after his present worries. **Dreaming about melons** is a sign of illness and business failures. **Eating them** means that the dreamer will experience anxiety as a result of hasty actions.

Memorial — Dreaming about a memorial means that the dreamer will have to be kind and patient to sick and unfortunate relatives.

Menagerie — This is a sign of all kinds of problems.

Mendicant — If a woman dreams about mendicants, her ambitions will be interrupted by unpleasant things.

Mending — If the **dreamer is mending dirty clothes**, he will choose the wrong time to put an injustice to rights. If **he is mending clean clothes**, he will be prosperous. If a **young**

woman dreams about mending, she will be of valuable assistance to her husband.

Mercury — **Dreaming about mercury** means that negative changes will occur in the dreamer's life due to the intervention of enemies. If a **woman suffers from mercury poisoning**, she will be abandoned by her family.

Mermaid — Dreaming about something that does not exist in reality signifies the search for impossible love.

Merry — A dream about being merry, or with merry people, means that the dreamer will enjoy life for a while, and his business will flourish.

Meshes — **Dreaming about being enmeshed** means that the dreamer will be attacked by enemies. If a **young woman dreams this**, she will go off the straight and narrow path, and eventually be abandoned. If **she succeeds in extricating herself**, she will not be the object of malicious gossip.

Message — **Receiving a message** in a dream is an indication of change. **Sending a message** foretells awkward situations for the dreamer.

Metamorphosis — This is a sign of changes in life, which can be good or bad.

Mice — A **dream about mice** predicts domestic strife, business problems and false friends. **Killing mice** is a symbol of defeating enemies. If a **young woman dreams about mice**, she has secret enemies, and is being deceived. A **mouse in her clothes** predicts a scandal in which she will be involved.

Microscope — This is a sign of failure in projects or business ventures.

Microwave Oven — Using a microwave oven

to prepare a meal means that the dreamer can expect a visit from unwelcome guests.

Midwife — **Seeing a midwife** is a sign of illness and near death. It is a bad sign of slander and distress for a **young woman**.

Milepost — If the **dreamer sees or passes a milepost** in a dream, he will have fears and doubts about love or business. To see a **fallen milepost** means that his affairs will be threatened by mishaps.

Milk — **Purchasing milk** portends good times. **Selling milk** indicates success and good luck. **Boiling milk** means success following great effort. **Sour and spoiled milk** signifies domestic problems, and distress caused by friends' suffering. **Spilt milk** indicates a temporary setback at the hands of friends. **Giving milk away** means over-generosity. **Big quantities of milk** symbolize health and wealth. **Drinking milk** is an excellent sign for farmers, women and travelers. **Bathing in milk** predicts pleasure and good times with friends.

Milking — Milking a cow with abundant milk means that success will be attained after a lot of trouble.

Mill — A **mill** is a sign of good fortune and prosperity. A **broken-down mill** signifies disease and bad luck.

Milldam — **Clear water pouring over a milldam** is a sign of social or business success. **Muddy water** implies losses and troubles instead of joy. A **dry dam** means reduced business.

Millstone — This represents hard work which is not sufficiently remunerated.

Miller — A **miller** in a dream signifies an improvement in the dreamer's environment. If a **woman** dreams about an **unsuccessful miller**, she will be disappointed by her lover's financial situation.

Mineral — Dreaming about minerals means that the dreamer's life will improve.

Mineral Water — Drinking mineral water means that the dreamer will succeed in his endeavors, and will be able to satisfy his cravings.

Mine — **Being in a mine** indicates business failure. **Owning a mine** means wealth. Working in **a gold mine** means that the dreamer will try to take the rights of others away from them. He should avoid scandals at home.

Minister — **Seeing a minister** means changes for the worse and undesirable trips. **Hearing a minister preach** means that the dreamer will be influenced to do wrong. **Dreaming about being a minister** indicates that he will try to take the rights of others away from them.

Mink — **Dreaming about a mink** indicates that the dreamer will have to defeat cunning enemies. If **he kills them**, he will be victorious. If a **woman dreams about loving mink furs**, she will fall in love with a madly jealous man.

Mint — Dreaming about mint means good news: the dreamer will soon receive a substantial inheritance from an unexpected source.

Minuet — **Seeing the minuet being danced** is the sign of a pleasant life with good friends. If the **dreamer himself dances a minuet**, he will have success in business and happiness at home.

Mire — Dreaming about going through mire means that the cherished plans of the dreamer will have to be put on hold due to changes occurring around him.

Mirror — If the **dreamer sees himself in a mirror**, he will encounter many obstacles; he will suffer losses and distress due to illness. A **broken mirror** foretells the sudden or violent death of someone close to the dreamer. For a **young woman to break a mirror**, it means that she will have an unhappy marriage. Seeing **others reflected in a mirror** means that the dreamer is about to be treated badly in order to bring about the advancement of other people.

Miser — **Dreaming about a miser** warns the dreamer that because of his selfishness, he will not find true love and happiness. If a **woman dreams about being befriended by a miser**, she will receive love and wealth because of her cleverness and tact. If the **dreamer dreams about being miserly**, it means that he will behave disgustingly toward others. If **his friends are misers**, he will be affected by other people's troubles.

Mist — If the **dreamer is shrouded in mist**, it means that his luck is not stable. If **the mist clears**, his troubles will pass. If **he sees others in a mist**, he will profit from their troubles.

Mistletoe — **Dreaming about mistletoe** is a very happy, festive dream, promising good times. If **bad signs appear with the mistletoe**, however, there will be disappointment instead.

Mixer — Dreaming about an electric mixer means that the dreamer is about to enjoy a more active social life.

Mockingbird — **Seeing or hearing a**

mockingbird means that the dreamer will be invited to friends for a pleasant visit. Business matters will go smoothly. If a **woman sees a dead or wounded mockingbird**, she will soon quarrel with her lover.

Models — **Dreaming about a model** means that the dreamer will waste his money on his social life, and this will lead to rows and recriminations. If a **young woman dreams about being a model**, it foretells a complicated love affair that will cause her anguish due to an egoistic friend.

Molasses — **Dreaming about molasses** means that the dreamer will receive a pleasant invitation which will lead to nice surprises. If **he eats molasses**, it means that he will be disappointed in love. If **it is smeared on his clothing**, he may suffer business losses and receive unwanted marriage proposals.

Mole (animal) — **Dreaming about moles** is a warning of danger hovering over the dreamer's head in the form of secret enemies. **Catching a mole** is a sign of the dreamer's victory and rise to power.

Moles (on the skin) — These are a sign of disputes and illness.

Molting (birds) — This indicates inhuman and unscrupulous treatment of the unfortunate and downtrodden by the wealthy.

Money — **Finding money** is a sign of minor worries but great joy. **Losing money** foretells domestic unhappiness and bad luck in business. **Counting money** and being short means that the dreamer will have trouble paying his debts.

Winning money means that the dreamer should consider his actions carefully. **Saving money** means future wealth. **Paying out money** means bad luck. **Receiving money** means wealth and pleasure. **Stealing money** indicates a fear of losing authority. Full **money boxes** indicate the end of money worries and a comfortable retirement.

Monk — **Seeing a monk** indicates that the dreamer has family problems and has to undertake unpleasant journeys. If a **young woman dreams about a monk**, she should watch out for gossip. Dreaming about **being a monk** portends bereavement and disease.

Monkey — **Dreaming about a monkey** means that the dreamer has a dishonest relationship with a close acquaintance, who wishes to exploit the dreamer for his own gain. **Seeing a dead monkey** means that the dreamer's worst enemies will disappear. **Feeding a monkey** is a sign of flattery and suspicions of infidelity.

Monster — A **monster appearing in different forms** in a dream signifies that the dreamer suffers from such extreme fear that he is paralyzed. **Being chased by a monster** is a sign of extreme bad luck and sorrow. **Killing a monster** means victory over enemies.

Moon — A **new moon** symbolizes wealth and success in love. **Seeing the moon in an ordinary sky** is a sign of success. A peculiar moon signifies domestic strife, bad luck in love and business disappointments. A **blood red moon** means that a woman's lover will go off to war.

Morgue — If the **dreamer visits a morgue**, he will

receive appalling news about the death of someone close. If he **sees many corpses in the morgue**, he will hear about a lot of grief and trouble.

Morning — **Seeing morning break** is a sign of good luck and pleasure. A **cloudy morning** signifies weighty issues that the dreamer will have to deal with.

Morocco — Dreaming about Morocco predicts plentiful assistance from unexpected quarters. The dreamer's love will be reciprocated with faithfulness.

Morose — If the **dreamer appears morose**, everything will be wrong for him when he awakes. If **others are morose**, disagreeable tasks and associates are his lot.

Mortgage — If the **dreamer takes a mortgage**, it means that he is in financial trouble which will cause him embarrassment. If **he gives a mortgage to others**, it means that he does not have enough money to pay his debts.

Mortification — Dreaming about feeling mortified about one's behavior means that the dreamer will suffer humiliation in front of those he wished to impressed. He will experience financial loss.

Moses — A dream about Moses is a sign of a happy marriage and prosperity.

Mosquito — **Seeing mosquitoes** is a sign that enemies are plotting evil against the dreamer, and he will suffer financially from this. **Killing mosquitoes** signifies prosperity and domestic happiness.

Moss — **Dreaming about moss** means that the dreamer will work as an employee. If, however, the **moss grows in fertile soil**, the dreamer will gain recognition.

Moth — **Seeing a moth** means that a relationship with someone close to the dreamer will become strained, causing quarrels. The dreamer will allow minor anxieties to trap him in unwanted situations. A **white moth** is a sign of inevitable illness. If a **woman sees a white moth flying around her room at night**, it is a sign of unfulfilled desires which will spoil other people's enjoyment. **Seeing a moth flying around and then either landing or disappearing** is a prediction of the death of a friend or a relative.

Mother — The nature of the relationship between the dreamer and his mother is of utmost importance. Usually, **dreaming about a mother** speaks of pregnancy in the near future. However, for a **woman**, it may also symbolize strong friendship, honesty, wisdom, generosity and a successful married life. Dreaming about a **dead mother** is a prediction of grief and dishonor. If **she cries out**, she may be ill, or the dreamer may be about to fall ill. If **his mother calls him**, it means that he is not doing what he is supposed to do.

Mother-in-law — If the **dreamer argues with a mother-in-law**, it means that he wants peace at home. There will be reconciliations after a quarrel. If a **woman dreams about quarreling with her mother-in-law**, she will encounter unpleasant, argumentative people.

Motor — This symbolizes the desire to be a leader and to be at the center of things.

Motorcycle — **Dreaming about riding a motorcycle** means that the dreamer will control his relationships. **Watching others ride** means that he is in a rut, while others are advancing in their personal and professional lives.

Mountain — If the **ascent is very difficult**, it portends encounters with obstacles that the dreamer will struggle to overcome. An **easy, fast ascent** means that the dreamer will have a swift rise to wealth and fame. If **he meets other people during the climb**, it signifies that the dreamer will have to seek help from others on his path to success. A **bald mountain** is a sign of famine and distress.

Mourning — **Wearing mourning clothes** symbolizes loss, sorrow and pain. If **others wear mourning**, certain dynamics among the dreamer's friends will cause him loss and unhappiness. For **lovers**, a dream of mourning portends a break-up. A **mourning veil** is a sign of trouble and sadness, as well as business embroilment.

Mouse — This warns of potential harm to the dreamer as a result of unnecessary interference and treachery by enemies in his life.

Mousetrap — **Seeing a mousetrap** means having to be careful of people who wish to take advantage of the dreamer. If there are **mice in the trap**, the dreamer will probably fall into the hands of his enemies. By **setting a trap**, he will defeat his rivals.

Mouth — A big mouth means great future wealth. A small mouth means financial problems.

Mud — Dreaming about **walking in mud** symbolizes dissatisfaction with friendships and domestic disharmony. **Extricating oneself from mud** or quicksand represents the ability to get out of difficult and complex situations. **Seeing others walking in mud** signifies that the dreamer will hear ugly rumors about a friend. **Mud on one's clothing** means that one's reputation is at stake. If the **dreamer scrapes it off**, he will escape the scandal.

Muff — **Wearing a muff** signifies protection against life's troubles. If a **lover dreams of his beloved wearing a muff**, someone else will win her away.

Mulberries — If **mulberries appear in a dream**, the dreamer will be prevented from realizing his desires by illness, and he will have to alleviate the suffering of others. **Eating mulberries** is a sign of bitter disappointment.

Mule — **Riding on a mule** signifies that the things in which the dreamer is involved are causing him huge anxiety. If **the ride is uneventful**, he will be successful. **Being kicked by a mule** is a sign of disappointment in love and marriage. A **dead mule** symbolizes break-ups and social ostracism. If a **woman dreams about a white mule**, she will marry a wealthy foreigner or some other wealthy, but incompatible, man.

Murder — **Seeing murder in a dream** signifies sorrow resulting from the actions of others. Business will suffer, and there will be more news of violent deaths. If the **dreamer commits murder**, it means that he is involved in some spurious enterprises that will ruin his reputation. **Being murdered** means that enemies are trying to cause the dreamer's downfall.

Muscles — If the **dreamer's muscles are developed**, he will encounter enemies, but will defeat them. **Undeveloped muscles** are a sign of the dreamer's inability to succeed in business. If a **woman dreams about muscles**, it foretells a life of hard work and difficulties.

Museum — **A dream about a museum** means

that the dreamer will experience a variety of things while seeking his perfect niche - things that will enrich him more than formal learning. If **he dislikes the museum**, it is a sign of irritating worries.

Mushrooms — **Seeing mushrooms** means that the dreamer has unsavory wishes and is in a rush to accumulate money, which will be lost in lawsuits. **Eating mushrooms** signifies embarrassment and scandalous love.

Music — **Harmonious and pleasant music** symbolizes success and a good life. **Discordant sounds and cacophony** signal domestic strife, undisciplined children, and disruptions during a journey or long trip.

Musk — This is a sign of unanticipated happy events, as well as harmony and fidelity between lovers.

Mussels — This is a sign of average prosperity, but a happy and contented domestic life.

Mustache — **Having a mustache** is a sign of impertinence and selfishness, which will cost the dreamer an inheritance; he will treat women very badly. If a **man dreams about shaving off his mustache**, it indicates that he is trying to reform himself and return to the path of decency. If a **woman dreams about admiring a mustache**, her moral standing is in jeopardy.

Mustard — **Seeing mustard growing** is a sign of prosperity for the farmer and wealth for sea travelers. **Eating mustard** is a warning against receiving bad advice, and of taking some unconsidered action which will cause the dreamer trouble.

Mute — This indicates that the dreamer is unable to

convince others to think like he does. He tries to exploit them by utilizing smooth talk.

Myrrh — Myrrh is a sign of satisfactory returns on investments. If a **young woman dreams about myrrh**, she will meet a wealthy person.

Myrtle — Dreaming about **blooming, verdant myrtle** signifies pleasures and fulfilled desires. If a **young woman dreams about wearing myrtle**, she will make a good marriage at a young age. However, if the **myrtle is dry**, she will miss out because of her own behavior.

Mystery — If **mysterious events perplex the dreamer**, it means that he will be bothered by strangers' problems and demands for assistance. It is a reminder of unpleasant duties, and foretells business embroilments. If the **dreamer contemplates the mysteries of creation**, his life is about to change and rise on to a higher plan, promising him joy and prosperity.

Nails (finger) — See **Fingernails**.

Nails — **Nails** symbolize hard work and small profit. **Dealing in nails** means that the dreamer will have a respectable job, even if it is not prestigious. **Rusty or broken nails** indicate disease and business failure.

Naked — **Dreaming about being naked** is a prediction of scandal. **Seeing others naked** means that the dreamer will succumb to bad temptations. If the **dreamer discovers that he is naked and tries to cover up**, it means that he wants to return to the right path, forgoing all his dubious pleasures. **Walking or swimming naked and alone** means that one's spouse is very loyal. **Walking naked among clothed people** also foretells a forthcoming period of scandal.

Name — If the dreamer hears someone calling his name, it is a sign that he will soon require help from someone close to him.

Napkin — **Dreaming about a napkin** is a prediction of happy events in which the dreamer will participate. For a **woman to dream about dirty napkins** means that she will be the victim of embarrassing circumstances.

Narrow Passage — A feeling of suffocation and a lack of air while dreaming abpit being in a narrow passage signifies the dreamer's very strong sexual passion or feelings of pressure and anxiety.

Navy — A **dream about the navy** signifies that the dreamer will have to cope with strange and serious obstacles, but he will overcome them and be prosperous. Enjoyable trips are predicted. If the **navy is in disarray**, the dreamer will have bad luck in love and business.

Nearsighted — A **dream about being nearsighted** means that the dreamer will experience humiliating failure, and can expect unwelcome visitors. For a **young woman**, it means unanticipated rivalry. If the **dreamer's sweetheart is nearsighted**, he will be disappointed in her.

Neck — If the **dreamer receives a compliment about his neck**, it signifies that he has a full love life. **Admiring someone else's neck** predicts domestic break-up. If **he sees his own neck**, his life will be disrupted by domestic strife. If a **woman dreams that her neck is thick**, it warns her that she will become shrewish if she does not watch herself.

Necklace — A **necklace** symbolizes the dreamer's desire to be at the center of things. If a **woman dreams about receiving a necklace**, she will have a loving husband and beautiful home. **Losing a necklace** indicates bereavement in the near future.

Necromancer — Dreaming about a necromancer and his practices means that the dreamer is in danger of being influenced by evil strangers.

Need — **Dreaming about being in need** means unsuccessful business ventures and bad news about friends. If **others are in need**, both the dreamer and other people will suffer from hard times.

Needle — **Finding a needle** in a dream predicts a strong friendship with a new acquaintance. **Using a needle** means that the dreamer can expect a hardship for which he will receive no sympathy. **Looking for a needle** signifies foolish anxieties. **Threading a needle** symbolizes the dreamer's responsibility for people other than his immediate family. A

broken needle is a sign of poverty and loneliness. **Sewing** means that the dreamer suffers from loneliness.

Needlefish — **Dreaming about needlefish** means unpleasantness with friends for reasons unknown to the dreamer. **Catching a needlefish** signifies that the dreamer will overcome an obstacle in his path. **Eating a needlefish** means the obstacle has been overcome.

Needlepoint — If the **dreamer is doing needlepoint**, it signifies that he wants to know what lies in store for him in the future. He will receive answers to many questions; his rivals will no longer hassle him, and his family will love having him around. **Practicing multicolored needlepoint** is an indication of a lively social life. **Seeing a monochrome needlepoint design** is a warning not to let fear of the unknown prevent the dreamer from realizing his ambitions. **Finding a cushion worked in needlepoint** predicts new opportunities. If a **woman dreams about holding a needlepoint purse**, romance and excitement are on the way.

Needlewoman — **Seeing a needlewoman** indicates a change from the outside that will cause a change in the dreamer's life, and foretells harmony at home. **Seeing a needlewoman at work** is a positive forecast. If **she is asking for work**, the dreamer should actively make a change before it simply happens to him. If the **needlewoman has come to demand payment for services rendered**, the dreamer should be careful when he gets up.

Negligee — **Dreaming about a negligee** foretells a daring love life with a partner with similar tastes. **Seeing a negligee in a box** means that old relationships are still satisfying.

Dreaming about a woman wearing a negligee foretells a love affair that will upset the dreamer's life.

Neighbor — **Seeing one's neighbors** in a dream means wasting a lot of time on quarrels and gossip. If the **neighbors are angry or upset**, this is a prediction of strife.

Nephew — **Dreaming about a handsome nephew** is a prediction of a windfall. If the **nephew is not handsome**, the dreamer will only have unpleasantness and disappointment.

Nervousness — Good news is on its way!

Nest — **Seeing birds' nests** means the possibility of a lucrative business proposition. For a **young woman**, it means moving house. An **empty nest** means sadness because a friend has left. A **nest with bad or broken eggs** is a sign of failure and disillusionment. **Doves building nests** signify domestic harmony and world peace.

Nets — If the **dreamer catches anything in a net**, it means that he has no scruples in his dealings with others. If he **dreams about a torn, old net**, it means that his property is mortgaged or otherwise entailed, a sign of trouble.

Nettles — **Dreaming about nettles** foretells insubordination by employees or children. **Walking through nettles without being stung** is a sign of prosperity. **Being stung** is sign of self-loathing and making others unhappy. For a **woman to dream about walking through nettles**, it means that she will be anxious about deciding which proposal of marriage to accept.

News — Strangely, **good news in a dream** warns of problems and worries. **Bad news,** however, heralds good luck and success in the near future.

Newspaper — This means that the dreamer's reputation is being compromised because of fraudulent actions.

Newspaper Reporter — If the **dreamer is not happy to see reporters in his dream**, he will be hassled by silly quarrels and small talk. If the **dreamer himself is a newspaper reporter**, he will experience a variety of adventures and trips, not all of them good, but overall will gain respect and profit.

New Year — **Dreaming about the New Year** is a symbol of prosperity and joy in love. If the **dreamer considers the New Year a drag,** he will undertake successful ventures.

Niece — If a woman dreams about her niece, it is a prediction of unanticipated problems and futile anxiety.

Night — **Darkness and night** symbolize a lack of mental clarity, as well as hardship, confusion and a lack of clarity in the dreamer's life. If the **light disappears**, there will be an improvement in his life and business. **Walking at night** means bad luck and fruitless striving for happiness.

Nightgown — **Dreaming about wearing a nightgown** is a sign of a minor illness. **Seeing others dressed in nightgowns** signifies bad news and business problems. If a **lover sees his beloved in a nightgown,** he will be dumped.

Nightingale — A **dream about a nightingale** causes an immediate association with melody and pleasant sounds. It means that romance will dominate the dreamer's life for a short while. The dreamer will have a pleasant and prosperous life. A **silent nightingale** denotes minor disagreements between friends.

Nightmare — A **dream about having a nightmare**

means disputes and business failure. For a **young woman**, it predicts disappointments and unjustified insults. It is a warning about her health.

Ninepins — A dream about ninepins is altogether bad. It warns the dreamer that he is wasting his time and energy. He should be more discriminating in his choice of friends.

Nobility — If the **dreamer associates with the nobility**, it means that he is aspiring to the wrong things — frivolous pleasures instead of higher spiritual issues. If a **young woman dreams about the nobility**, it means that she will choose a man for his looks instead of for his inner qualities.

Noise — If there is a **lot of noise around the dreamer**, it means that he will play the role of arbiter and peacemaker in a quarrel between two people close to him. If he hears a **strange noise**, it is a sign of bad news. If the **noise wakes him up**, there will be a sudden change in his life.

Nomad — If the dreamer or another person appears as a nomad or a wanderer, the dreamer has a burning desire for change in his life.

Noodles — This is not a good dream, as it indicates desires and appetites which are not normal.

Nose — If the **dreamer sees himself with a large nose**, it indicates great wealth and economic prosperity. A **small nose** means that one of the dreamer's immediate family members or relatives will disgrace the family. **Seeing his nose in a dream** means that the dreamer is aware of his abilities and his strong character. If there is **hair growing on his nose**, he will accomplish incredibly difficult things through sheer will power. A **bleeding nose** foretells disaster.

Notary — **Dreaming about a notary** means that the dreamer has unfulfilled desires, and will probably be involved in lawsuits. If a **woman has dealings with a notary**, she risks her reputation in return for fleeting pleasures.

Note — If the dreamer receives a note, it means that he will require his friends' help, but they will not extend it.

Notebook — The dreamer has problems breaking away from his past.

November — This is an indication of very mediocre success in all spheres.

Numbers — This is a sign of instability in business which causes the dreamer anxiety and discontent.

Numbness — If the dreamer begins to feel numbness, it is a prediction of illness and anxieties.

Nun — If a **religious person dreams about nuns**, it means that there is a conflict between material pleasures and matters of the spirit. For a **woman**, this dream foretells widowhood or separation from her lover. If **she dreams that she is a nun**, it reflects her unhappiness with her life. A **dead nun** indicates the dreamer's despair about his loved ones' infidelity and his financial losses. If a **nun dreams about discarding her habit**, it means that she is unsuitable for her calling.

Nuptials — If a woman dreams about her nuptials, it is a forecast of pleasant events which will give her joy and respect.

Nurse — If a **nurse appears in a dream,** it suggests good things to come — mainly success at work or an improvement in one's economic situation. If a **nurse is employed in the**

dreamer's home, it is a sign of illness or unfortunate visits with friends. If the **nurse leaves the dreamer's home**, it is a sign of good health. If a **young woman dreams about being a nurse**, she will be admired for her self-sacrifice.

Nursing (babies) — A **woman who dreams about nursing her infant** will enjoy what she does. A **young woman who has the same dream** will have responsible, respectable jobs. If a **man dreams that his wife is nursing their infant**, everything he does will go smoothly.

Nutmeg — This is a sign of financial success and good journeys.

Nuts — Dreaming about gathering nuts predicts success in business and love. **Eating nuts** means that the dreamer will be wealthy enough to have anything he wants. If a **woman dreams about nuts**, she will have her heart's desire.

Nymph — Seeing nymphs in clear water means that intimate desires will be realized in a shower of ecstasy and pleasure. If the **nymphs are not in water**, it is a sign of disillusionment. If a **young woman sees nymphs bathing**, she will have pleasure and joy, but they will not be pure; she will use her charms to corrupt men.

Oak — The **oak tree** is a symbol of health, prosperity and a good quality of life. If **the oak tree is full of acorns**, it means a professional promotion.

Oar — **Handling oars** is a sign of disappointment for the dreamer, as he will have to make many sacrifices for the well-being of others. A **dream about losing an oar** portends that the dreamer will not be able to realize his ambitions. A **broken oar** means that some event to which the dreamer was looking forward will be postponed.

Oath — Taking an oath in a dream forecasts disputes and arguments in waking life.

Oatmeal — **Eating oatmeal** in a dream means that the dreamer deserves to enjoy the wealth he has worked so hard for. If a **young woman dreams about preparing it**, she will soon be responsible for the fate of others.

Oats — **Seeing oats** is a good omen, especially for farmers. **Rotten oats** is a sign of sorrow that will replace joy. A **horse eating oats** indicates that the dreamer has unfinished tasks at hand.

Obedience — **Being obedient** to someone else predicts a normal, pleasant period in life. If **others are obedient** to the dreamer, it is a sign that he will have wealth and power.

Obelisk — **Seeing an obelisk** means that sad news is imminent. If **lovers stand next to an obelisk**, they will break up.

Obituary — **Dreaming about writing an obituary** means that the dreamer will soon have to perform unpleasant tasks. **Reading one** means that disconcerting news will arrive soon.

Obligation — If the **dreamer obligates himself** in any situation, he will be distressed by the complaints of others. If **others obligate themselves to him**, he will earn the esteem of friends and family.

Observatory — **Observing the skies from an observatory** predicts the dreamer's meteoric rise to prominence. If the **sky is cloudy**, the dreamer's highest aspirations will not be realized. A **young woman dreaming about an observatory** can look forward to material pleasures.

Occultist — Dreaming about listening to the teachings of an occultist means that the dreamer will try to raise other people to higher levels of tolerance and justice.

Ocean — Dreaming about the ocean signifies a desire for a new beginning, or for withdrawal and inner contemplation. A **calm sea and a clear horizon** represent a rosy, lucky and prosperous future; a **stormy sea** predicts imminent danger, domestic strife and business worries. If the **ocean is so shallow** that the dreamer can see the sea bed, a mixture of joy and prosperity with sorrow and hardship is predicted.

October — This is a sign of success in all ventures. New friendships will be cemented.

Oculist — Dreaming about consulting an oculist means that the dreamer is not satisfied with his progress in life, and will try to advance by other means.

Odor — **Sweet odors** in a dream mean that the dreamer is being taken care of by a beautiful woman, and is prospering. **Revolting odors** foretell bitter quarrels and irresponsible employees.

Offense — If the **dreamer is offended**, he will be angry at having to justify himself for minor misdemeanors. If **he gives offense**, his path to success will be full of obstacles. If a **young woman is offended or offends**, she will be sorry for having disobeyed her parents or jumped to hasty conclusions.

Offerings — Making an offering means that the dreamer will be servile and obsequious until he raises his level of responsibility.

Office (workplace)— If the **dreamer is working in an office**, financial problems are predicted. **Managing an office** symbolizes ambitiousness and the ability to overcome obstacles.

Office (public) — If the **dreamer holds office**, his ambitions prompt him to take risks sometimes, but he will be successful. If **he dreams about failing to be appointed to a certain position**, it means that he will suffer serious disappointments in his business. If **he is dismissed from office**, he will lose valuable possessions.

Officer — This indicates that the dreamer needs an authoritative figure in his life to map a path for him.

Offspring — **Seeing one's own offspring** is a sign of happiness and cheerfulness. **Seeing the offspring of domestic animals** means increased prosperity.

Oil — If the **dreamer sees large quantities of oil**, it means that he has exaggerated his pleasures. A **man's dream about oil dealings** represents a warning against difficult times, fraught with disappointments and frustration. If a **woman dreams about oil**, she will be respected and have a happy marriage. If **she is anointed with oil**, she will be privy to indecent propositions. **Sweet oil** means that the dreamer will not be treated with consideration in a troubling event.

Oilcloth — **Dreaming about oilcloth** is a symbol of aloofness toward and betrayal of the dreamer. **Dealing in oilcloth** means spurious business.

Ointment — A dream about ointment signifies that the dreamer will form warm and profitable friendships.

Old Man or Woman — This is a sign of sad burdens.

Olive — A **dream about olives** is a symbol of happiness and wealth for the dreamer. A **dream about harvesting olives** or about **black olives** predicts a birth in the family. **Breaking a bottle of olives** predicts that pleasure will be preceded by disappointment. **Eating olives** means happiness and good friends.

Omelet — **Seeing an omelet served** in a dream is a warning of false flattery and deceit at the expense of the dreamer. If **he eats it**, he will have demands made of him by someone he thought he trusted.

One-eyed — This is a huge warning of plots and intrigues against the dreamer's happiness and luck in life.

Onion — **Seeing quantities of onions** is an indication of difficulties, economic concerns, fear of losses. **Peeling an onion** symbolizes renewed efforts to try and achieve a coveted objective. **Eating onions** means that the dreamer will overcome all resistance. **Seeing them growing** means that the dreamer's affairs will be spiced with a little rivalry. **Cooked**

onions are a sign of tranquillity and minor profits. If **the dreamer cuts up onions** and his eyes burn, he will suffer defeat at the hands of his competitors.

Opera — **Attending an opera** means that the dreamer's friends will entertain him, and his business will be profitable. A **dream about an opera that is unpleasant** to the dreamer's ears is a sign of crises and failure, conflict and inner struggles. If the **dreamer participates in an opera**, it symbolizes a desire to reveal a hidden talent that is not being expressed.

Opium — This dream means that strangers will sabotage the dreamer's chances of success by subtle measures.

Opponent / Rival — If the dreamer dreams about an opponent, it is a sign that his wishes will soon come true.

Opulence — If a young woman dreams about incredible, gorgeous opulence, she should be warned not to be deceived and find herself in a bad and shameful situation.

Orange — **Eating or seeing an orange** in a dream suggests a significant improvement in one's lifestyle. However, a **young woman dreaming about eating an orange** risks losing her lover. **Healthy orange trees**, bearing ripe fruit, signify health and prosperity. **Slipping on an orange peel** predicts the death of a family member.

Orangutan — **Dreaming about an orangutan** signifies that the dreamer is being used to further someone else's selfish schemes. It is a sign of an unfaithful lover for a **young woman**.

Orator — If the dreamer is influenced by the words of an orator, it means that his head will be turned by flattery, and he will help undeserving people.

Orchard — **Lovers walking through blossoming, leafy orchards** predict the consummation of the courtship. If the **orchard is full of fruit**, it means that faithful employees will be rewarded for their services, owners of businesses will be successful, and homes will be happy and harmonious. If the **orchard is surrounded by a fence**, it means that the dreamer yearns for something unattainable. If the **orchard is afflicted with blight**, it foretells wretchedness despite joy and wealth. If the **dreamer becomes entangled in brambles** in an orchard, he has a jealous rival; it also indicates a terrible domestic quarrel. A **barren orchard** indicates that the dreamer will take no notice of opportunities to advance in life. If an **orchard is beaten by a storm**, it is a prediction of unwelcome guests.

Orchestra — **Listening to an orchestra playing music** indicates that the dreamer will be very famous. A **dream about playing in an orchestra** predicts a significant promotion at work. **Dreaming about playing in an orchestra** is a sign of enjoyable entertainment events, and a cultured, faithful partner.

Orchid — This attests to the dreamer's strong sexual desires.

Organ — **Hearing powerful organ music** signifies solid wealth and good friends. **Seeing an organ in a church** is a sign of despair due to death or separation in the family. If the **dreamer plays the organ competently**, he will enjoy prominence and good fortune. **Gloomy singing accompanied by an organ** means that unpleasant tasks are imminent, as well as the loss of friends or a job.

Organist — **Seeing an organist** indicates that the dreamer will have trouble because of a friend's careless behavior. A **young woman who dreams about being an organist** should be warned against being so demanding in love that her lover abandons her.

Ornament — **Wearing an ornament** means that the dreamer will receive a wonderful honor. **Receiving ornaments** is a sign of luck. **Giving them away** is a sign of carelessness and wastefulness. **Losing them** predicts the loss of a job or a lover.

Orphan — **Dreaming about comforting orphans** will cause the dreamer to sacrifice his own pleasures in order to help them. If the **orphans are the dreamer's relatives**, he will have new obligations which will cause him to lose friends.

Orphanhood — If the dreamer or another person is orphaned, it means that a new and positive personality will enter the dreamer's life, constituting a highly dominant force.

Ostrich — **Dreaming about an ostrich** means that the dreamer will become rich secretly, but will conduct immoral affairs with women. If **he catches an ostrich**, he will be wealthy enough to enjoy a life of knowledge and travel. An **ostrich hiding its head in the sand** is a sign that the dreamer or a family member has health problems. If a **woman sees an ostrich feather**, it means that she will advance in society by very dubious means.

Otter — **Seeing otters playing in clear springs** is a sign of happiness and good luck. A **single person** might marry soon after this dream, and **spouses** may be particularly affectionate.

Ottoman — If the dreamer and his sweetheart are lounging on an ottoman and enjoying a conversation about love, rivals are sure to make mischief to demean him in the eyes of his sweetheart, and he will have to marry her quickly.

Ouija — Dreaming about working on an ouija board predicts failed plans and partnerships. If the **dreamer does not work on one**, it is a warning of neglecting business for pleasure. If the **board writes fluently**, there will be good results.

Oven — The **dreamer who sees an oven** is in need of warm and loving human contact. If a **woman dreams that her oven is hot**, she will be universally loved for her sweet nature. If **she is baking**, she will experience passing disappointments. A **broken oven** indicates aggravation from employees and children.

Overalls — If a **woman sees a man wearing overalls**, she will be taken in as to the true nature of her lover. If **she is married**, she will be deceived by her husband's frequent absences, which stem from infidelity.

Overcoat — Dreaming about an overcoat means that others will cross the dreamer. If **he borrows one**, he will suffer for other people's mistakes. If **he sees or wears a new overcoat**, he will be extremely lucky in having his wishes come true.

Owl — Hearing the mournful hooting of an owl symbolizes sad things: death, pain, loss, melancholy, etc. A **dead owl** means that the dreamer or someone else will narrowly escape a serious disease or death. **Seeing an owl** is a warning that the dreamer will be in danger from enemies.

Oxen — **Seeing a fat ox** means that the dreamer will become a leader and win the admiration of women. **Seeing fat oxen grazing** predicts incredible advancement and wealth. **Thin oxen** signify that the dreamer's assets will decrease, and he will lose his friends. A **dead ox** is a sign of bereavement. If **oxen are drinking from a clear pond or stream**, the dreamer will finally own something he long coveted — possibly a lovely woman. If the **dreamer is a woman**, she will gain her lover's affection. **Yoked, well-matched oxen** symbolize a happy and wealthy marriage.

Oysters — **Dreaming about eating oysters** means that the dreamer will discard all his sense of decency and morality for the sake of pursuing base pleasures. He will also pursue financial gain shamelessly. If **he deals in oysters**, he will employ any means to win a woman or wealth. **Seeing oysters** predicts wealth and children. **Oyster soup made of fresh milk** indicates disputes and some trouble, but there will be a reconciliation. **Oyster soup made of buttermilk** means that the dreamer will have to do some distasteful things. There is a threat of quarrels, bad luck and break-up of friendships. Only if the **dreamer wakes up while eating the soup** can this be prevented.

Oyster Shells — Seeing these indicates that the dreamer will not be able to lay his hands on somebody else's assets.

Pacify — If the **dreamer tries to pacify people in pain**, it testifies to his good nature. For a **young woman**, this dream means that she will have a good husband or friends. If the **dreamer is pacifying other people's anger**, it means that he will work toward other people's progress. If a **lover is pacifying the jealousy of his sweetheart**, it is a sign that he is loving the wrong person.

Package — Receiving a package means that there are positive changes in store for the dreamer or for those close to him.

Packet (cargo ship) — **Seeing a packet docking** is a sign of a treat in store for the dreamer. If **it departs**, he will have minor losses and disappointments.

Packing — **Dreaming about packing** indicates a yearning for change. If the **dreamer does not finish packing**, it is a sign of frustration.

Page — **Seeing a page** means that the dreamer will marry an unsuitable person too hastily. If a **young woman dreams about being a page**, she is going to make a fool of herself in some dubious affair.

Pages — **Pages of paper** signify restlessness and a lack of clarity. The **cleaner and lighter the pages**, the greater the chance of extricating oneself from the problematic situation and turning over a new leaf.

Pagoda — **Seeing a pagoda** means that the dreamer will go on a long-awaited trip. If **a young woman is in a pagoda with her lover**, there will be many obstacles on the way to marriage. An **empty pagoda** is a warning of a break-up.

Pail — **Full pails of milk** in a dream mean happiness and prosperity. An **empty pail** signifies hunger and crop failure. If a **young woman carries a pail**, she will be employed in a home.

Pain — A **dream about pain** shows that the dreamer is surrounded by a supportive and loving environment. The **stronger the pain**, the more significant the dreamer is to those around him. If the **dreamer is in pain**, he will have to face unhappiness and regrets. **Seeing others in pain** warns of other people's mistakes. **Foot pains** predict family disputes. **Heart pains** indicate business problems and losses due to a mistake made by the dreamer.

Paint / Painting — **Seeing something freshly painted** indicates that something the dreamer has long been wishing for will come true. **Paint stains on clothes** mean that other people's criticism will hurt the dreamer. If the **dreamer himself holds the paint brush and paints**, it means that he is pleased with his job.

Paint and Painting — **Dreaming about seeing beautiful paintings** is an indication of the falseness of the dreamer's friends. If a **young woman dreams about painting a picture**, her lover will be unfaithful to her and leave her for another.

Palace — If the **dreamer finds himself in a palace** or great hall, it is a sign of unexpected problems. If the **dreamer did not see the entrance to this palace**, it means that good news is coming his way regarding romance. **Wandering through a palace and admiring it** is a sign that he is advancing.

Palisade — Seeing palisades means that the dreamer will change carefully laid plans to please strangers, but will suffer from doing so.

Pall — **Seeing a pall** is a sign of grief and bad luck. **Raising the pall from a corpse** portends the death of a loved one.

Pallbearer — **Dreaming about a pallbearer** means that an enemy is trying to get a rise out of the dreamer by doubting his honesty. **Seeing a pallbearer** means that the dreamer will make a nuisance of himself to institutions and friends.

Pallet — **Dreaming about a pallet** means that the dreamer will worry about his love affairs. For a **young woman**, a pallet is a symbol of a rival.

Palmistry — If a **young woman dreams about palmistry**, suspicion will be directed against her. **Having her palms read** means popularity with men, but condemnation from women. If **she reads palms**, it is an indication of her smartness.

Palms (of the hands) — If **the hands are far from the body**, it shows that the dreamer and those around him do not understand each other. **Hairy palms** indicate that the dreamer has a wild imagination. **Dirty palms** indicate jealousy. **Folded hands** mean emotional stress. **Bound hands** show that the dreamer is very restrained.

Palm Tree — **Palm trees** are a very optimistic symbol. If a **young woman goes down a palm-lined avenue**, she will have a happy home and good husband. If the **palm trees are dry**, her joy will be marred by a sad event.

Palsy — If the **dreamer has palsy**, he is making uncertain deals. If **his friend has palsy**, his fidelity is in question, and the dreamer's life might be affected by disease.

Pancake — **Eating pancakes** is an excellent dream meaning success in all endeavors. **Making pancakes** means a well-run, economical household.

Pane of Glass — **Handling a pane of glass** signifies that the dreamer's affairs are uncertain. If **he breaks it**, it is a sign of failure. **Talking to someone through a pane of glass** means that there are troublesome obstacles in the dreamer's path.

Panorama — This dream implies a change of job or address.

Panther — If the **dreamer sees a panther and is frightened**, business and love agreements may fall through unexpectedly because of people who want his downfall. **Killing the panther** means success. **Being threatened by a panther** means business disappointments and broken promises. The **frightening roar of a panther** means bad news.

Pantomime — **Seeing a pantomime** means betrayal by friends. **Participating in one** means that the dreamer will be offended and unsuccessful.

Pants — **Seeing pants** means that the dreamer will tempted to do unsavory things. **Putting pants on inside out** means that the dreamer will be totally mesmerized by something.

Paper or Parchment — **Handling these** is a sign

of losses, as they could be a lawsuit. **Paper or parchment** often predicts domestic strife. For a **young woman**, it means a quarrel with her lover.

Parables — Dreaming about parables means the inability to make a decision pertaining to a business dilemma. **Parables** are also a symbol of infidelity and misunderstandings.

Parachute — Dreaming about a parachute floating earthward means that the dreamer wants to get out of a personal or professional relationship.

Parade — See **Procession**.

Paradise — Dreaming about Paradise indicates loyal friends and a change for the better in life. The transition will manifest itself in a move from preoccupation with the material world to preoccupation with the spiritual world. For **mothers**, it means good children. For **lovers**, fidelity and wealth.

Paralysis — Dreaming about paralysis portends disappointments in business and in literary pursuits. For **lovers**, it foretells a break-up.

Parasol — Seeing a parasol if the dreamer is married is a sign of illicit pleasures. If a **young woman dreams about a parasol**, she will have many affairs on the side, and will enjoy concealing them from her lover.

Parcel — Dreaming about the delivery of a parcel means that someone dear to the dreamer will return unexpectedly. **Carrying a parcel** means an unpleasant task that has to be done. **Dropping a parcel on the way to delivering it** means that the dreamer neglected something important.

Pardon — If the **dreamer seeks a pardon for a crime he never committed**, it means that he is worried about business, but it will work out. If **he is guilty**, he will have hassles. If **he receives a pardon**, things will work out after a lot of trouble.

Parents — **Seeing happy parents** is a sign of harmony and good friends. **Seeing dead parents** is a warning of impending trouble. If **they are alive and living happily in the dreamer's home**, positive changes are in the offing. **Happy, healthy parents** mean a good life for the dreamer, while **sad, ill parents** mean bad luck.

Parks — **Walking through a well-maintained park** means happy leisure. If the **dreamer is with his lover**, it predicts a happy marriage. A **neglected park** is a sign of serious setbacks.

Parrot — A **parrot which is tied up** suggests that the dreamer enjoys gossiping or is a victim of gossip. A **chattering parrot** indicates idle gossip in the part of the dreamer's friends. A **sleeping parrot** means a time-out in family disputes. If a **young woman dreams of owning a parrot**, her lover will think that she is shrewish. **Teaching a parrot** is a sign of business problems, while a **dead parrot** signifies losing friends.

Parsley — **Parsley** is a sign of success after struggle. **Eating parsley** signifies good health, but also responsibility for a large family.

Parsnips — These denote business success but trouble in love.

Parting — **Parting from dear ones** predicts minor

hassles, while **parting from enemies** signifies good luck in love and business.

Partner — If the **dreamer's partner breaks goods**, it means that he will cause damage to the business. If the **dreamer scolds him for the breakage**, the loss will be recouped to some degree.

Partnership — **Forming a partnership with a man** predicts unstable money matters, while **forming a partnership with a woman** means that the dreamer will want to conceal some venture from his friends. **Dissolving a disagreeable partnership** foretells happiness, but if **it was a good partnership**, there will be bad luck.

Partridge — **Seeing partridges** is a sign of good luck in the near future. **Killing them** means accumulation of wealth and distributing it to others. **Eating them** symbolizes enjoying the fruits of a high position. **Flying partridges** predicts a good future. **Trapping partridges** means that the dreamer's hopes will be realized.

Party (group) — If the **dreamer is mugged by a party of strangers**, it means that his enemies are uniting against him. If **he is unscathed**, he will surmount any obstacles in business or love.

Party (celebration) — A **party** is a sign of a happy life. A **happy party on a lawn** means an active social life and plenty of business.

Passenger — **Seeing incoming passengers** foretells positive things for the dreamer, while **outgoing passengers** are a sign of a missed business opportunity. If the **dreamer is one of the departing passengers**, he is displeased with what he does and will attempt to change it.

Password — This means that the dreamer will be helped during some imminent trouble.

Pastry — **Dreaming about pastry** means that the dreamer will be taken in by a con artist. If **he eats pastry**, he will have true friendships. If a **young woman cooks it**, her intentions will be clear to others.

Patch — **Having patches on one's clothing** means that the dreamer will do his duties humbly. If **others have patches**, poverty and wretchedness are imminent. If a **woman patches her family's clothing**, it signifies a lot of love but a lack of money. If a **young woman tries to hide her patches**, it means that she will attempt to conceal flaws in her character from her lover.

Patent — **Dreaming about securing a patent** means that the dreamer takes a lot of trouble with everything he does. If **he does not secure a patent**, he will fail in ventures which are beyond his capabilities. If he **buys a patent**, he will have to undertake a futile journey.

Patent Medicine — If the **dreamer takes patent medicine** in order to cure himself, it signifies his determination to succeed, which he will, much to the chagrin of his rivals. If **he sees or produces patent medicines**, he will enjoy a meteoric rise to prominence.

Path — A **narrow, rough, rocky path** means adversity for the dreamer. If **he is searching for his path**, it means that he cannot accomplish a task that he hoped to complete. **Walking along a grass- and flower-lined path** indicates emotional freedom.

Paunch — A **large paunch** means great wealth together with total lack of finesse. A **shrunken paunch** means hardship and disease.

Pauper — **Dreaming about being a pauper** presages bad things for the dreamer. **Seeing paupers** means that he will have to be generous.

Peach — If the **peaches are growing on leafy trees**, opportunities to enjoy pleasurable experiences and advancement can be expected in the future. **Seeing or eating peaches** signifies sick children, canceled trips and business set-backs. **Dried peaches** mean that enemies will steal from the dreamer. If a **young woman dreams of gathering ripe, juicy peaches**, she will marry a rich, wise, well-traveled man. If the **peaches are hard and green**, her relatives will treat her badly, and she will become ill and lose her looks.

Peacock — **Peacocks** warns against conceit and excessive pride. **Dreaming about one** warns the dreamer that superficial wealth and glitter conceal poverty and failure. To **hear the call of peacocks** means that a handsome, well-dressed person will humiliate the dreamer.

Peanuts — These signify that the dreamer is sociable and will be blessed with many friends.

Pearls — **Dreaming about pearls** predicts successful business and a good social life. If a **young woman's lover sends her pearls**, they will have a wonderful, harmonious relationship.

Pears — **Seeing pears** indicates that others are gossiping and talking about the dreamer, his friends, or relatives, behind his back. **Eating pears** means poor health and business failure. **Seeing golden pears on trees** foretells improved business success. **Gathering pears** means that disappointments will be followed by happy surprises. **Baked pears** are a sign of lukewarm friendships.

Peas — **Eating peas** heralds a good period, bringing prosperity and economic growth. **Seeing peas growing** means business success. **Planting them** will lead to prosperity. **Gathering them** means the successful implementation of plans. **Canned peas** mean that the dreamer's hopes are stagnant for a while, but finally come true. **Dried peas** means neglected health. **Eating dried peas** signifies a slight decrease in pleasure and wealth.

Pearls — If a **young woman dreams about pebbles**, it shows that she is egoistic and unforgiving. **Seeing a path strewn with pebbles** means that she can expect to have lots of worthy rivals.

Pecans — **Eating pecans** in a dream means the totally successful implementation of a plan. **Seeing them grow on the tree** means a long, happy life. If **they are rotten**, there will be failure in business and love. If the **dreamer has difficulty cracking them**, and then finds small nuts, it means that success will be his, but in a minor way.

Peddler — This predicts financial success occurring in an unusual manner.

Pelican — A **dream about pelicans** symbolizes a mixture of success and failure. Failure can be overcome **by catching one**. **Killing one** means that the dreamer rides rough-shod over the rights of others.

Pen — If the **dreamer is writing with a pen**, he will hear from a person with whom he has been out of touch for a long time. If the **pen does not write**, the dreamer will face accusations of immorality. **Seeing a pen** means that the dreamer's love of living on the edge is leading him into trouble.

Penalties — If the **dreamer has penalties imposed on him**, it means that he is rebelling against duties he has to perform. **Paying a penalty** is a sign of disease and financial loss. **Beating a penalty** is a sign of the dreamer's triumph.

Pencil — **Seeing a pencil** is a symbol of good positions. If a **young woman writes with a pencil**, it means that she will marry well. If **she erases what she has written**, her lover will let her down.

Penguin — This signifies that the dreamer has an adventurous character and aspires to go on journeys.

Penis — Dreaming about a penis or vagina has a sexual interpretation which depends on the character of the dreamer.

Penitentiary — **Dreaming about a penitentiary** signals that the dreamer will become involved in ventures that will be to his detriment. If **he is an inmate**, it signifies an unhappy home and business failure. If **he escapes**, he will overcome problems.

Penny — **Dreaming about pennies** means that the dreamer is wasting his time, damaging both his business and his relationships. **Losing pennies** means failure. **Finding them** means good prospects of advancement. **Counting them** implies a sense of economy.

Pension — If the **dreamer draws a pension**, friends will help him. If the **dreamer is not awarded a pension**, his ventures will fail and he will lose friends.

Pepper — If the **dreamer's tongue is burnt by pepper**, it means that his predilection for gossip will cause him anguish. If he sees **red pepper growing**, it means that he will marry an economical and independent woman. **Seeing pods of red pepper** means that he will jealously defend his rights. **Grinding black pepper** means that he will be taken in by slippery people. **Putting it on food** is a sign of treachery by friends.

Peppermint — **Dreaming about peppermint** predicts interesting business developments, and pleasant leisure time. **Seeing it growing** indicates a fun activity with some romance in it. If there is **peppermint in a beverage**, the dreamer will have an encounter with an interesting and attractive person.

Perfume — A **dream about inhaling perfume** is a sign of good news, particularly concerning love relationships. **Perfuming one's body and clothing** means that the dreamer seeks admiration — and will get it. If the **scent is so strong that it is stupefying**, it attests to the fact that the dreamer will indulge in excessive pleasures to the detriment of clear thinking. **Spilling perfume** means a loss of something the dreamer enjoys. **Breaking a bottle of perfume** is a sign of real bad luck, the dashing of one's greatest hopes. If a **woman perfumes her bath**, she will experience the ultimate joy.

Perspiration — If the dreamer is perspiring, it means he will overcome some scandal with flying colors.

Pest — If **the dreamer is anxious about any kind of pest**, it means that he will have worries. If **others are bothered by pests**, the dreamer will be upset by negative developments.

Pestering / Bothering — Any kind of pestering means that nonsense, useless chatter and small talk are liable to cause harm.

Petticoat — **Seeing new petticoats** means that people will mock the dreamer for taking pride in his possessions. **Dirty or torn petticoats** warn of a threat to the dreamer's good name. If a **woman has clean, silk petticoats**, it means that she has a good, attentive husband. If **she forgets to wear a petticoat**, it is a sign of bad luck. If her **petticoat falls down while** she is in public, she will lose her lover.

Pewter — This is a dream signifying financial difficulties.

Phantom — **Being pursued by a phantom** is a forecast of peculiar and disturbing experiences. If a **phantom flees from the dreamer**, it means that his troubles will diminish.

Pheasant — A **dream about pheasants** symbolizes well-being and good friends. **Eating a pheasant** means that the dreamer's wife will prevent contact between the dreamer and his friends. **Shooting pheasants** is a sign of the dreamer's refusal to give up on one pleasurable activity for the sake of making his friends feel good.

Phosphorus — **Dreaming about phosphorus** symbolizes fleeting happiness. For a **woman**, it is a symbol of great but transient success with admirers.

Photographs — **Seeing photographs** is a sign of imminent deception. If the **dreamer is being photographed**, it means that he will unwittingly cause himself and others trouble. If the **dreamer receives a photograph of his lover**, it is a warning of infidelity. If **married people have photographs of others**, it means that bad things about them will be made public.

Photography — A **dream about any sort of photography** indicates a long journey. If a **woman dreams about a camera**, it means that she will soon have a heart-warming meeting with a man.

Physician — If a **young woman dreams about a physician**, it means that she is ruining her good looks on superficial pleasures. If **she is ill and dreams about a physician**, she will soon be well. If **he appears anxious**, her troubles will increase.

Piano — **Seeing a piano** predicts a happy event. **Hearing beautiful piano music** is a sign of success and health. **Cacophonous sounds** signify annoyance. **Sad music** indicates bad news. A **broken, out-of-tune piano** means that the dreamer is generally dissatisfied with his own achievements, as well as those of his children and friends.

Pickax — **Dreaming about a pickax** indicates that an enemy is seeking the dreamer's social downfall. A **broken pickax** is a sign of very bad luck.

Pickles — If the **dreamer sees pickles**, he will waste his time on worthless things if he does not use his judgment. If a **young woman eats pickles**, she will have a mediocre job, as well as rivals who will defeat her unless she uses her discretion.

Pickpocket — **Dreaming about a pickpocket** means that

an enemy will cause the dreamer damage. If a **young woman falls victim to a pickpocket**, it means that she will be the butt of someone's jealousy and malice. If **she picks someone's pockets**, she will be ostracized for her crude behavior.

Picnic — **Attending a picnic in a dream** portends success and pleasure. If the **picnic is spoilt by a storm or another interruption**, there will be temporary setbacks in business and love.

Picture — **Being surrounded by artistic masterpieces** shows a strong desire to succeed and avoid failure. **Seeing pictures** is a portent of envy and deception on the part of others. **Painting a picture** means that the dreamer will get involved in a poorly paid project. **Buying pictures** warns of bad business ventures.

Pier — **Standing on a pier** signifies that the dreamer will overcome obstacles and receive the highest honors and prosperity. If **he tries to walk on a pier**, but fails to do so, he will lose the honor he values so much.

Pies — **Dreaming about eating pies** warns the dreamer to watch out for his enemies, who wish him harm. If a **young woman dreams about making pies**, she will flirt habitually.

Pig — In **Western culture**, a pig symbolizes a difficult personality, one that does not get on well with others. In the **Far East**, it is a sign of economic abundance. **Pigs wallowing in mud** mean bad business partners and dubious business ventures. A **young woman** dreaming about a wallowing pig will have a jealous and possessive male friend.

Pigeon — **Seeing and hearing pigeons** is a sign of

domestic harmony and good children. For a **young woman**, it means a happy marriage at a young age. If **pigeons are shot for sport**, it shows a cruel streak in the dreamer's nature. He should be careful of pursuing immoral pleasures. **Flying pigeons** foretell harmony and news from faraway acquaintances.

Pilgrim — **Dreaming about pilgrims** means that the dreamer will undertake a long journey, leaving his dear ones behind, in the erroneous belief that it is in everyone's best interests. If **he is a pilgrim**, it is a sign of poverty and uncaring friends. If a **young woman is approached by a pilgrim**, she will be conned. If **he goes away**, she will become aware of her weakness of character and will try to improve herself.

Pillow — **Dreaming about a pillow** is a sign of comfort and affluence. **Sleeping on a pillow** is a warning against an inappropriate action by the dreamer that may cause concern, embarrassment and a lack of confidence. If a **young woman makes a pillow**, she will have a happy life.

Pills — If the **dreamer sees pills in a package or a bottle**, it means that he will soon embark on a journey or a trip. **Taking pills** means unhappy and unrewarding responsibilities. **Giving pills to other people** predicts that the dreamer will be unpopular.

Pimple — **Pimply flesh** means niggling worries. **Other people with pimples** means that the dreamer will be bothered with the hassles of others. If a **woman's beauty is spoilt by pimples**, her behavior will be condemned by her friends.

Pincers — If the **dreamer is pinched by pincers**, he will have to cope with infuriating worries. **Dreaming about pincers** is a bad sign.

Pineapple — **Dreaming about pineapples** is an indication of days of very good luck, happiness and joy, especially in the company of close friends. **Pricking one's finger** while preparing a pineapple is an indication of obstacles that will be overcome, leading to success.

Pine Cone — A closed pine cone symbolizes a tight-knit family; an open pine cone — a family that has separated and drifted apart.

Pine Tree — **Seeing a pine tree** is a symbol of constant success. A **dead pine** foretells bereavement.

Pins — **Dreaming about pins** is a sign of domestic strife and lovers' tiffs. **Swallowing a pin** is a warning of accidents and dangers. **Losing a pin** means minor losses and arguments. **Seeing a bent or rusty pin** means a loss of respect by others because of the dreamer's sloppy habits. **Being pricked by a pin** signifies being bothered by someone.

Pipe (smoking) — **Seeing a pipe** means peace after struggles. If the **dreamer smokes a pipe**, he will have a pleasant visit with an old friend. There will be a reconciliation.

Pipes (drain, etc.) — **Various utility pipes** are an indication of a caring and prosperous community. If the **pipes are old and broken**, it is a sign of illness and lack of advancement in business.

Pirate — **Dreaming about pirates** means that false friends will conspire against the dreamer. If the **dreamer is a**

pirate, it foretells his drop in society. If a **young woman's lover is a pirate**, she should be warned of his treachery and worthlessness. If **pirates capture her**, she will be tricked into leaving her home.

Pistol — If the **dreamer owns a pistol**, it is an indication of his base nature. If **he hears one go off**, one of his ventures will fail. **Shooting a pistol** means that the dreamer will be jealous of someone unjustifiably and will persecute them.

Pit — **Looking into a deep pit** indicates that the dreamer will take ridiculous business risks. **Falling into a pit** is a sign of sorrow and disaster — unless the dreamer wakes as he falls. If **he goes down into a pit**, he knowingly risks health and property for greater gains.

Pitcher — **Dreaming about a pitcher** is an indication of the dreamer's pleasant and giving nature. He will be successful. A **broken pitcher** signifies losing friends.

Pitchfork — **Dreaming about a pitchfork** is a sign of the dreamer's struggle for self-improvement and prosperity. If **he is attacked by a pitchfork-brandishing person**, it means that he has enemies who want to harm him.

Plague — **Dreaming about a plague epidemic** means extreme business failures and domestic misery. If the **dreamer has the plague**, he will have to make enormous efforts to keep his business afloat. **Attempting to flee the plague** means that a serious problem is pursuing the dreamer.

Plain — If a **young woman crosses a green, fertile plain**, she will have a good life. If the **plain is arid and barren**, her life will be lonely and unpleasant.

Planet — If the dreamer visits other planets, he will soon experience new and fascinating things.

Plank — If a young woman is crossing murky water on a rotten plank, she will suffer from an inattentive lover, have many troubles and be in danger of risking her good reputation.

Plaster — **Undecorated, plastered walls** mean a fragile success. If **pieces of plaster fall on the dreamer**, it is a sign of total catastrophe. **Seeing plasterers working** means enough money to live fairly comfortably.

Plates — If a **woman dreams about plates**, she is thrifty and will marry a good man. If **she is married**, she will keep her husband happy by managing the house well.

Play — If a **young woman sees a play**, she will marry for money and the pursuit of pleasure. If **she has trouble getting to or from the play**, or if **there are ugly scenes**, she will have an unexpectedly rough time ahead of her.

Pleasure Boat — This indicates that the dreamer longs to go on a vacation and to let his hair down.

Plow — **Dreaming about a plow** is a sign of unprecedented success. If the **dreamer plows**, it is a sign of joy and prosperity. **Watching people plow** means increased knowledge and property. If a **young woman watches her lover plow**, she will have a good, wealthy husband and a happy life.

Plum — **Green plums** are a clear sign that the dreamer has enemies of whom he is not aware, and will suffer harm. **Ripe plums** signify happy but brief events. Eating plums is a sign of flirtation. **Gathering plums** means fulfillment of wishes — but not for long. If among the **plums gathered there are some rotten ones**, it is a reminder to the dreamer that life is not a bed of roses.

Pocket — A **pocket** symbolizes the womb. The dream is interpreted according to the context in which the pocket appeared. It may indicate the dreamer's desire to return to the womb, or, alternatively, his desire to storm back into life. **Dreaming about a pocket** also means evil schemes against the dreamer.

Pocketbook — **Finding a pocketbook** stuffed with money indicates good luck. If it is empty, the dreamer will suffer a grave disappointment. **Losing a pocketbook** indicates that the dreamer will quarrel with a good friend, much to his detriment.

Poison — If the **dreamer or his children or relatives are poisoned**, he will be hurt. If **he wants to poison people**, everything will go wrong. To **discard poison** or **to dream that an enemy is poisoned** means surmounting obstacles. **Handling poison** means being surrounded by bad things. If the **dreamer recovers after being poisoned**, he will succeed after a struggle. If a **physician prescribes some poison**, it means that the dreamer will undertake a very risky venture.

Poker (cards) — **Dreaming about playing poker** is a warning against falling into bad company. **Young women dreaming about poker** will compromise their moral integrity.

Poker (for the fire) — **Seeing a red-hot poker** or **fighting with one** means that the dreamer will face his problems courageously.

Polar Bear — **Dreaming of polar bears** means that the

dreamer will be taken in by bad luck that resembles something positive, including enemies pretending to be friends. A **polar-bear skin** means that the dreamer will overcome all opposition.

Police — **Any dream involving the police** on all levels will extricate the dreamer from the crisis he is now going through. A **dream about a confrontation with a police officer** or **about arrest** means that the dreamer will soon receive assistance which shows that he is suffering from confusion and guilt. **Being arrested while innocent** means that the dreamer will overcome rivalry. **Seeing patrolling police officers** means worrying business vacillations.

Polishing — If the dreamer polishes something, his achievements will lead him to lofty positions.

Politician — **Dreaming about a politician** signifies bad friends and time- and money-wasting events. If the **dreamer dabbles in politics**, his friends will behave angrily and unpleasantly toward him. For a **young woman**, dreaming about being interested in politics is a warning against being conned.

Polka — Dancing the polka signifies agreeable pastimes.

Pomegranate — A **pomegranate given by the dreamer's beloved,** or **a pomegranate tree**, suggests that the dreamer fears sexual infidelity on the part of his partner. **Dreaming about pomegranates** implies that the dreamer will exploit his talents for enriching his mind rather than for superficial pleasures. **Eating one** means falling desperately in love.

Pond — **Seeing a pond** signifies a calm, smooth-running life. A **muddy pond** is a sign of domestic strife.

Pony — This is a sign of success in business ventures.

Poor — If the dreamer or his friends are poor, it signifies trouble and loss.

Poorhouse — This is a sign of disloyal friends who associate with the dreamer only so that they can get hold of his money and possessions.

Pope — If the **dreamer sees a pope but does not speak to him**, it means that he will be servile to a master. If he **speaks to the pope**, he can expect great honors. If the **pope looks sad or upset**, it warns the dreamer against sorrow and immorality.

Poplars — **Blooming or leafy poplars** are a good sign. If a **young woman** stands under such a tree with her lover, all of her wildest dreams will come true. If the **trees are bare and dry**, she will experience disappointment.

Poppies — **Dreaming about poppies** is a sign of transient, baseless pleasures and business successes. **Inhaling the scent of a poppy** means that the dreamer will fall victim to arch flattery.

Porcelain — **Dreaming about porcelain** means favorable business conditions. **Broken or dirty porcelain** is a sign of mistakes that will have serious consequences.

Porch — **Dreaming about a porch** means that the dreamer will begin new ventures which will make him feel very unsure. **Standing on a porch** means that day-to-day worries are bothering him. **Building a porch** is a sign of undertaking new obligations. If a **young woman is on a**

porch with her lover, it means that she suspects the purity of someone's intentions.

Porcupine — **Seeing a porcupine** indicates the dreamer's unwillingness to undertake any new ventures or make new friends. If a **young woman dreams about a porcupine**, she will be afraid of her lover. **Seeing a dead porcupine** means that the dreamer discards anger and relinquishes his possessions.

Pork — **Eating pork** is a sign of awful trouble, but **seeing it** portends triumph for the dreamer.

Porpoise — Seeing a porpoise means that the dreamer is incapable of retaining other people's interest, so his enemies are pushing him aside.

Porridge — See **Cereal**.

Port / Harbor — This symbolizes worries, conflicts with others, dissatisfaction and a lack of serenity.

Porter — **Seeing a porter** is a sign of bad luck and tumultuous events. If the **dreamer sees himself as a porter**, it is a sign of a reduction in his status. **Hiring a porter** means success and its attendant joys. If the **dreamer sends a porter away**, charges will be made against him.

Portfolio — This indicates displeasure with the dreamer's job, and his desire to make a change.

Portrait — Dreaming about looking at a portrait of a handsome person warns the dreamer that certain joys have a treacherous side to them. This dream brings bad luck.

Postman — This is a sign that the dreamer is worried about financial, business-related, or social difficulties.

Post Office — Dreaming about a post office indicates that the dreamer has a guilty conscience concerning an outstanding debt or commitment. It is a sign of bad news and luck.

Postage — **Dreaming about postage stamps** means lucrative and organized business affairs. **Attempting to use canceled stamps** means a bad reputation. **Torn stamps** are a sign of obstacles in the dreamer's path to success.

Postcard — Dreaming about receiving a postcard means that sudden tidings will generally be bad.

Pot — **Dreaming about a pot** means that the dreamer will be bothered with minor hassles. A **boiling pot** in a woman's dream is a sign of happy duties. A **broken or rusty pot** signifies disappointment.

Potatoes — **Dreaming about potatoes** symbolizes calm, stability and satisfaction with one's life. **Planting potatoes** foretells wishes come true. **Digging up potatoes** is a sign of success. **Eating them** is a sign of profit. **Cooking them** implies a good job. **Rotting potatoes** signify the end of good things.

Potsherds — These portend a period of happiness and joy, as well as of economic prosperity.

Potter — **Dreaming about a potter** is a sign of satisfaction with work. If a **young woman sees a potter**, she will have a good social life.

Poultry — **Dreaming about poultry** is a warning to the dreamer against a profligate lifestyle. If a **young woman chases poultry**, it means that she will pursue superficial pleasures.

Powder — This is a sign of amoral people

who are in contact with the dreamer. He can beat them at their game if he is alert.

Prairie — **Dreaming about a prairie** indicates a comfortable, affluent lifestyle, and smooth advancement. A **grassy, flower-filled, undulating prairie** is a sign of happy events. An **arid prairie** means that the absence of friends will cause the dreamer loss and unhappiness. **Being lost on a prairie** is a sign of sadness and bad luck.

Prayer — If the **dreamer is praying**, it is a sign that a good period, filled with happiness and joy, is approaching. If **prayer takes place without the dreamer**, it is a sign that the dreamer's deeds are harmful to others, and can lead to failure.

Preacher — **Dreaming about a preacher** means that the dreamer is not perfect, and he will have problems. **Dreaming about being a preacher** predicts business losses. **Hearing a preacher** is an omen of bad luck. A **dispute with a preacher** means losing a contest. If a **preacher leaves the dreamer**, business will be more lively. If the **preacher looks sad**, the dreamer will suffer recriminations.

Precipice — **Standing over a gaping precipice** is a sign of catastrophe. **Falling over a precipice** means disaster for the dreamer.

Pregnancy — For a **woman to dream about being pregnant** is an indication of dissatisfaction with her husband and children. If a **woman is really pregnant and has this dream**, it portends a safe delivery and speedy recuperation. If a **virgin has this dream**, it is a sign of scandal and trouble.

Presents —Receiving presents indicates that the dreamer will be extremely lucky.

President of the United States — Dreaming about speaking to the President of the United States means that the dreamer has political leanings and ambitions.

Priest — This is a sign of bad luck. If a **woman is in love with a priest**, her lover has no conscience and no morals. **Confessing to a priest** predicts grief and humiliation. **Any dream about a priest** means that the dreamer will be the cause of unpleasantness to the people close to him.

Primrose — This is a portent of happiness, comfort and serenity.

Printer — If a **printer** appears in a dream, it means that the dreamer will suffer from economic difficulties if he is not careful. If a **woman dreams about some kind of relationship with a printer**, it means that her choice of friends will not be approved of by her parents.

Printing Press — **Being at a printing press** signifies gossip and slander. **Running a printing press** foretells bad luck. If a **woman's lover is associated with a printing press**, it means he has neither time nor money for her.

Prince / Princess — This indicates that the dreamer possesses the hidden ability to fulfill his urgent need to improve his social status.

Prison — **Dreaming about imprisonment** warns about a change for the worse in physical health. A **dream about an unsuccessful attempt to escape from prison** is an indication of an obstacle that must be overcome in one's life. A **dream about a successful**

escape from prison suggests success and the fulfillment of hopes. **Seeing someone freed from prison** is a sign of overcoming obstacles.

Privacy — If the **dreamer's privacy** is disturbed, he will be bothered by inconsiderate people. A **woman** who has this dream should take care of her private affairs and not interfere with those of her partner.

Prize — Winning a prize signifies the opposite: Heavy financial losses can be expected.

Prize Fight — Seeing a prize fight in a dream symbolizes difficulty controlling one's affairs.

Prize Fighter — If a woman dreams about a prize fighter, it means that she will lead a wild life.

Procession / Parade — A **festive procession or parade** indicates changes that will usher in a period of anxiety about unfulfilled hopes as well as sorrow and stormy events. A **torch-lit procession** is an indication of frivolous pastimes.

Profanity — **Dreaming about profanity** symbolizes the dreamer's coarse, tactless behavior. If he dreams about **others using profanities**, he will soon be offended.

Profit — **Dreaming about profits** is a sign of imminent success. If the **dreamer receives a large sum of money**, this is a sign of deception, denial and being led astray by one of his close friends.

Promenade — **Dreaming about promenading** predicts pleasant, profitable pastimes. If **others promenade**, it is a sign of rivalry.

Property — Dreaming about owning a lot of property is a sign of financial and social success.

Prostitute — If the **dreamer is with a prostitute**, it means his friends will be justifiably angry at him. A **married woman dreaming about a prostitute** will suspect her husband and quarrel with him. If a **young woman has this dream**, it signals that she will not be honest with her lover.

Psychiatrist — **Dreaming about a psychiatrist** means that the dreamer will soon receive advice and counseling. If the **dreamer is a psychiatrist's patient**, it foretells emotional turmoil.

Publisher — If a **dreamer sees a publisher**, it means he has literary aspirations. If a **woman dreams that her husband is a publisher**, she will be jealous of his female acquaintances. If a **publisher rejects the dreamer's manuscript**, disappointment is imminent. If the **publisher accepts the manuscript**, the dreamer's hopes will be realized. If the **publisher loses the manuscript**, the dreamer will be hurt by unknown parties.

Puddings — **Dreaming about puddings** symbolizes disappointingly small profits. **Eating pudding** denotes disappointments. **Making a pudding** means bad luck in love.

Puddle — If the **dreamer steps into a puddle of clear water**, he will have some minor hassle that will disappear later. If the **puddle is muddy**, the hassle will not disappear so soon. If the **dreamer's feet get wet because of stepping into a puddle**, it means that good luck will turn sour.

Pulpit — A **pulpit** is a sign of trouble and sadness. If the **dreamer is in a pulpit**, he is warned of illness and bad luck in business.

Pulse — **Dreaming about one's pulse** warns the dreamer to watch out for his health and business, both of which are in jeopardy. **Feeling someone else's pulse** is a sign of debauchery.

Pump — If a **pump** appears in a dream, it is a sign of prosperity following hard work. It is also a sign of health. A **broken pump** means that the dreamer has no chance of prospering because of family worries. **Working a pump** means a good life.

Punch — If the **dreamer has punched someone**, he should expect to lose a court case. If the **dreamer has been punched**, he should expect to win.

Punch (beverage) — Dreaming about drinking punch indicates a preference for a selfish, immoral life to a respectable one.

Pups — **Dreaming about pups** and their innocence signifies a good, pleasant life. If the **pups are strong and healthy**, the dreamer will enjoy prosperity close friendships. The opposite is true if **they are weak and sickly**.

Purchases — A sign of prosperity and career success.

Purse — If the dreamer's purse is stuffed with money bills and diamonds, he will enjoy harmony and love in life.

Putty — This warns of risking one's fortune.

Pyramid — A **pyramid** is a symbol of changes. **Climbing the pyramids** signifies waiting a long time before realizing one's hopes and desires. **Dreaming about studying the mysteries of the pyramids** means that the dreamer will enjoy nature's mysteries, and will become knowledgeable.

Quack (bogus doctor) — This foretells the incorrect treatment of a disease.

Quack Medicine — **Dreaming about quack medicine** means that the dreamer is sinking under the weight of some problem, but by working hard can get out of it. If the **dreamer sees an ad for this medicine**, he will be hurt by bad associates.

Quadrille — This is an indication of a good social life.

Quagmire — **Being in a quagmire** is a sign that the dreamer is incapable of fulfilling his obligations. If **he sees others in a quagmire**, it means that he will suffer from their failures.

Quail — **Live quails** in a dream are an excellent sign. **Dead ones** foretell bad luck. **Shooting quail** means that friends will be angry at the dreamer. **Eating quail** is an indication of a wasteful lifestyle.

Quaker — **Dreaming about Quakers** indicates true friends and honest business dealings. If the **dreamer is a Quaker**, he will treat his enemies decently. If a **young woman is present at a Quaker meeting**, it signifies that she will have a good and faithful husband.

Quarantine — Dreaming about being in quarantine means that the dreamer's enemies will place him in an impossible position through their scheming.

Quarrel — If the **dreamer is involved in a quarrel**, it means that someone is fiercely jealous of him. It is a sign of unhappiness. For a **woman**, it can mean strife and separation.

Quarry — If the **dreamer is in a quarry**, watching people work hard, it means that he will be promoted by means of hard work. A **non-operational quarry** is a sign of bad luck, failure and even death.

Quartet — **Participating in a quartet** means happy times, prosperity and good friends. **Hearing a quartet** means new and high aspirations.

Quay — A **dream about a quay** predicts a long trip. If the **dreamer sees ships** while he is on a quay, it is a sign that things will work out for him.

Queen — **Dreaming about a queen** indicates that the dreamer will soon receive help or aid from those close to him. If the **queen is old or tired**, the dreamer will not enjoy his leisuretime activities.

Question — If the **dreamer questions something's worth**, it means that he suspects a loved one of infidelity. **Asking a question** means a serious search for the truth, as well as success. If the **dreamer is questioned**, he will not be treated justly.

Quicksand — If the **dreamer is trapped in quicksand**, it is a sign that his social and economic status will collapse. If the **dreamer sees another person trapped in quicksand**, it is a sign that others will stand in the way of his attempts to achieve his objectives. If the **dreamer cannot get out of the quicksand**, he will be devastated by bad luck.

Quills — If the **dreamer is a person of letters**, this dream means success. If the **quills are for decoration**, business will boom.

Quilts — **Dreaming about quilts** is a sign of good fortune. For a **young woman**, it means that her down-to-earth, clever nature will appeal to a man, who will want to marry her. If the **quilt is clean but has holes in it**, she will have a husband who values her, but she will not be attracted to him. If the **quilt is dirty**, this will be a reflection on her own conduct, and she will not marry a good man.

Quinine — A **dream about quinine** is a sign of great happiness, but not of wealth. If the **dreamer takes quinine**, his health will improve, as will his social and business life.

Quitting (a job) / **Resignation** — Dreaming about quitting a job, especially if the dreamer has a senior position, indicates that his plans will be realized in the near future.

Quiz — **Dreaming about taking a quiz or exam** portends an imminent important opportunity in business. **Failing a quiz** means business losses. **Getting a good score on a quiz** is a sign of good fortune and a peaceful life. **Blanking out during a quiz** means that the dreamer cannot progress, nor can he surmount obstacles on his path.

Quoits — **Playing quoits** means getting fired from a good job. **Losing the game** is a sign of bad luck.

Rabbi — See **Saint**.

Rabbit — **Dreaming about rabbits** is a sign of improvement in life. If the **rabbit is white**, it means that the dreamer is sexually unfulfilled and is dissatisfied with his sex life. **Dreaming about rabbits running about happily** means joy from one's children.

Rabies — See **Hydrophobia**.

Raccoon — Dreaming about a raccoon means that the dreamer's enemies are conning him by pretending to be friends.

Race — **Dreaming about being in a race** means that the dreamer has rivals for the things he wants. If he **wins the race**, however, he will beat his rivals.

Rack (torture) — Dreaming about a rack means that the dreamer is unsure of the outcome of something which he is very worried about.

Racket — A racket in a dream signifies disappointment in something the dreamer was looking forward to.

Radio — **Listening to the radio** means that the dreamer will make a nice new friend with whom he can have fun. **Hearing a radio** means good fortune.

Radish — **Dreaming about a bed of radishes** is a sign of good luck from the point of view of friends and business. **Eating radishes** means that someone close to the dreamer will offend him. **Seeing or planting radishes** is an indication of wishes coming true.

Raffle — This is generally a sign of disappointment. At a **church raffle**, the dreamer will be disappointed. For a **young woman**, she can forget her hopes.

Raft — **Dreaming about a raft** means that there will be opportunities for good deals. If the **dreamer is sailing on a raft**, his journey is not totally safe. If **he arrives safely**, he will be lucky. If a **raft comes apart**, there will be illness and accidents for the dreamer or his friend.

Rage — **Being in a violent rage** in a dream means strife and violence among friends. If **others are in a rage**, bad luck in social and business life will ensue. If a **young woman's lover is in a rage**, they will experience misunderstandings and quarrels.

Raging — See **Wildness**.

Railing — **Seeing a railing** is a symbol of barriers in the dreamer's path. If **he is holding on to a railing**, it means that he will take a huge chance in order to attain his heart's desire — either in love or in business.

Railroad — **Dreaming about a railroad** is a warning to the dreamer to guard his affairs from his enemies. If the **railroad is blocked**, it is a sign of dirty business. If a **young woman dreams of a railroad**, she will go on a successful journey.

Rain — **Gentle, light rain** indicates that the dreamer will have to face disappointment and frustration; **heavy, pounding rain** means that the dreamer will have to cope with situations that will cause him despondency and depression. **Being out in a shower of clear rain** is a sign of youthfulness and prosperity. If the **rain comes from dark clouds**, the dreamer is worried about the seriousness of his business. **Watching a heavy shower from inside** is a sign of passionate love and wealth. **Hearing rain on the**

roof is a sign of domestic happiness and moderate prosperity. **Storms** never bode well. If the **dreamer sees others out in the rain**, it means that he is not taking his friends into his confidence. If **it rains on cattle**, there will be bad luck in business and social life.

Rainbow — A **rainbow** is always a good sign: Happiness, joy, tranquillity and pleasure will come the dreamer's way. It is an excellent sign for **lovers**. If the **rainbow appears low over green trees**, the dreamer will be successful in anything he does.

Raisins — **Seeing raisins** symbolizes wastefulness and extravagance that need to be curbed. **Eating raisins** means disappointed hopes.

Rake (the tool) — **Seeing a rake** is an indication of great effort and hard work that must be expected on the road to glory. **Using a rake** means that the dreamer cannot rely on others to do work which he delegated to them. A **broken rake** predicts illness and accidents. If **others are raking**, the dreamer will be happy for their good fortune.

Ram — If a **ram chases the dreamer**, it is a sign of bad luck. If the **dreamer sees a ram grazing tranquilly**, he will enjoy the intervention of powerful friends in his behalf.

Ramble — If the **dreamer is on a country ramble**, he will have a comfortable life, but will experience unhappiness because of separation from loved ones. For a **young woman**, it means that her home will be pleasant, but she will lose a loved one at a young age.

Ramrod — A **ramrod** is a sign of bad events. A **young woman who sees a bent ramrod** will be disappointed by a friend or lover.

Ranch — See **Farm**.

Ransom — If a **ransom is paid for the dreamer**, it is a sign of deception. For a **woman to dream of a ransom** is a sign of evil unless the ransom is paid.

Rape — If a **woman dreams of being raped**, it indicates a warped relationship with her partner. If the **dreamer dreams of a rape within his circle**, he will hear terrible news about some of them.

Rapids — If the dreamer is being swept over rapids, it means that he is neglecting his affairs for the sake of superficial pleasures and will pay for this in huge financial losses.

Raspberry — This symbolizes a strong desire for passionate sexual relations.

Rat — **Dreaming about rats** is a sign that a person very close to the dreamer is conspiring against him and deceiving him. If a **pack of rats appears**, it means that the dreamer's health is very poor. **Killing a rat** means success. **Catching rats** means defeating enemies by means of excellent conduct.

Rattles — If a **baby plays with a rattle in a dream**, it is a sign of a happy, prosperous household. If a **young woman dreams of a rattle**, she will marry young. **Giving a baby a rattle** means unsuccessful deals.

Rattrap — If the **dreamer gets caught in a rattrap**, he will be mugged. A **broken rattrap** signifies the end of unfortunate relationships. An **empty rattrap** means freedom from rivalry and gossip. If the **dreamer sets a rattrap**, he will be aware of his enemies' bad designs and therefore foil them.

Raven — **Seeing a raven in a dream** signifies mystical beliefs or black magic. **Dreaming about a raven** means bad luck. For a **young woman**, it is a sign of infidelity by her lover.

Razor — **Dreaming about a razor** is a sign of bad luck and troubles. If the **dreamer cuts himself with a razor**, he will make a bad deal. A **broken or rusty razor** means great unhappiness. **Fighting with a razor** means dealing with an extremely aggravating person.

Reading — **Reading in a dream** means that the dreamer will do very well at a task which looks difficult. To see **others reading** is a sign of very good friends. If the **dreamer discusses reading**, he will become more erudite. If the **reading is incomprehensible or inaudible**, it is a sign of cares and let-downs.

Reapers — Seeing **reapers working in a dream** is a sign of happiness and prosperity. If the **field is stubbly and dry**, business will be bad. If the **reapers are not working**, there will be a setback in business. If a **reaping machine has broken down**, people will be fired.

Reception — **Dreaming about being at a reception** predicts enjoyable social events. If there is **an unpleasant incident at a reception**, the dreamer will have anxieties.

Recipe — Dreaming about a recipe book indicates that the dreamer is blessed with good physical and mental health.

Recitation — Learning a text by heart is a sign of problems that the dreamer must face and that he will overcome. This dream is a sign of the extraordinary success the dreamer will enjoy on any path that he might choose.

Reconciliation — If the dreamer effects a reconciliation with a person with whom he has fought and broken off relations, this suggests good tidings.

Record Player — This signifies happiness and prosperity as well as a peaceful domestic life.

Red Pepper — Dreaming about a red pepper growing symbolizes an independent and economical spouse.

Refrigerator — If the **dreamer puts ice into the refrigerator**, he will fall out with people. **Dreaming about a refrigerator** means that the dreamer will behave selfishly and offensively with someone who does not deserve it.

Reindeer — A **dream about a reindeer** means that the dreamer does his duties well, and is a faithful, steadfast friend. If the **dreamer is driving a team of reindeer**, he will have a lot of hassles, but his friends will help him through.

Religion — **Dreaming about a religious event** signifies a positive and successful future: the dreamer will enjoy good times. **Discussing religion** in a dream, however, means that the dreamer's serenity will be disturbed, and business will not flourish.

Religious functionary — The appearance of a religious functionary indicates hard times filled with problems, disappointments, anxiety and frustration.

Religious Revival — **Being present at a religious revival** portends bad luck in business and family affairs. If the **dreamer participates in a religious revival**, he will anger his friends as a result of his wayward behavior.

Remote Control — Dreaming about using a remote control predicts that the dreamer will get involved in a manipulative relationship.

Rent — **Renting a house** predicts profitable deals. If the **dreamer does not succeed in renting out property**, he will experience stagnation in business. If he **pays rent**, he will have nothing to complain about his financial affairs. An **inability to pay rent** means financial failure.

Reprieve — If the **dreamer is reprieved**, he will overcome some tiresome obstacle. If a **young woman's lover is reprieved**, it is a sign of good luck for him which is significant to her.

Reptiles — **Any kind of reptile** is usually a sign of conflicts or obstacles awaiting the dreamer. If a **reptile attacks him**, serious troubles lie ahead. If **he kills the reptile**, he will surmount the difficulties. If the **dreamer holds reptiles without getting hurt**, he will suffer from the negative behavior of his friends, but will eventually overcome this. If a **young woman dreams about reptiles**, she will have many troubles, including a lover with roving eyes. If **any reptile bites her**, she will be dropped in favor of another woman.

Rescue — If the **dreamer is rescued**, it indicates that he was misled or mistaken, and warns against making any momentous decisions. If **he rescues others**, his good deeds will be acknowledged and appreciated.

Resign — If the **dreamer resigns**, it means that he will be unlucky in any new endeavors he undertakes. If **others resign**, it portends bad news.

Restaurant — **A dream about a restaurant** usually symbolizes love and romance. **Seeing a restaurant** may also indicate that the dreamer lacks a warm family relationship. In addition, a **restaurant** may symbolize hedonism and love of the good life.

Resurrection — **Dreaming about being resurrected from the dead** is a sign of enormous worries which will be overcome. If **others are resurrected**, it means that the dreamer's friends will help him overcome his worries.

Resuscitation — If the **dreamer is being resuscitated**, he will sustain heavy losses, but he will overcome them and attain prosperity and happiness. If **he resuscitates someone else**, he will experience new and satisfying friendships.

Revelation — A **positive revelation** foretells good things in business and love, whereas a **negative revelation** is a sign of worries and bad luck.

Revenge — **Any sort of revenge** in a dream signifies that the dreamer will be guilty of having caused a quarrel. **Dreaming about taking revenge** denotes the dreamer's petty and weak character, which can cause trouble for himself, as well as losing friends. If the **dreamer suffers revenge by others**, he has a lot to fear from his enemies.

Revolver — If a young woman dreams about her lover holding a revolver, she will quarrel fiercely with a friend and may well break up with her lover.

Rheumatism — If the **dreamer falls victim to rheumatism**, his plans will suffer an unforeseen delay. If **others suffer from rheumatism**, the dreamer will suffer disappointments.

Rhinestones — **Dreaming about rhinestones** means short-lived pleasures. **Dreaming that a rhinestone actually**

turned out to be a diamond means that a seemingly unimportant action led to good luck.

Rhinoceros — Dreaming about a rhinoceros signifies a longing for male potency, as a result of sexual problems. **Seeing a rhinoceros** warns of the threat of enormous losses and secret hassles. **Killing a rhinoceros** is a symbol of overcoming obstacles.

Rhubarb — Seeing rhubarb grow means enjoyable events for the dreamer. If the **dreamer cooks it**, he will fall out with a friend. **Eating it** means dissatisfaction with the dreamer's present job.

Rib — This is a sign of poverty and unhappiness.

Ribbon — A **ribbon** is a sign of extravagance. Dreaming about a **bride wearing ribbons** indicates that the groom's intentions are not honorable. **Ribbons on clothing** mean that the dreamer will have jolly friends and will not take anything too seriously. If a **young woman sees other women wearing ribbons**, she will have rivals over the affections of a man. **Buying ribbons** means a good domestic life for a woman.

Religion — Dreaming about discussing religion or feeling religious means that the dreamer's serenity will disappear. If a **young woman dreams of being overly religious**, her false piety and sanctimoniousness will repel her lover. If **she is not religious**, but is a decent and honest person, she will be universally loved. If **she is not religious**, but is also not a decent person, she will be ostracized. If the **dreamer sees the power of religion waning**, his life will be more harmonious and less prejudiced.

Rice — Rice in a dream means that good things can be

expected in one's personal or family life: an improvement in one's sex life, finding the perfect partner or domestic harmony. In addition, **seeing rice** in a dream signifies prosperity. **Eating rice** means domestic bliss. **Dirty, impure rice** is a sign of illness and separation from friends. Rice is a good sign for a **young woman**, as she will be wealthy and will enjoy a useful life.

Riches — If the dreamer dreams of possessing wealth, it means that he will go far as a result of his diligence and hard work.

Riddles — **Riddles** are a sign of confusion and discontent. If the **dreamer is attempting to solve riddles**, it means that he will undertake a project that will tax his patience and waste his money.

Ride — **Dreaming about riding** does not bode well: It often forecasts illness. **Riding slowly** means disappointing outcomes of business dealings. **Riding fast** means prosperity at the risk of danger.

Riding School — This warns of the treacherous behavior of a friend. The dreamer will overcome the bad effects, however.

Ring — **Wearing a ring** is a sign of success in new endeavors. **Seeing others with rings** symbolizes increasing wealth and lots of new friends. A **broken ring** is a sign of strife, conjugal unhappiness, and break-ups. If a **young woman dreams about receiving a ring**, she need no longer worry about her lover, who will now be attentive to her.

Ringworms — **Dreaming about seeing ringworms on one's body** means that the dreamer will soon suffer a mild illness and aggravating hassles. If the **dreamer sees ringworms on other people**, he will be plagued by requests for charity.

Riot / Tumult — Displays of violence, rage or wild behavior indicate that the dreamer's conscience is not clear, and that he is advised to reevaluate his actions carefully. **Seeing riots** is a sign of business disappointments. If the **dreamer sees a friend killed in a riot**, it is a sign of bad luck, illness or death.

Rising — Dreaming about rising to some high position means that the dreamer will become wealthy as a result of learning and promotion. If the **dreamer rises into the air**, he will enjoy himself greatly and receive unforeseen wealth, but he should beware of unwelcome publicity.

Rival — If the dreamer dreams of a rival, he will not be assertive enough and will be overlooked by important people. For a **young woman**, it is a warning to stick with her present love and not risk making mistaken choices. If the **dreamer is tricked by a rival**, it means that he is not paying sufficient attention to his business. If the **dreamer himself is the successful rival**, he will have luck in his career and his love life.

River — If the dreamer sees a smooth-flowing river, he will have a pleasurable and prosperous existence. If he is sitting on the bank of a river whose **waters are clear**, he will soon travel or go on a long trip. A **stormy river with muddy water** indicates obstacles on the dreamer's path to success, as well as jealousy. If the **dreamer is trapped by a river overflowing its banks**, he will have temporary business setbacks, as well as hassles caused by gossip. **Dry river-beds** are a sign of real bad luck and illness.

Road — Dreaming about a difficult road, winding and full of potholes, is a sign of success in the personal and business realms. Traveling along a **rough, strange road** means new projects that will waste the dreamer's time and energy. **Mistaking the road** means that the dreamer will suffer financial losses due to an error of judgement. A **smooth, straight road** indicates family quarrels. A **tree- and flower-lined road** is a sign of unforeseen good luck in financial matters, as well as happiness with spouse and children.

Roadblock — This predicts a good period in life. The dreamer can expect a promotion at work and will succeed in attaining his objectives.

Roast — Eating or seeing roast meat signifies unhappiness and infidelity in the home.

Robbery / Theft — This is an indication of fears and anxieties stemming from economic difficulties.

Robin — Dreaming about this bird is usually connected to its red color — the color of sex and love — or suggests an attempt to make amends with a person one loves.

Rock — A **rock** symbolizes disagreements, danger and difficulties. The **larger the rock**, the greater the danger. A **steep rock** signifies imminent difficulties and unhappiness.

Rocket — Dreaming about a rocket is a sign of dissatisfaction with one's partner, as well as the desire for change or movement in the

relationship. **Seeing a rocket launch** means that
the problems will be solved. **Watching a rocket
ascending** means promotion, winning one's
sweetheart, and a solid marriage. **Seeing a
rocket plummeting** means a bad marriage. If
the **dreamer flies a rocket**, he can overcome his
problems.

Rocking-chair — An **empty rocking-chair** is a sign that
sadness and pain are coming the way of the dreamer as a
result of separation from a beloved person, possibly by
death. **Someone sitting in a rocking-chair** — especially a
wife, mother or lover — is a sign of material and economic
stability, as well as personal happiness.

Rogue — If the **dreamer sees himself as a rogue**, he may
become ill, or he may act in a way that causes his friends
embarrassment and unhappiness. If a **woman dreams that
her husband or lover is a rogue**, it is a sign that a close
friend will hurt her badly.

Rogue's Gallery — Dreaming about **being in a rogue's
gallery** means that the dreamer will not be appreciated by his
associates. If **he sees his own picture in a rogue's gallery**, it
means that he will suffer at the hands of an enemy.

Roller-skates — If the dreamer is roller-skating, it is a
warning: He may be involved in an accident in the near
future, and should be careful.

Roman Candles — **Seeing a Roman candle** means a
meteoric rise to success and pleasure. **Finding that the
Roman candle is empty** signifies disappointment with a
long-coveted object.

Roof — If the **dreamer is on a roof**, it is a sign of great success. If **he is afraid of falling**, he may not keep hold of that success. If the **repair or the construction of a roof** appears in a dream, it shows progress and prosperity in his life. **Climbing onto a roof** is a sign that his ambitions will be fulfilled. **Climbing on to a roof quickly** indicates that success will arrive even more quickly. Dreaming about a **roof caving in** means a sudden disaster. **Sleeping on a roof** denotes safety from enemies and good health. A **penthouse apartment** indicates success and prosperity.

Rooks — This means that although the dreamer has true friends, their aspirations are far more modest than his, so they will never be able to provide him with the level of pleasure and happiness he craves.

Room (a closed room) — This symbolizes the dreamer's repressed fears, or his unfulfilling relationship with his partner.

Rooster — **Dreaming about a rooster** is a sign of success and fame, but the dreamer will let this go to his head. **Seeing fighting roosters** is a sign of strife and competitors.

Roots — **Seeing roots of trees or plants** is a sign of bad luck in health and business. **Taking roots in the form of a medicine** warns of imminent grief and illness.

Rope — If the **dreamer sees himself tied up with a rope**, it is a sign that he has broken (or is about to break) a promise to a friend, or betray a confidence. **Climbing a rope** suggests difficulties or enemies on the road to success, but eventual triumph. **Tying a rope** is an indication of the need to control others. **Climbing down a rope** is a sign of disappointment. **Walking a rope** signifies risks followed by success. **Others walking ropes** means that the dreamer will profit from others. **Jumping rope** with children is a sign of selfishness, bossiness, and cruel parents.

Rosebush — A **leafy rosebush without buds** is a sign of approaching prosperity. A **dead rosebush** is a bad sign, predicting bad luck and illness.

Roses — **Seeing roses** is a sign of prosperity and success in all areas of life, particularly romance. A **young woman dreaming about picking roses** will soon receive a much-wanted proposal of marriage. **Dried-up roses** means a lack of love. **White roses**, sunless and dry, are a sign of a serious illness.

Rosette — If the dreamer or someone else wears a rosette, it symbolizes superficiality. It may provide initial joy, but it will soon be a disappointment.

Rouge — **Dreaming about using rouge** means deceiving someone in order to get something. If **others have rouge on their faces**, the dreamer is the victim of deceit. If there is **rouge on the dreamer's hands or clothes**, he will be caught out in something unsavory. If the **rouge comes off the dreamer's face**, he will be embarrassed in front of a rival and will lose his lover.

Rowboat — If the **dreamer is in a rowboat with other people**, he will have a merry and lively social life. If the **boat overturns**, he will experience financial setbacks. If **he wins a rowing race**, he will have luck in love and in business. If **he loses**, his rival will win his beloved.

Rubber — **Wearing rubber clothes** means that the dreamer will be honored because of his moral character. If the **clothes are torn or shabby**, he should take care, because his reputation is in jeopardy. If the **dreamer's limbs are as flexible as rubber**, he is in danger of becoming ill. He may also be dishonest in his business practices.

Rubbish — Dreaming about rubbish symbolizes mismanagement of one's business.

Ruby — **Dreaming about a ruby** is a sign of good luck in love and finances. If a **woman loses one in a dream**, it signifies that her lover no longer cares about her.

Rudder — A **dream about a rudder** symbolizes an enjoyable trip abroad and new friends. A **broken rudder** is a sign of illness and disillusionment.

Rudeness — If the dreamer was rude to someone in his dream, this shows that the dream concerns his relationship with his partner.

Ruins — **Dreaming about ruins** is a bad sign: destroyed crops, bad health, broken love relationships, failure in business. A **dream about ancient ruins** signifies a lot of travel, but along with the excitement goes sadness at the absence of someone close.

Ruler — This indicates the dreamer's need to be objective and honest when judging others, although in reality, this is not possible.

Rum — Drinking rum predicts wealth without taste. It is a sign of moral coarseness.

Running — **Seeing himself run** means that during a trip in the near future, the dreamer will meet someone who will have a profound influence on his life. **Running with other people** means that the dreamer is approaching some celebration and that his business is flourishing. If **he trips or falls**, he will suffer financial losses and damage to his good name. If **he runs alone**, he will beat his friends up the ladder of success and status.

Running away / Fleeing— If the **dreamer is running away from something**, it means that a close friend is conspiring against him and joining forces with his enemies. If a **person who is close to the dreamer is running away**, it signifies that the dreamer's family will soon increase in size. An **unsuccessful attempt to run away** indicates that certain problems have not been solved. **Running away from danger** warns of unavoidable losses. If **others are running like that**, the dreamer will be distraught by his friends' troubles. **Seeing cattle running** warns the dreamer to be cautious when making deals or entering new endeavors.

Rupture — **Dreaming of suffering from physical ruptures** means that the dreamer will get ill or have quarrels. If **others have physical ruptures**, the dreamer runs the risk of bitter strife.

Rust — **Rust** symbolizes disappointment in the realm of romance. **Seeing rust on tin or iron objects** means that the dreamer's environment is run-down. He is generally weighed down by ill-health, financial worries and unfaithful friends.

Rye — **Seeing rye** is a sign of prosperity and a good future. If **cattle go into a field of rye**, it is also a sign of wealth.

Rye Bread — Seeing or eating rye bread in a dream symbolizes a happy and attractive home.

Saddle — Dreaming about saddles is a superb dream, predicting good news, as well as a successful trip accompanied by a surprise, such as an unexpected guest.

Sadness — A feeling of sadness, and even depression actually means the exact opposite: The dreamer may expect a period filled with happiness and joy in the near future.

Safe (deposit box) — **Dreaming about a safe** symbolizes marriage. **Breaking into a safe** predicts that the dreamer will marry someone he has not yet met. An **empty safe** means an early marriage. A **full safe** indicates a late marriage. If the **dreamer is trying to open a safe,** he will be anxious about the failure of his plans.

Saffron — **Saffron seen in a dream** symbolizes futile hopes as a result of the conspiracy of serious enemies, who will sabotage the dreamer's plans. **Eating or drinking food flavored with saffron** is a sign of family strife.

Sage (the herb) — **Dreaming about sage** symbolizes the recovery from a serious disease, whether it is the dreamer's illness or the illness of someone close to him. If a **woman dreams about using too much sage** in her cooking, she will realize that she is too lavish with money and with love.

Sailing — **Sailing on calm waters** is symbolic of a good and happy future and a variety of opportunities open to the dreamer. **Sailing on a small boat** means that the realization of the dreamer's hopes is possible.

Sailor — **Dreaming about a sailor** or seaman indicates long, interesting voyages, as well as sexual infidelity. If a **young woman dreams about a sailor**, she will break up with her lover because of a trivial flirtation. If in her dream **she is a sailor**, she will lose her true lover because of her behavior.

Saint — This indicates that the dreamer relies on a higher power for help.

Salad — **Seeing a salad** indicates that one of the dreamer's hidden talents will soon manifest itself and bring him glory. If **he eats a salad**, it is a sign of unpleasant people and illness. A **young woman preparing a salad** will quarrel with her lover.

Salary — If a person dreams of receiving a raise, it is a warning about an upcoming incident.

Salmon — The **salmon** can symbolize an obstacle that the dreamer will encounter, but one that he will eventually overcome through will power. **Seeing a salmon** means happiness for the dreamer. For a **young woman**, it means that she will marry a nice man who can support her well.

Salt — **Dreaming about salt** is a very positive dream which heralds good luck and success in many areas of life. If **meat is salted**, however, the dreamer will have money problems. If a **young woman dreams of eating salt**, her lover will leave her for a more beautiful woman.

Saltpeter — This is a very bad omen, foretelling grief and loss.

Salve — Despite negative conditions, the dreamer will flourish, and his enemies will become his friends.

Samples — **Receiving samples of goods** signifies improved business. If a **salesman mislays his samples**, he will have trouble in business and love. If a **woman looks at samples** she has received, she will have a variety of options.

Sand — Dreaming about sand indicates famine, losses, conflicts and quarrels with family members.

Sapphire — This indicates good luck in business and in choosing a lover.

Sardines — **Eating sardines** signifies that bad things will happen out of the blue. If a **young woman puts sardines on the table**, she will be bothered by somebody's unwelcome attentions.

Sardonyx — **Dreaming about sardonyx** means that the dreamer will improve his wretched surroundings by improving his financial situation. A **woman who dreams of sardonyx** will enjoy increased wealth. If **she throws them away or loses them**, she will ignore the chance to improve her lot.

Sash — **Dreaming about wearing a sash** means that the dreamer is trying to get a fickle person to fall in love with him. If a **young woman buys one**, it is a sign of her fidelity and the respect she will earn in the future.

Satan — **Dreaming about Satan** signifies dangerous undertakings that will jeopardize the dreamer's respectability. **Killing Satan** means abandoning dubious company for more moral pursuits. If **Satan is disguised as wealth or power**, the dreamer will abuse it rather than exploit it for the good of others. If **Satan comes as music**, he will seduce the dreamer. If **he takes the shape of a beautiful woman**, the dreamer will succumb to her caresses at the expense of his better nature. If the **dreamer tries to escape Satan**, he will overcome his selfishness to help others.

Sausage — **Dreaming about making sausage**

is an indication of success in most of the dreamer's endeavors. **Eating a sausage** is a sign of a modest but attractive home.

Saw — If a **man dreams that he is sawing** something, it is a sign that he is reliable, energetic and happy. If a **woman saws something** in a dream, it means that one of her friends will soon offer her helpful advice. **Seeing big industrial saws** means that the dreamer will run a large concern. **For a woman**, it is a sign that she will be respected and listened to. **Broken or rusty saws** are a sign of bad luck and mishaps. **Finding a rusty saw** means recovering one's property. **Carrying a saw** means substantial responsibilities accompanied by wealth. **Hearing a saw** indicates economy and prosperity.

Sawdust — This symbolizes serious errors that will lead to domestic strife and unhappiness.

Scabbard — **Dreaming about a scabbard** means resolving a quarrel amicably. **Losing a scabbard** is a sign of overwhelming problems.

Scaffold — **Dreaming about a scaffold** heralds failure to win the heart of the person the dreamer loves. If the **dreamer goes up to the scaffold**, it means that he has been judged unfairly by his friends for a misdemeanor he never committed. If **he goes down from the scaffold**, it is a sign of the dreamer's guilt, for which he will be punished. If **he falls from the scaffold**, he will be caught while conniving against others.

Scaffolding — This is a sign that an incorrect step taken by the dreamer may cause a lover's quarrel and even a break-up.

Scalding — If the dreamer is scalded, it means that something he was looking forward to will be spoilt by a negative event.

Scale (measuring) — **Using a scale** indicates an affinity for justice and the ability to judge properly. Occasionally, a **scale appearing in a dream** suggests conjugal conflict. If a **young woman uses a scale to weigh her lover**, she will find him faithful.

Scandal — **Dreaming about being the subject of scandal** means that the dreamer prefers the company of frivolous, immoral people to more solid companions. After this dream, business will slow down considerably. If a **young woman discusses a scandal**, she will be taken advantage of by a man who is not worthy of her.

Scar — This indicates the inability of the dreamer to break away from his past.

Scarcity — This is a bad sign, predicting sadness at home and bad business.

Scarf — **Dreaming about a scarf** is not a good sign. If the **dreamer sees himself wrapped in a scarf**, it means that he has a tendency toward depression. If a **woman dreams about a scarf that bothers her when she wears it**, it means that an intimate secret concerning her life will soon be revealed.

Scarlet Fever — **Dreaming about scarlet fever** is a portent of illness or of enemies. If a **relative of the dreamer dies of scarlet fever**, the dreamer will be destroyed by treacherous behavior.

Scepter — If the **dreamer holds a scepter**, it means that he will be elected to a weighty, responsible position as a result of his abilities, and he will not let anyone down. If **others hold a scepter**, it means that the dreamer will always be an employee, rather than self-employed.

School — Dreaming about school indicates anxiety about failure. If the **dreamer is an adult**, the dream indicates frustration and a feeling of missed opportunities and failure. If the **dreamer is a young person**, it means that he is avoiding responsibility. An **adult dreaming that he is young and at school** will have sorrows and troubles that will make him yearn for the simplicity of his school-days. **Teaching at school** means that the dreamer has literary inclinations, but the practical aspects of earning a living prevail. **Dreaming about one's old school** means that there are problems in the dreamer's life. A **dream about a schoolteacher** means that the dreamer does not seek ostentatious and noisy forms of entertainment.

Scissors — A **dream about scissors** is a bad sign. It portends strife between husbands and wives, and between lovers. Business will not boom. **Dreaming about having scissors sharpened** indicates loathsome work. **Broken scissors** signal break-ups and fights. **Lost scissors** mean that the dreamer is trying to avoid doing something he does not want to do.

Scorpion — A **dream about a scorpion** warns of enemies who want to harm the dreamer. If **he does not destroy the scorpion**, he will sustain losses from the enemy's onslaught.

Scrapbook — This predicts that the dreamer will soon meet unpleasant people.

Scratch — If the **dreamer scratches another person**, it is a sign that he has a very irascible and critical nature. If the **dreamer is scratched**, he will be hurt by the actions of a false, conniving person. If the **dreamer is scratched by a cat**, an enemy will snatch a good transaction that he has spent a lot of time on away from him.

Scratching — This symbolizes unfounded concerns.

Scratching One's Head — Strangers will flatter the dreamer, much to his annoyance, as he knows they are trying to get something out of him.

Screech Owl — Dreaming about hearing the cries of the screech owl portend terrible news about the terminal illness or death of a close friend.

Screen — This indicates that the dreamer suffers from emotional problems.

Screw — **Seeing screws** is a sign of boring tasks and bad-tempered associates. **Screws also warn the dreamer** to be economical and attentive to detail.

Sculptor — **Dreaming about a sculptor** means that the dreamer will get a job which pays less, but is of higher status. If a **woman dreams that her lover or husband is a sculptor**, it means that she will have influence with people in high places.

Scum — The dreamer will be badly let down by failures in his social life.

Scythe — **Dreaming about a scythe** means that the dreamer will be unable to concentrate on his business or travel because of illness or mishaps. **Seeing an old or damaged scythe** means business losses or partings from old friends.

Sea — Dreaming about the sea is a sign of hopes unrealized, mainly in the spiritual realm. A **young woman who dreams of skimming over the sea with her lover** will be  experience bliss in marriage. If the **dreamer hears the dull roar of the sea**, it means that he is destined to have a lonely, loveless life.

Sea Foam — For a **woman, dreaming about sea foam** signals lascivious behavior. If **she decorates herself with sea foam**, it symbolizes her quest for material things rather than spiritual, self-improving ones.

Seagull — The seagull is a sign of bad news: the dreamer is likely to hear news that will cause him sadness and distress.

Seal — Dreaming about seals means that the dreamer is an over-achiever, usually unhappy with his present situation, and aspiring to bigger and better things.

Seamstress — Seeing a seamstress means that the dreamer will not do something he wants to do due to unforeseen circumstances.

Seaport — If the dreamer goes to a seaport, it means that he will have the chance to travel and study, but someone will try to prevent him from doing so.

Search — Searching for something warns that the dreamer is acting in haste, not paying attention to important and meaningful details. The search for a person signifies fear of loss.

Seat — If the **dreamer's seat is taken** in a dream, it means that he will have no respite from people soliciting his help. If the **dreamer gives up his seat for a woman**, it means that someone is taking advantage of him.

Secret Order — **Dreaming about any secret order** warns the dreamer not to be selfish and scheming. If the **leader of the order dies**, great difficulties will eventually be resolved.

Seducer — If a **man dreams about seducing a woman**, it warns him to watch out for people who are keen to frame him. If **he dreams about trying to seduce his sweetheart**, and she protests angrily, it means that she is pure and blameless. If **she acquiesces**, he is being exploited for his money. A **young woman who dreams about being seduced** can easily fall under dubious influences.

Seeds (to plant) — Dreaming about seeds means that the dreamer's elaborate plans for the future will indeed be realized and prosperity will follow, despite current difficulties.

Seeds — A dream about any kind of seed always signifies good things. The dreamer will find happiness and blessings through his efforts.

Selling — A **dream about selling one's private property** is a sign that the dreamer will have financial difficulties in the near future. **Selling butter** or **fruit** means very little profit. **Selling iron** means very little success and unworthy friends.

Sentry — Seeing a sentry is a sign of benevolent protectors and a peaceful life.

Separation — Dreaming about separation means that the dreamer will have to make concessions in his life.

September — This predicts good luck.

Serenade — If the **dreamer hears a serenade**, he will receive good news from faraway friends, and his hopes will be realized. If **he is serenading**, wonderful things await him in life.

Serpents — Dreaming about serpents is an indication of gloomy and depressed feelings and environment, and usually precedes disappointments. **Hearing Eve in conversation with the serpent** means that women will cause the dreamer to lose his money and good name. **Dreaming about bronze serpents** is a forecast of destruction and envy. **Seeing serpents crawling in the grass** means that the dreamer will be devastated by treachery and slander. A **young woman who sees a serpent on her lap** is in danger of being humiliated by dangerous rivals.

Servant — If the dreamer has a servant in the dream, it means that his standard of living will increase and he will be financially successful. If **he fires a servant**, remorse and loss will be his lot. **Dreaming of quarreling with a servant** predicts a dispute with someone about their non-performance of duties. If a **servant steals**, it means that a person close to the dreamer does not care about the rules of possession.

Sewage — Sewage in a dream is indicative of an unsuccessful marriage, of hidden enemies or of a bad business connection.

Sex — Dreaming about enjoyable sex is a sign of happiness and contentment in the dreamer's personal life. **Watching other people have sex** indicates that the dreamer is incapable of having a good relationship. **Indulging in perfunctory, meaningless sex** warns the dreamer of doing something which will result in shame and guilt.

Shadows — Dreaming about shadows indicates that there will be a great improvement in the dreamer's economic status as well as significant monetary profits.

Shakespeare — **Dreaming about Shakespeare** means that important undertakings will be marred by gloom and sadness, and the passion will disappear from love. **Dreaming about reading the works of Shakespeare** is a sign that the dreamer will be involved in literary pursuits.

Shaking Hands — **Shaking hands with people of a lower station in life** means that the dreamer will gain love and respect for his benevolent conduct. If, however, he thinks that **one of the side's hands is dirty**, friends will turn out to be enemies. If **he dreams about shaking hands with someone who has done him wrong**, he will fall out with a close friend. A **young woman who shakes hands with an important leader** will win respect and wealth. If **she has to reach upward to do so**, competition and obstacles await her. However, if **she is wearing gloves**, these will be avoided.

Shampooing (the hair) — **Seeing shampooing being done** is an indication of gossip and revealed secrets as well as lowly pursuits. If the **dreamer's hair is being shampooed**, it is an indication of a secret trip which will be excellent if its secret nature is hidden from family and friends.

Shanty — **Dreaming about a shanty** means that the dreamer will abandon his home in order to improve his state of health. **Seeing a shanty** is a warning of financial loss.

Shark — **Dreaming about sharks** is a symbol of terrifying enemies. If a **shark chases and attacks the**

dreamer, he will be plagued by serious worries. If **he sees sharks swimming in clear water**, it means that other people's envy of his happy lot will cause him damage. **Seeing a dead shark** means regaining his wealth and making up with people from whom he was estranged.

Shave — If the dreamer considers getting a shave, it means that he has grandiose plans for developing his business, but will be unable to muster the energy to bring them to fruition.

Shaving — Dreaming about being shaved means that con-men will rip the dreamer off. If the **dreamer shaves himself**, it means that he is in charge of his business and household, despite a bossy wife. If **his face is smooth**, he will lead a serene life. If **it is rough and craggy**, domestic strife is in the offing. A **blunt razor** means that the dreamer will cause his friends to criticize his personal life. If the **dreamer's beard is gray**, he will show no justice. If a **woman sees men shaving**, she will pursue coarse pleasures. If **she dreams about being shaved**, it means that she will be so masculine that she will repel men.

Shawl — Dreaming about a shawl signifies being flattered and admired. **Losing a shawl** predicts sadness and unpleasantness. A **young woman** who dreams this may be dumped by a handsome man.

Shearing — Dreaming about shearing lambs means that the dreamer lacks the milk of human kindness, and deals straightforwardly, but coldly and calculatedly, with others. **Shearing sheep** predicts big financial gains.

Shears — Seeing shears means that the dreamer will

become cantekerous and tight with money. **Damaged shears** foretell the loss of friends due to the dreamer's peculiar behavior.

Sheaves — Dreaming about sheaves means happy events and prosperity.

Sheep — **Seeing sheep** means that it will be worthwhile for the dreamer to stick to his chosen path tenaciously. **Flocks of sheep** symbolize good times for farmers. **Thin, sickly sheep** predict anguish at the failure of plans which promised financial gain. **Eating sheep's meat** means that the dreamer will be aggravated by unpleasant people.

Sheet Iron — **Seeing sheet iron** means that the dreamer is taking the criticism of others seriously, to his detriment. **Walking on sheet iron** symbolizes unpleasant meetings.

Sheets — See **Bed-linen**.

Shells — **Seeing shells** means that good and positive things are on their way: happiness, joy, financial and business success. **Walking among shells and collecting them** signifies wastefulness. The results of pleasure will be frustrating memories.

Shelter — **Looking for a shelter** means that the dreamer is very fearful of enemies. **Building a shelter** signifies the desire to escape from one's enemies. **Seeking shelter** means that the dreamer will be caught cheating and will attempt to explain himself.

Shelves — **Empty shelves** indicate that there will be losses and failures. **Full shelves** are a sign of great financial and material success.

Shepherd — **Dreaming about a shepherd** symbolizes the dreamer's hidden need to be involved in spiritual matters.

Watching shepherds looking after their sheep is a prediction of a good harvest, as well as of happiness and prosperity. **Idle shepherds** signify death and illness.

Sheriff — Seeing a sheriff signifies fear of change. If the **dreamer is chosen to be sheriff**, it means that he will take part in something that will result in neither respect nor gain.

Ship — A dream about ships foretells promotion and a rise in status. **Dreaming about a ship's captain** indicates success in most areas of the dreamer's life. A **shipwreck** means business disasters, as well as betrayal by women. If the **dreamer perishes in a shipwreck**, it means that he will have a narrow escape from death or dishonor. **Seeing a ship sailing through a storm** means business failure, as well as a conspiracy to hide some unsavory deal from the public — a deal which his partner threatens to reveal. If **other people are shipwrecked**, the dreamer will attempt to shield a friend from shame and bankruptcy. **Abandoning ship** means failure in business, but a safe landing means that he will overcome it.

Shirt — If the **dreamer puts on his shirt**, he will lose his lover because of his infidelity. A **torn shirt** means bad luck and wretched conditions. A **dirty shirt** is a warning of contagious diseases. **Losing one's shirt** means humiliation in love or business.

Shirtwaist — If a **young woman dreams about a shirtwaist**, it means that her pleasant conduct will win her esteem. If **her shirtwaist is torn**, she will get into trouble for immoral behavior. If **she tries on a shirtwaist**, there will be a rival for the man she loves. If **she gets it to fit her properly**, she will win the man she loves.

Shoemaker — **Seeing a shoemaker** in a dream means that the dreamer will not be promoted. If a **woman dreams that her husband or lover is a shoemaker**, she will get whatever her heart desires.

Shoes — If the **dreamer's shoes are dirty and scuffed**, he will make enemies because of his critical nature. If the **dreamer has his shoes shined**, business will pick up. **New shoes** are a sign of change for the better. If **shoes pinch**, the dreamer will be the victim of his friends' practical jokes. **Shoes with laces untied** signify strife, illness and losses. **Losing shoes** means abandonment and divorce. If a **young woman's shoes are admired while she is wearing them**, she should be wary of people she meets, particularly men.

Shooting — **Hearing or seeing shooting** means that couples are unhappy because of insuperable selfishness. Business will not be very good because of carelessness. If **someone shoots the dreamer**, it means that he fears significant losses in the future.

Shop — This means that the dreamer will be thwarted at every turn by friends who begrudge his advancement.

Shore — See **Beach**.

Short (physique) — If the dreamer or one of his friends appears as a short person, it means that the dreamer will make progress in most areas of his life.

Shortage / Hunger — This predicts particularly good things and indicates a positive turnabout in the dreamer's life.

Shot — If the dreamer **dreams that he is dying after**

being shot, it means that his friends will show unprecedented and sudden animosity toward him. If **he outwits death and wakes up**, he will effect a reconciliation with his friends.

Shotgun — Dreaming about a shotgun presages domestic problems and anxiety from employees and children. If the **dreamer shoots with both barrels of a double-barreled shotgun**, it means that he will have been provoked to such an extent by the attitude of people in his professional life that he will drop all courtesy and etiquette and vent his anger.

Shoulder — **Seeing bare shoulders** is a sign of positive changes and a new outlook on life. If the **dreamer sees his own shoulders as scrawny**, he will need other people to provide him with amusement and enjoyment.

Shovel — **Seeing a shovel in a dream** symbolizes hard but not unpleasant work. A **damaged or old shovel** means that hopes will not be realized. **Stoking a fire with a shovel** indicates that the dreamer can expect good times.

Shower (bathing) — **Dreaming about a shower** symbolizes the desire for sexuality and love. A **dream about taking a shower with a partner** indicates a good sex life.

Shower (rain) — Dreaming about being in a shower means that the dreamer will greatly enjoy devising and indulging in hedonistic pleasures.

Shrew (animal) — Seeing a shrew in a dream means that the dreamer will have to make an effort to cheer a friend up. The dreamer will no longer be able to cope with daily life.

Shroud — A **dream about shrouds** predicts illness and

worry, as well as the malevolent scheming of false friends and a fall-off in business. **Seeing shrouded corpses** is a sign of enormously bad luck. If the **shroud is taken off a corpse**, there will be irreconcilable rifts.

Sickness — **Dreaming about sickness** is truly a sign of distress and illness in the family. Strife will also play a part. If the **dreamer himself is sick**, he is warned to take care of himself. If **he sees any member of his family looking ill and wan**, a sudden and negative event will occur. This dream usually foretells sickness.

Side — **Seeing only the side of something** means that a straightforward suggestion by the dreamer will be rejected. If the **dreamer's side hurts him**, his patience will be tried by hassles and anxieties. If **he dreams that his side is healthy and strong**, he will be lucky in love and business.

Siege — If a young woman dreams of being in a siege, she will have to overcome all kinds of obstacles on her way to pleasure, but when she does, it will be worth it.

Sieve — **Dreaming about a sieve** means that the dreamer is about to make a deal which will be harmful to him. If the **sieve is very fine**, the dreamer may be able to stop something that is bad for him from happening. If the **sieve is very coarse**, the dreamer will lose newly-acquired assets.

Sigh — A dream in which the **dreamer sighs because of something bad or troubling** is indicative of sudden sadness which will be alleviated by something good. It means that the dreamer does not owe other people anything. If the **dreamer hears other people sigh**, he will be upset by the bad behavior of close friends.

Silk — **Dreaming about wearing clothes of silk** means the realization of aspirations, and reconciliations. If a **woman dreams about silk,** it symbolizes that she is happy with her family and love life. If the **dreamer is a man,** it is a sign that he will be highly successful in business. If a **young woman dreams about old silk,** she will be proud of her forefathers, and courted by a rich, old man. **Dirty or torn silk** means that she will bring disgrace to her respected family.

Silkworm — **Dreaming about a silkworm** is an indication of an excellent, well-paid, prestigious job. **Dead silkworms,** or cut cocoons, signify bad luck and difficulties.

Silver — **Dreaming about silver** warns against relying on money for happiness. If the **dreamer finds silver money,** he will be too critical and hasty in his judgment of others.

Silverware — **Dreaming about silverware** is a sign of anxiety and unfulfilled yearnings. **Using silverware** represents a marriage in the family or of a close friend of the dreamer.

Singing — If the **dreamer is singing in happy surroundings,** it is a prediction of a jealousy that will spoil joy. If the **song is sad,** there will be obstacles and problems in business. If the **dreamer hears singing,** it is a sign of cheerfulness and merry friends, as well as news from faraway friends. **Bawdy songs** are a sign of wastefulness.

Single — If a married person dreams of being single, it predicts that his marriage will not be happy.

Sister — See **Brother.**

Skating — **Ice-skating** predicts the loss of a job or a valuable possession. If the **ice breaks,** the dreamer will be advised by unqualified friends. If the **dreamer sees other people skating**, his name will be negatively linked by unpleasant people with that of someone he admires. **Seeing skates** means strife among his acquaintances. **Watching youngsters on roller-skates** is a sign of health, as well as of joy at being able to make others happy.

Skeleton — **Seeing a skeleton** predicts illness, arguments and damage caused by enemies. If the **dreamer himself is a skeleton**, it means that he worries about non-existent problems and should make an effort to calm down. If the **dreamer is plagued by a skeleton**, it is a prediction of death or a terrible mishap — either physical or financial.

Skin — If a dreamer sees his skin, it indicates a non-spiritual, materialistic personality.

Skull — **Dreaming about leering skulls** is a symbol of domestic problems. If the dreamer touches skulls, his business will suffer. **Seeing a friend's skull** means that a friend will be jealous that the dreamer succeeded where he did not, and will hurt him. If the **dreamer sees his own skull**, he will be conscience-stricken.

Sky — A **clear sky** is an indication of high honors, as well as fascinating trips with knowledgeable people. If the **sky is not clear**, problems in love will occur, and hopes will be dashed. If the **sky is red**, it is a sign of civic unrest and violence.

Slander — If the **dreamer is the victim of slander**, he is taking advantage of people's ignorance in order to deceive them. If he **slanders someone**, his egoism will cause him to lose friends.

Slaughterhouse — This indicates that the dreamer will be accused of embezzlement, and his wife or lover will fear rather than love him.

Sleep — If the **dreamer sees himself sleeping**, it warns of others who aim to harm him. **Sleeping in a clean bed** is a sign of love and harmony. **Sleeping in peculiar places** predicts break-ups and illness. **Sleeping next to a child** means domestic harmony and love. **Seeing others sleeping** means that the dreamer will win the heart of a woman despite the disapproval of others. **Sleeping with someone disgusting** means that the dreamer will suffer as a result of his lascivious behavior when his love for his partner disappears. If a **young woman dreams of sleeping with her lover**, she should be warned not to succumb to him.

Sleigh — **Seeing a sleigh** is a sign of failure in love and a fight with a friend. **Riding in a sleigh** is a sign of unwise meetings. A **young woman who is in a sleigh** will encounter disapproval of her choice of a lover.

Sliding — A **dream about sliding** warns of a decline in business and infidelity in love. **Sliding down a grassy slope** means that the dreamer will be ruined because of flattery and false promises.

Slighting — If the **dreamer slights someone,** he will not find contentment, and his nature will become irascible and obnoxious. If the **dreamer is slighted**, his complaints will be justified.

Slippers — **Dreaming about slippers** signifies that the dreamer is about to embroil himself in some plot or negative association — possibly with a married person, probably leading to hassles and scandal. If **people admire the dreamer's slippers**, he will become involved in a love affair that will bring him humiliation.

Slot Machine — Dreaming about a slot machine predicts good luck and wealth. If the **dreamer uses a slot machine**, he will soon have financial problems which he will not be able to solve.

Smallpox — Seeing people ill with smallpox signifies a sudden, terrible illness, possibly contagious, as well as disappointed aspirations.

Smoke — Dreaming about smoke predicts anxiety and deliberations. **Black smoke** warns of possible problems in family life. If the **dreamer is overcome with smoke**, he is being flattered by unscrupulous people.

Smoking — This predicts an unfavorable period accompanied by frustration and anxiety.

Snail — Seeing snails means unsavory surroundings. **Treading on snails** warns of dealings with unpleasant individuals.

Snake — Dreaming about a snake is a warning against all forms of evil and falsehood. A **writhing mass of snakes** predicts grappling with remorse. A **dream about a snake bite** means that someone close to him is lying to him and deceiving him, and enemies are causing him harm. **Killing a snake** in a dream indicates triumph over enemies. **Stepping over snakes** means fear of illness, and of rivalry for the affections of the dreamer's lover. If a **snake coils itself around the dreamer**, he will be at the mercy of his enemies, and will succumb to ill-health. If **snakes rear up behind the**

dreamer's friend, it means that there is a conspiracy against him and the friend. If the **friend controls the snakes**, someone in a high position will afford the dreamer protection. **Handling snakes** means overcoming opposition. If the **dreamer steps on a snake while bathing**, unexpected trouble will occur instead of pure enjoyment. If **snakes bite other people**, the dreamer will hurt or criticize a friend. **Small snakes** mean that people to whom the dreamer is being friendly will slander and sabotage him. **Seeing children playing with snakes** means that the dreamer will not be able to distinguish between friends and enemies. If a **child places a hissing snake on a woman's head,** she will be tricked into relinquishing something of value. If a **woman hypnotizes a snake**, the dreamer's rights will be in jeopardy, but powerful friends and the law will be on his side. **Illuminated snakes** means that the dreamer will be victimized mercilessly and cruelly by his enemies.

Sneeze — If the **dreamer sneezes**, it means that unexpected news will cause him to change his plans. If **other people sneeze**, it is a prediction of tedious social engagements.

Snouts — This is a sign of perilous times for the dreamer. He is plagued by vicissitudes and besieged by enemies.

Snow — Any type of snow in a dream indicates extreme fatigue. **Seeing snow** means fairly bad luck, but not disastrous. **Dirty snow** means fallen pride, and attempting to find favor with someone the dreamer had previously despised and scorned. **Melting snow** means that worries will become happiness. **Being snowbound** is a sign of never-ending ill fortune. A **snowstorm** symbolizes sadness and disappointment because some long-anticipated pleasure does not materialize. **Throwing snowballs** means that the dreamer will face unpleasant moral dilemmas which will ruin him if he does not exercise wise judgment. If the **dreamer sees big snowflakes** through the window, he will quarrel with his lover and experience financial difficulties. **Gazing at distant, snow-capped mountains** means that the dreamer's aspirations will never be realized. **Looking at a sun-drenched, snowy scene** promises the dreamer that he will triumph over the obstacles in his path.

Snuff — **Dreaming about snuff** means that the dreamer's enemies are prejudicing his friends against him. If a **woman uses snuff**, it predicts a situation which will lead to her falling out with a good friend.

Soap — **Dreaming about soap** means that the dreamer will enjoy himself doing unusual things with his friends. If a **woman dreams about making soap**, she will have a comfortable life.

Socialist — If the dreamer sees a socialist, he will lose the affection of his friends. He will throw himself into fantasized tasks at the expense of his real business.

Soda Fountain — If the **dreamer is at a soda fountain**, he will finally have obtained good things after endless frustrations. If **he treats others to sodas**, it means that he will ultimately be successful in his endeavors, however unlikely that may seem at the moment.

Sold — If the dreamer has sold anything, it predicts hassles as a result of unsuccessful deals.

Soldier — Dreaming about a soldier indicates that the dreamer is involved in conflicts or quarrels. **Seeing soldiers marching** predicts extravagance, but also promotion to a high position. If the **dreamer sees wounded soldiers**, he will empathize with the troubles of others to the point of losing his sense of judgment. If the **dreamer is a good soldier**, he will live up to his highest moral aspirations. If a **woman dreams about soldiers**, her reputation is in jeopardy. A **married woman who dreams about being in a soldiers' camp** may disgrace her husband, who may divorce her.

Somnambulist — This means that the dreamer may agree to a plan, in all innocence, that will later cause him worry and bad luck.

Son — If the **dreamer sees his son as obedient and good-looking**, the dreamer will have a lot of joy from him, as well as pride in his achievements. A **dream about a lost, maimed or sick son** warns about the future. If a **mother hears her son crying out because of the grave danger he is in,** there will be illness, bereavement and sorrow. If **she rescues him**, any risks or danger will disappear immediately.

Soot — Seeing soot in a dream is a sign of bad luck in business, and a prediction of quarrels between lovers.

Sorcerer — This foretells that the dreamer's aspirations will not be realized, and will undergo a transformation.

Sores — If the **dreamer sees sores**, he will experience mental anguish and losses because of a disease. If the **dreamer puts a dressing on a sore**, it means that he will forgo his own enjoyment for the good of others.

Soul — If the **dreamer sees his soul departing from his body**, it means that he is about to indulge in futile, time-wasting pursuits that will erode his moral sense and make him materialistic and miserly. If the **dreamer sees another person's soul inside him**, it means that an as yet unknown individual will enter his life and help him. **Discussing the immortality of one's soul** means that the dreamer will have the chance to increase his knowledge and enjoy erudite conversations with intelligent people.

Soup — **Dreaming about soup** is a prediction of good news and pleasant things. If the **dreamer sees others eating soup**, there is every likelihood that he will get married. If a **young woman dreams about making soup**, she will marry a rich man and will not have to deal with the mundane details of housekeeping.

Sovereign — This is a sign of improvement in one's financial situation as well as in one's social life.

Sowing — If a **farmer sows seeds in freshly plowed earth**, a good harvest is predicted. **Sowing lettuce** means that the dreamer will be responsible for his own illness or death at a young age.

Space — If the dreamer is voyaging through outer space, he will soon be liberated from a restrictive situation, and will enjoy the exhilaration of self-sufficiency and liberty.

Spade — Dreaming about a spade symbolizes nuisance and annoying tasks that the dreamer has to perform.

Sparrow — If the **dreamer sees sparrows**, it means that he is cocooned in love and happiness, and this means that he will have the patience and sympathy to deal with other people's misfortunes. If the **sparrows are injured or dead**, unhappiness or grief might ensue.

Specters — See **Spirits**.

Spice — If the **dreamer sees spice**, it means that he is likely to ruin his name as a result of his hedonistic pursuits. If a **young woman smells or eats spice**, she will be taken in by a con artist.

Spider — In the **context of European culture**, the spider symbolizes a woman. **Dreaming about a spider** means that a woman will control the dreamer's life (even if the dreamer is a woman). **Dreaming about a spider** symbolizes diligence and thrift. **Dreaming about a spider spinning a web** indicates a happy domestic life. **Killing a spider** is an indication of domestic quarrels. If the **dreamer is bitten by a spider**, his enemies will sabotage his business, and he will be the victim of treachery. **Seeing lots of spiders and spider-webs** is a symbol of luck, health, happiness and sociability. **Facing a large spider** means a meteoric increase in wealth. **Running away from a large spider,** however, means that the dreamer will suffer financial losses. **Seeing golden spiders** is a sign of improved finances and social life.

Spider-web — **Seeing spider-webs** is a prediction of lucrative deals and a good social life. A **spider-web being woven around the dreamer** means that the dreamer will achieve his objectives despite obstacles along the way.

Spinning — If the dreamer is spinning, he will undertake a project that suits him perfectly, in every way.

Spinning Top — This means that the dreamer will experience minor hassles.

Spirits — **Seeing spirits in a dream** or **hearing them knock at the door** foretells sudden vicissitudes for the dreamer. If they are **clothed in white**, the health of one of the dreamer's good friends is in jeopardy. If they are **wearing black**, deceit and infidelity will be the dreamer's lot. **Hearing a spirit speak** is a warning to listen to advice in order to prevent bad things from happening. If the **spirits hide behind the curtains**, the dreamer is warned not to give vent to his emotions, in order not to behave foolishly. **Seeing his friend's spirit gliding in the house** means that the dreamer will suffer from disillusionment and lack of confidence.

Spitting — **Dreaming about spitting** means that endeavors that looked favorable at the outset will end very badly. If **someone spits on the dreamer**, quarrels and break-ups are predicted.

Spleen — Dreaming about spleen foretells a disagreement with someone who will cause the dreamer damage.

Splendor — **Dreaming about living in splendor** means that the dreamer will advance to a much higher status in life. If **others live in splendor**, the dreamer will be pleased with the fact that his friends are very concerned with how he feels.

Splinter — If the **dreamer is suffering from the discomfort of splinters**, it means that his family or competitors will cause him a lot of trouble. If the **dreamer gets a splinter in his foot while paying a visit**, it is a prediction of an especially awful visit, as well as damage to business because the dreamer did not pay enough attention.

Sponge — If the **dreamer sees a sponge**, he is being conned. If **he uses one to erase a blackboard**, someone else's stupidity will cause him to suffer.

Spools of Thread — Dreaming about spools of thread indicates unhappy feelings resulting from the dreamer's inability to cope with the tedious tasks at hand. **Empty spools** symbolize disillusionment.

Spoon / Teaspoon — Dreaming about a spoon attests to a good and happy family life. **Losing a spoon or teaspoon** represents the dreamer's feeling that others are suspicious of him although he has not done them any wrong. If the **dreamer steals a spoon**, he will be severely upbraided for his stinginess at home. **Bent or dirty spoons** are a sign of hassles and losses.

Spring (season) — **Dreaming about the approach of spring** is a sign of good fortune and a happy social life. If **spring appears at the wrong time of the year**, it is a prediction of trouble and loss.

Spur — Dreaming about wearing spurs is an indication of involvement in a highly disputed topic. If **others wear spurs**, it means that enemies are conspiring against the dreamer.

Spy — If **spies are bothering the dreamer**, he can expect serious fall-outs and unpleasantness. If the **dreamer sees himself as a spy**, it predicts an unsuccessful adventure.

Spyglass — If the **dreamer peers through a spyglass**, there will be alterations in his lifestyle that will be detrimental to him. A **broken or non-functional**

spyglass is a sign of quarrels and falling-out with friends.

Squall— This is a prediction of gloom and bad business.

Squinting — If the **dreamer sees a person who squints**, he will be irritated by disagreeable individuals. If he dreams of **his lover or a beautiful woman squinting at him**, he will be pursued by troubles if he goes after women. If a **young woman has this dream**, her good name may be jeopardized.

Squirrel — **Seeing squirrels** predicts good times accompanied by success in all areas of life. If the **dreamer kills a squirrel**, he will be cold and unpopular. **Stroking a squirrel** means domestic bliss. If a **dog chases a squirrel**, there will be disputes and awkward moments between friends.

Stable — **Dreaming about a stable** is a sign of good luck and profitable business. A **burning stable** may presage the actual event, or indicate changes that will be to the dreamer's benefit.

Stag — Seeing stags in a dream means that the dreamer's friends are faithful and straightforward, and he will have good times with them.

Stage Driver — This foretells a peculiar journey that the dreamer will undertake in search of wealth and contentment.

Stains — **Stains on the dreamer's clothing or hands** indicate difficulties, frustrations and fears. The **same stains on others** mean that the dreamer will be betrayed by someone.

Stairs — **Going up stairs** is a sign of excellent luck. **Going down stairs** is a sign of bad luck in business and love. **Falling down stairs** means that the dreamer will be despised and envied. **Sitting on the stairs** means a general improvement in the dreamer's life. **Seeing a broad, elegant staircase** foretells wealth and higher status. If the **dreamer sees other people going down the stairs**, happy things will soon give way to unhappiness.

Stall — Dreaming about a stall is an indication of the dreamer's unrealistic expectations of a particular situation.

Stallion — **Dreaming about a stallion** predicts prosperity and status for the dreamer. If the **dreamer rides a handsome stallion**, he will enjoy a meteoric rise to fame and fortune, but his new situation will corrupt him. If the **stallion is rabid**, the dreamer's wealth will cause him to become arrogant, thus alienating his friends.

Stammer — If the **dreamer stammers**, it means that his joy in life will by jeopardized by hassles and ill-health. If **other people stammer**, it means that the dreamer will be bothered and aggravated by unpleasant people.

Standard Bearer — If the **dreamer is a standard bearer**, he will have an enjoyable and multifaceted occupation. If **others are standard bearers**, the dreamer will envy a friend.

Stars — **Bright, shining stars** are a sign of good health and fortune. **Dull, reddish stars** foretell bad luck. A **shooting star** is a forecast of grief. If a **star falls on the dreamer**, he will suffer the loss of a close family member. If **stars appear and disappear** in a strange way, there will be changes in the dreamer's life. It is a dangerous sign to see **stars circumventing the earth**.

Starving — If the **dreamer is starving**, he will lack work and friends. If **others are starving**, the dreamer's present job and friends will bring nothing but unhappiness.

Statue — **Looking at a statue in a dream** is a sign of a self-imposed change in the dreamer's life. **Seeing a statue** means a break-up with the dreamer's lover.

Stealing — If the **dreamer or someone else steals**, it is a sign of bad luck and reputation. An **accusation of stealing** means that the dreamer's actions will be misinterpreted, but the situation will turn to his advantage later. If the **dreamer accuses someone else of stealing**, it means that he will be totally inconsiderate to somebody.

Steeple — **Seeing a steeple of a church** foretells ill-health and misfortune. A **broken-down steeple** is a sign of death among the dreamer's group of friends. If the **dreamer climbs up a steeple**, it signifies difficulties that the dreamer will overcome. If **he falls off a steeple**, he will suffer from illness and business losses.

Steer (animal) — **Seeing a steer** indicates the dreamer's honesty and fairness, which are his most outstanding character traits. If **more than one steer appears in a dream**, it shows that this is the right time to take risks. (A steer, as opposed to a bull or cow, is characterized by his horns; see **Bull**.)

Steps — **Going up steps** means an improvement in the dreamer's fortune. **Going down steps** means the opposite. If he **falls down steps**, he will experience sudden business setbacks.

Stepsister — Dreaming about having a stepsister is a sign of inevitable worry and responsibility.

Stethoscope — Nothing good comes of this dream —

only bad luck, dashed hopes, and trouble in love.

Sticks — This is a sign of bad luck.

Stillborn — Dreaming about a stillborn baby means that the dreamer will be informed of a sad event.

Stilts — If the **dreamer walks on stilts**, it means that his financial situation is shaky. If **he falls, or they break**, he will have serious trouble as a result of entrusting his business to other people.

Sting — If the **dreamer is stung by an insect**, there are troubles and bad things in store for him. If a **young woman is stung**, it foretells sadness and guilt as a result of some relationship with a man.

Stockings — **Dreaming about stockings** is a sign that the dreamer will enjoy bad company. If a **young woman's stockings are worn or full of runs**, her behavior will not be judicious — it could even be immoral. If **she wears fancy stockings**, she should be careful of how she behaves in the company of men. If **she wears white stockings**, bad luck awaits her.

Stone Mason — **Watching stone masons working** is a sign of disappointment. If the **dreamer is a stone mason**, his job will be unrewarding and his associates uninspiring.

Stones — **Seeing stones** is a sign of trouble. **Walking through stony or rocky terrain** means that the dreamer's path in life will be rough. **Small stones** mean that the dreamer will be plagued by minor worries. If **he throws a stone**, he will have to reprimand someone. If **he throws a stone at a violent person**, it means that the dreamer's strong sense of justice will prevent some bad thing from happening.

Store / Shop — If the **dreamer is actually a storekeeper**, it indicates business problems. If the dreamer does not own a shop, and he **dreams that he is walking amongst the products on sale**, it is a sign that he can expect good, pleasure-filled times. A **store filled with goods** means good profits. An **empty store** means losses and disputes. If the **store is on fire**, the dreamer will have a sudden revival in enjoyment and business. A **department store** is a symbol of several lucrative areas. If the **dreamer sees merchandise in a department store**, he will advance as a result of his own and his friends' efforts. If a **woman dreams that someone sells her shabby merchandise**, the man she likes will reject her advances.

Storeroom — A **tidy storeroom** is a sign of economic prosperity, pleasure and abundance. An **empty storeroom** is a warning against incorrect decisions, especially in the monetary sphere.

Stork — This symbolizes renewal and a change for the better in the dreamer's life.

Storms — If the **dreamer sees and hears an approaching storm,** he will have bad luck in everything: business, health, friendships. If the **storm passes**, things will improve somewhat.

Stranger — Dreaming about a stranger, especially one wearing a black suit, represents a warning about a bad period and depression in the life of the dreamer.

Strangled — **Dreaming about being strangled** is a prediction of a confining and draining relationship. If the **dreamer is strangled by an unseen strangler**, it means that he will be injured by someone near to him.

Straw — **Dreaming about straw** reflects the dreamer's bad feelings about the futility of his life. He sees his end and his destruction. **Seeing bales of straw on fire** signals prosperity. **Feeding straw to cattle** is a sign that the dreamer will not provide properly for his dependants.

Strawberries — **Dreaming about strawberries** is a good sign — promotion, enjoyment, and fulfillment of wishes. **Eating strawberries** means happy love. **Buying and selling strawberries** means that there will be good crops and joy.

Street — If the **dreamer walks down a brightly illuminated street**, he will experience an unsatisfactory and fleeting enjoyment. If **he is in a familiar street in a faraway town**, it means that he will soon go on a trip which will not be as enjoyable or worthwhile as was previously thought. **Walking in a street** foretells cares, bad luck, and failure to realize ambitions. If the **dreamer is in a street and is afraid of being mugged**, it means that he is taking perilous risks in his business or social life. **Seeing a crowd in a street** is a sign of excellent business and sales.

Streetcars — **Seeing streetcars** means that the dreamer is being plotted against and sabotaged. **Riding a streetcar** means that the dreamer's well-being will be undermined by jealousy and envy. If the **dreamer rides on the platform**, it means that he will take an enormous risk in some affair. If **he rides without mishap**, he will succeed. A **high platform** means more serious danger, but a **low one** means a very low degree of success.

Stretcher — If a **stretcher appears in a dream**, it predicts bad news. If the **dreamer is using a stretcher**, it means that he will have to do disagreeable work.

Struggle — **Struggling** symbolizes difficulties. However, **triumph over another person in a struggle** is a sign that the dreamer will overcome difficulties that stand in his way in life.

Strychnine — Consuming strychnine under a physician's orders signifies taking huge risks in some affair.

Stumbling — **Stumbling while running or walking** foretells disapproval of the dreamer, as well as obstacles in his path, and damage to assets and good reputation. **Avoiding stumbling** means overcoming the obstacles.

Stumps — **Dreaming about a stump** means troubles and a change in lifestyle. **Fields of stumps** attest to the dreamer's helplessness in the face of attack. **Uprooting stumps** shows the dreamer's practical determination to cast off poverty, defeat rivals and get on in life.

Submarine — **Dreaming about a submarine** symbolizes an unsavory secret which will be revealed unexpectedly and harm the dreamer. If the **dreamer is in a submarine**, he will accidentally reveal bad news, causing chaos.

Subway — **Dreaming about riding in a subway** is a sign of imminent troubles, mostly of a psychological and emotional nature. **Being stuck in the subway symbolizes** a struggle with a moral issue which will necessitate consideration and time.

Suckle — To see a mother suckling an infant means that the dreamer will have success and happiness.

Suffering — Contrary to what might be expected,

dreaming about pain or suffering is actually an indication of happiness, joy and laughter coming the way of the dreamer in the near future.

Suffocating / Choking — Dreaming about suffocating expresses aggression as well as the fear of being humiliated as a result of a loved one's conduct. If the **dreamer is suffocating another person**, it means that he feels hatred towards him. If the **dreamer is being suffocated by another**, it means that he deeply fears the person who is suffocating him in the dream.

Sugar — Dreaming about sugar symbolizes a good period in the dreamer's domestic life accompanied by feelings of wholeness and harmony with his environment. If the **dreamer eats sugar**, he will have to cope with disagreeable things, but they will resolve themselves satisfactorily. If the **dreamer asks the price of sugar**, he is being threatened by his enemies. If the **dreamer's business is sugar**, and a large shipment is brought to him, he risks a huge business loss. If a **big sack of sugar falls and breaks**, he will suffer a minor loss.

Sugar Tongs — The dreamer will get to hear of bad deeds committed by others.

Suicide — Dreaming about suicide indicates the dreamer's desire to extricate himself from a difficult situation. If the **dreamer commits suicide**, he will have bad luck. If others commit suicide, other people's losses will affect the dreamer. If a **young woman's lover commits suicide**, she is very aware of his infidelity to her.

Suitcase — If the **suitcase belongs to the dreamer**, it indicates that he will soon have to deal with problems. If the **suitcase belongs to someone else**, it means that he will embark on a trip in the near future.

Sums (addition) — An incorrect sum warns against unsuccessful commercial negotiations.

Sulfur — **Dreaming about sulfur** warns against the evil plots of others. **Burning sulfur** means that the dreamer should safeguard his wealth. **Eating sulfur** is a sign of health and enjoyment.

Sun — **Dreaming about a bright, lucid sunrise** is a sign of happiness and wealth. The **midday sun** symbolizes ambitions which are satisfactorily realized. **Sunset** is a symbol of being past one's prime, with the attendant health worries. If the **sun shines through clouds**, the dreamer's troubles will soon disappear, and good luck will replace them. A **peculiar-looking sun**, or an **eclipse**, foretells perilous things ahead, but they are temporary.

Sunflower — This signifies sunshine, light and warmth.

Sunshade — **Seeing young women carrying sunshades** is a sign of good fortune and happiness. A **broken sunshade** is a sign of bad luck and untimely death.

Surgeon — **Dreaming about a surgeon** means dangerous business enemies. A **young woman who dreams about a surgeon** will come down with a bad disease.

Surgical Instruments — Seeing these in a dream means that the dreamer will feel miffed that a friend is holding back on something.

Swallow (bird) — **Dreaming about a swallow** signifies a happy and serene home. A **dead or injured swallow** is a sign of deep sorrow.

Swamp — **Walking through swamps** means bad luck in money matters — especially bequests — and in love. If the **swamp has green vegetation and limpid water**, the dreamer will enjoy money and good times — but with a lot of risk.

Swan — **Seeing white swans swimming on calm waters** is a sign of prosperity and pleasure. A **black swan** symbolizes a good and generous spouse; a **white swan** indicates a happy marriage and successful progeny. A **dead swan** means a feeling of surfeit and dissatisfaction. **Flying swans** means that something long awaited will come to fruition.

Swearing (oaths) — A **lover who dreams about swearing** will no longer have faith in his beloved. **Dreaming about swearing** means a setback in business. If the **dreamer swears in the presence of his family**, there will soon be a quarrel because of his bad conduct.

Sweeping — A **woman who dreams that she is sweeping** will be appreciated by her family. If the **floors need sweeping, but they are not swept**, there will be troubles and severe disillusionment. If **employees dream about sweeping**, it gives them cause to doubt the sincerity of other people's intentions.

Sweetness — A dream about eating something sweet means that the dreamer possesses a high level of inner awareness and self-control.

Sweets — See **Candy**.

Sweet Taste — If the **dreamer has a sweet taste in his**

mouth, he will behave with control and kindness during a period of turmoil, and people will appreciate this. If **he tries to dispel a sweet taste**, it means that he will act scornfully and tyrannically toward his friends.

Sweetheart — If the **dreamer sees his sweetheart as pleasant and good-looking**, he will find a lovely and well-established woman. If his **sweetheart does not look so good**, the dreamer will have serious doubts about his future with her. If **his sweetheart is ill**, it means that he will have both happiness and sadness. If he dreams that his **sweetheart is dead**, it predicts a lot of bad luck.

Swelling — If the **dreamer sees his body as swollen**, it means that he will be prosperous, but his selfishness will be a stumbling-block. If **he sees others swollen**, his rise in life will be viewed with envy.

Swimming — If the **dreamer sees himself swimming**, it is a warning against taking unnecessary risks or gambling which will bring about significant losses. If **he starts sinking while swimming**, he will be very discontent. **S w i m m i n g underwater** is a prediction of worries and hassles. A **young woman swimming with a female friend** will be popular because of her lovely nature.

Swiss Cheese — Dreaming about Swiss cheese is a sign of great wealth about to be acquired by the dreamer, as well as wholesome enjoyments.

Switch — **Dreaming about a switch** symbolizes reverses of fortune and discouragement. A **broken switch** is an indication of humiliation and hassles. **Dreaming about a**

railroad switch indicates losses resulting from journeys.

Sword — If the **dreamer wears a sword**, it means that he will hold a position of great dignity and respect. If his **sword is confiscated**, he will be outwitted by rivals. If **others carry swords**, it is a warning of serious disputes. A **broken sword** is a sign of desperation.

Symphony — This is an excellent dream of pleasurable amusements.

Synagogue — **Dreaming about a synagogue** is an indication of powerful enemies who are preventing the dreamer's advancement. If **he climbs to the top of a synagogue from the exterior**, he will overcome the enemies and be successful. **Reading the Hebrew words** on a synagogue is a warning of financial catastrophe which will eventually be overcome.

Syringe — **Seeing a syringe** means that the dreamer will be unjustifiably shocked at bad news concerning a relative's health. A **broken syringe** signifies minor health setbacks and business worries.

Table — **Dreaming about a table** symbolizes a person's accomplishments in life. A **set table** signifies a comfortable, happy family life. A **bare table** is a sign of disputes and lack of money. **Clearing the table** signifies the transformation of happiness into coldness and worry. A **work table, operating table, desk**, etc., are interpreted according to the context of their appearance in the dream. **Eating off a table with no tablecloth** is indicative of an independent nature, unaffected by the behavior or situation of others. A **dirty tablecloth** means troublesome children or employees, and bad times. A **broken table** denotes loss of wealth. If the **dreamer sees someone standing or sitting on a table**, that person will soon behave foolishly.

Tacks — **Dreaming about tacks** is a sign of hassles and disputes. If a **woman hammers in a tack**, she will overcome opponents. If **she hits her finger in the process**, she will be upset about disagreeable things she has to do.

Tadpole — **Seeing tadpoles** means that the dreamer has made deals which are causing him anxiety. If a **young woman sees tadpoles swimming**, she will become involved with a rich but unscrupulous man.

Tailor — **Seeing a tailor** is a sign that the dreamer is indecisive and easily influenced by others. **Dreaming about a tailor** indicates anxiety about a trip. **Arguing with a tailor** foretells the dreamer's let-down about the results of one of his endeavors.

Tail — If the **dreamer has an animal's tail**, he will suffer from strange events and trouble as a result of his own wickedness. If **he cuts off an animal's tail**, it means that his own lack of care will cause him losses. **Seeing only an animal's tail** is a sign of aggravation when happiness was expected. **Trimming a horse's tail** means success in business or agriculture.

Talisman — **Wearing a talisman** signifies good friends and patronage from wealthy people. If a **young woman receives a talisman from her lover**, she will marry the man she desires.

Talking — **Dreaming about talking** predicts ill health in the dreamer's family and business worries. If **other people talk loudly**, it means that the dreamer will be accused of meddling. If **the dreamer thinks he is being spoken about**, it is a warning of illness and unhappiness.

Tambourine — This is an indication of an extraordinary occurrence which the dreamer will enjoy.

Tank (water) — **Dreaming about a tank** is a prediction of unprecedented contentment and prosperity for the dreamer. A **leaking tank** is a symbol of business losses.

Tannery — **Dreaming about a tannery** indicates contagious diseases and financial losses. If the **dreamer is a tanner**, he will have to do unpleasant work because of his dependants. If the **dreamer purchases leather from a tanner**, his financial status will be good, but his social life will not.

Tape — **Dreaming about tape** is a symbol of a job which is actually poorly paid drudgery. If a **woman purchases tape**, she will be the victim of bad luck.

Tape Recorder — Dreaming about a tape recorder

recording means that things said by the dreamer will return to torment and incriminate him, especially if the wrong people get to hear them.

Tapestry — **Dreaming about a lavish tapestry** means that the dreamer will enjoy a life of wealth and ease. If the **tapestries are in good condition**, he will attain his wishes. If a **young woman dreams of tapestries decorating her room**, she will marry someone rich and of an elevated social status.

Tapeworms — Dreaming about seeing or being afflicted with a tapeworm is a sign of approaching ill health and ruined pleasures.

Tar — **Tar on a road** signifies good health. **Tar on the soles of shoes or floating in water** means that the dreamer will soon embark on a trip. **Boiling tar** means personal problems. **Tar on the hands or clothing** is a sign of sadness and illness. **Seeing tar** is a warning against the traps set by dangerous enemies.

Tarantula — **Killing a tarantula** means success after massive failure. **Seeing a tarantula** means total defeat by the dreamer's enemies.

Target — **Dreaming about a target** means that the dreamer will have to deal with an unpleasant issue instead of enjoying himself. If a **young woman considers herself a target**, she may be badmouthed by acquaintances.

Tassels — **Seeing tassels** means the realization of the dreamer's loftiest aspirations. **Losing tassels** warns of an impending trauma.

Tattoo — If the **dreamer has a tattoo**, he will have cause to go on a long and unpleasant journey. If **he sees tattoos on**

others, he will be envied because of love. If **he is a tattoo artist**, his friends will reject him because of his predilection for weird experiences.

Taxes — If the **dreamer pays taxes**, he will overcome the forces of evil in his vicinity. If **he cannot pay taxes**, his endeavors will not succeed. If **other people pay taxes**, the dreamer will have to ask friends for help.

Taxi — If the **dreamer hails a taxi which drives past him without stopping**, it is a warning against being naive. If the **dreamer hails a taxi uneventfully**, he can expect a letter with good news in the near future.

Tea — **Seeing tea** suggests that the dreamer could be more resolute in his opinions and more decisive in his manner. **Making tea** indicates that the dreamer will not be circumspect, and will suffer pangs of conscience as a result. **Drinking tea** warns of problems in love and social life. **Spilt tea** is a sign of domestic strife. If the **dreamer is thirsty for a cup of tea**, it means that unexpected guests will arrive.

Teacher — This indicates that the dreamer must examine his financial and social situation and act cautiously.

Teacups — **Seeing teacups** predicts enjoyable events. **Breaking teacups or seeing broken teacups** means the interruption of good luck and happiness by some problem. **Drinking wine from a teacup** means that the dreamer will soon have both wealth and pleasure.

Teapot — **Seeing a teapot** is an indication of bad news. **Pouring fresh, cold water from a teapot** is a sign of sudden good fortune.

Tear — A tear indicates extreme emotional changes.

Tears — If **tears arc shed**, it means that the dreamer will enjoy a rosy future and happy events. If the **dreamer is in tears**, it foretells a problem. **Others shedding tears** means that the dreamer's problems will have an effect on other people.

Teasing — **Teasing someone** means that the dreamer will be popular because of his extrovert nature and sense of humor. Success in business will also follow. If the **dreamer is teased**, he will be liked by cheerful, wealthy people. If a **young woman is teased**, she will fall in love quickly without getting married.

Teaspoon — See **Spoon**.

Teeth — **Dreaming about teeth or about a dentist** warns of health problems; the dreamer should look after himself in the near future. **Loose teeth** symbolize lack of success and bad news. **Having a tooth pulled** means a serious but not fatal illness. **Having false teeth made** means struggling with troubles. **Losing teeth** symbolizes devastating troubles: If **one tooth falls out**, it signifies bad news; **two teeth** mean huge troubles which the dreamer did not bring upon himself; **three teeth** imply serious diseases and accidents. If **all the teeth fall out**, even because of caries, it is a sign of catastrophe and death. **Having teeth filled** means finding lost valuables after a lot of trouble. **Brushing teeth** indicates a battle to maintain one's financial status. **Dreaming about imperfect teeth** is a terrible dream, warning of accidents, losses, failure to implement plans, illness and depression. **Beautiful white teeth**, however, are a sign of happiness and wishes come true. If **tartar or**

plaque falls off the teeth, leaving them white and clean, it means that troubles will pass. If the **dentist cleans the dreamer's teeth**, but the next day they are stained again, it means that he will be betrayed and outwitted.

Telegram — Receiving a telegram foretells imminent bad news concerning a friend's distortion of the facts pertaining to something important to the dreamer. If **he sends a telegram**, he will fall out with someone close to him, and suffer business losses. If the **dreamer is in a telegraph office**, he will have unfortunate meetings.

Telephone — Dreaming about a telephone means that the dreamer will come into contact with unknown factors who will wreak havoc in his business. If the **dreamer is speaking on the telephone**, he can expect success in the area under discussion. A **ringing telephone** in a dream means that a friend needs help. A **silent telephone** indicates that the dreamer feels discriminated against. If a **woman dreams that she is speaking on the telephone**, a lot of envy will be directed at her, but she will deflect it. If **she has trouble hearing the party at the other end of the line**, she should beware of malicious gossip.

Telescope — Dreaming about a telescope indicates possible negative changes in the dreamer's professional life, as well as domestic problems. **Looking through a telescope** at the heavens means that the dreamer will take enjoyable trips, for which he will pay dearly later on. **A non-functioning telescope** means that things will not go smoothly, and there will be problems.

Television — If the **dreamer watches television** and does not feel happy with what he is seeing, it means that others can influence him too easily. **Dreaming about being on television** means that the dreamer is overly involved with his looks, and will be hurt as a result of this superficiality.

Tempest — This foretells catastrophic events for the dreamer, and uncaring friends.

Temptation — If the **dreamer is being enticed by another person to perform a criminal act**, the dream is a test and warning: Do not be tempted to walk forbidden paths in real life! If **he succeeds in resisting the temptation**, he will finally prevail in an undertaking which many people oppose.

Tenant — If a **landlord dreams about his tenant**, he will have hassles. If the **dreamer is a tenant**, he will suffer losses in business due to trying out ideas. If a **tenant pays the dreamer**, this is a sign of success.

Tennis — This is a sign that the dreamer feels the need to be popular and socially successful.

Tent — **Seeing a tent** symbolizes protection and security. In the future, the dreamer will not face worry or disappointment. **Being in a tent** is a sign of change in the dreamer's life. **Torn or shabby tents** symbolize trouble. **Seeing several tents** warns of trips with disagreeable people.

Terror — **Experiencing terror in a dream** predicts setbacks and disillusionment. If **other people are in terror**, the dreamer will be adversely affected by his friends' troubles.

Text — **Hearing a clergyman reading a text** foretells a dispute and a breakup with a friend. **Arguing about a text**

means bad luck. **Attempting to remember a text** is a sign of unforeseen problems. **Studying, rereading and thinking about a text** signifies overcoming many pitfalls on the way to realizing one's wishes.

Thatch — **Dreaming about a straw-thatched roof which leaks** means that there is a possibility of danger, but if the **dreamer is quick-witted enough,** he can avoid it. If the **roof is thatched with bad materials**, the dreamer will experience unhappiness.

Thaw — **Seeing the ground thawing** following a long period that it was frozen predicts prosperity. If the **dreamer sees ice thawing**, a problem which bothered him greatly will be solved satisfactorily and lucratively.

Theater — **Dreaming about a theater** shows that the dreamer has a strong desire to break his routine and bring his talents and creativity to the fore. **Being at the theater** means that the dreamer is enjoying new friendships and good business. If **he is acting**, his enjoyment will not be enduring. If **he dreams of clapping and laughing during a performance**, he will forget serious things and give himself over to superficial pleasures. **Watching an opera** is a sign of success and fulfilled aspirations. If a **fire or some other disaster occurs in a theater**, and the dreamer attempts to escape, it symbolizes something dangerous that the dreamer will undertake.

Theft — See **Robbery**.

Thermometer — **Looking at a thermometer in a dream** is a sign of poor business and domestic strife. If the **mercury is falling**, business will deteriorate. If the **mercury is rising**, the dreamer will overcome difficulties. If the **thermometer is broken**, illness is on the horizon.

Thermos Flask — This is a sign of an imminent disaster.

Thief — **Dreaming about being a thief who is pursued by the police** means problems in business and in social life. If the **dreamer catches a thief**, it is a sign that he will defeat his enemies.

Thigh — **Dreaming about a thigh** signifies recovery from a disease or the end of health problems. **Seeing one's own thigh smooth and pale** is a sign of very good fortune. If the **thigh is injured**, betrayal and disease will follow. If a **young woman admires her thighs**, she should avoid going overboard in her extrovert behavior.

Thimble — **Dreaming about a thimble** symbolizes unrealistic, unrealizable ambitions. **Using a thimble** means being accountable to many other people. If a **woman uses a thimble**, she will have to support herself. **Purchasing or receiving a new thimble** signifies pleasurable new relationships. **Losing a thimble** predicts distress and poverty. **Seeing an old, battered thimble** warns of an injudicious decision in an important matter.

Thirst — **Dreaming about being thirsty** means that the dreamer's aspirations are too high. If **he quenches his thirst**, he will realize his aspirations. If **others are thirsty and quench their thirst**, the dreamer will benefit from the patronage of rich people.

Thorn — A **dream about thorns** signifies that someone in the dreamer's environment is plotting against him and seeking to harm him. If the **thorns are camouflaged by green leaves**, the dreamer's financial security is being tampered with by invisible enemies.

Thread — **Dreaming about thread** means that the dreamer's path to wealth is long and convoluted. A **torn thread** indicates disappointment or loss brought about by the compassionate character of the dreamer and the betrayal of friends.

Threshing — **A dream about threshing grain or wheat** is a sign of flourishing business and domestic bliss. If there is **much more straw than grain**, there will be business failures. If there is **an accident or breakdown** during threshing, the dreamer will suffer a tragedy.

Throat — **Dreaming about a lovely throat** means promotion. A **sore throat** means that a friend has not turned out to be quite what the dreamer expected, much to his chagrin.

Throne — If the **dreamer is sitting on a throne**, he will enjoy increased wealth and status. **Getting off a throne** means disillusionment. **Seeing others on a throne** means that the dreamer will prosper as a result of the intervention of other people.

Thumb — **Seeing a thumb** means that the dreamer will be popular with unsavory people. A **sore thumb** is a sign of business losses and unpleasant associates. **Being thumbless** is a sign of isolation and poverty. An **extremely small thumb** means temporary enjoyment. An **extremely large thumb** means meteoric success. A **dirty thumb** symbolizes the gratification of base urges. A **long thumbnail**

warns of getting into wicked habits as a result of the quest for unnatural pleasures.

Thunder — **Hearing thunder** is a warning of setbacks in business. **Being out in a thunderstorm** predicts distress and grief. **Hearing deafening thunderclaps** is a sign of disillusionment and loss.

Ticket — Buying, receiving or handing someone a ticket indicates that a problem that has been bothering the dreamer lately will soon be solved.

Tickle — **Dreaming about being tickled** signifies anxieties and disease. If the **dreamer tickles other people**, he will sacrifice happiness and joy because of his own stupidity and weakness.

Ticks — **Seeing ticks crawling on one's body** signifies poverty and disease. If the **dreamer squashes a tick on his body**, it means that dangerous enemies are plaguing him. If **he sees huge ticks on his livestock**, it means that enemies are trying to abscond with his possessions.

Tiger — If a **tiger stalks the dreamer**, he will be stalked by enemies. If **the tiger attacks**, the dreamer's failure will cause him to sink into depression. **Chasing the tiger away or killing it** signifies success in all the dreamer's endeavors. If a **tiger flees from the dreamer**, he will defeat his opponents and achieve high status. If **tigers are caged**, the dreamer will outwit his opponents.

Till — If the **dreamer sees money and jewelry in a till**, success is predicted in love. An **empty till** promises nothing but disappointment.

Timber — **Seeing timber** is a symbol of peace and

prosperity. If the **timber has dried up and warped**, disillusionment is in the offing.

Tin — This is a warning that deceitful people surround the dreamer.

Tipsy — **Dreaming about being tipsy** is a sign of a jolly, carefree disposition which can ignore life's vicissitudes. If **others are tipsy**, the dreamer does not care about the behavior of people around him.

Toad — **Dreaming about a toad** is a symbol of corruption and mishaps. The dream warns against being tempted to engage in impure acts. If a **woman dreams about a toad**, it warns of becoming embroiled in a scandal. **Killing a toad** means that the dreamer's judgment will be scathingly questioned. **Touching a toad** means that the dreamer will cause the downfall of a friend.

Toast — This is a sign of a successful and enjoyable family life.

Toaster — This means that a wish will soon come true.

Tobacco — **Tobacco in any form** indicates that the dreamer's problems will soon be solved, and that his character is conciliatory and moderate. **Dreaming about tobacco** means success in business but not in love. **Using tobacco** is a warning against rivals and wastefulness. **Seeing tobacco grow** is a sign of successful undertakings. **Dry tobacco** is a good sign for farmers and dealers. If the **dreamer or another person is smoking**, it means pleasant friendships.

Tocsin — **Dreaming about the sound of a tocsin** denotes a battle which the dreamer will win. **For a woman to hear a**

tocsin, it is a sign of a breakup with her husband or lover.

Toddy — Dreaming about drinking a toddy means that the dreamer's lifestyle will be altered by fascinating occurrences.

Tomato — **Seeing tomatoes** means that the dreamer has a need for social involvement. **Eating tomatoes** is a sign of good health. **Seeing tomatoes growing** means contentment at home. If a **young woman sees a firm, ripe tomato,** she will be happily married.

Tomb — **Seeing tombs** signifies unhappiness and business letdowns. If the **tombs are shabby and broken,** it is a sign of serious illness and death. If the **dreamer sees his own tomb,** he will suffer disease or disappointment. **Reading tombstones** is a prediction of the dreamer's illness.

Tongue — If the **dreamer sees his own tongue,** his associates will view him with distaste. If he **sees another person's tongue,** he will be harmed by slander. If there is **anything wrong with his tongue,** it means that speaking without thinking will get him into trouble.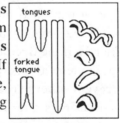

Toothless — A **dream about being toothless** means that the dreamer is incapable of advancing, and is threatened by illness. If **others are toothless,** it means that enemies are attempting unsuccessfully to slander the dreamer.

Toothpicks — **Dreaming about toothpicks** means that the dreamer will be bothered by trifling worries and hassles, if he permits it. **Using a toothpick** means that the dreamer will do a friend harm.

Topaz — **Seeing a topaz** means excellent luck and good friends. If a **woman loses a topaz**, she will suffer injury at the hands of envious friends. If she **receives a topaz**, she will get involved in a fascinating love affair.

Tops — See **Spinning Tops**.

Torch — **Seeing torches** is an indication of enjoyment and good business. **Carrying a torch** means success in love and intrigues. **An extinguished torch** is a sign of worry and failure.

Tornado — Dreaming about being in a tornado means that the dreamer will be devastated about the failure of plans for enrichment to materialize.

Torrent — Watching a swift torrent means extraordinary distress and hassles.

Torture — **Dreaming about torture** expresses a vague fear or unbridled feelings of jealousy. **Being tortured** means suffering anguish and disillusionment at the hands of false friends. If the **dreamer tortures others**, it indicates his failure to implement his plans to attain wealth. **Attempting to prevent others from being tortured** predicts success in love and business after overcoming obstacles.

Tourist — **Dreaming about being a tourist** means that some enjoyable matter will take the dreamer out of his routine. **Seeing tourists** means hassles in love and erratic business.

Tower — **Seeing a tower** is a symbol of great ambition. If the **dreamer sees himself standing at the top of a high building**, it means that he will suffer financial difficulties, but will have a life full of happiness. **Climbing a tower** in a dream indicates the fulfillment of wishes, while a collapsing tower is an indication of problems in business and dashed hopes. **Climbing down a rope from a tower** means economic success and prosperity.

Toys — Dreaming about clean, well-kept toys is a sign of happiness and joy for the dreamer. **Broken toys** signify difficult and sad times — even death. **Seeing children playing with toys** symbolizes a happy marriage. If the **dreamer gives toys away**, he will be ostracized socially.

Trade — Dreaming about trading is a sign of reasonable success. **Failure in trade** means hassles and anxieties.

Tragedy— Dreaming about a tragedy means dusionment and misunderstandings. **Being involved in a tragedy** foretells a catastrophe that will cause grief and danger for the dreamer.

Trailer — Dreaming about traveling in a trailer is a forecast of a trip which causes the dreamer anxiety. **Living in a trailer** means bad luck.

Train — If the **dreamer is in a smoothly-moving train that is not on tracks,** he will have worries that will be resolved to his advantage. **Freight trains** indicate positive changes. **Sleeping-cars** signal that the dreamer's desire to attain wealth is motivated by lust and other impure urges. If the **dreamer is sleeping on top of a sleeping-car,** it means he has a disagreeable companion on whom he is wasting time and money. If the **dreamer is on the wrong train,** he is warned that he has chosen the wrong path in life and should rectify the error.

Traitor — Seeing a traitor in a dream indicates that the dreamer is threatened by enemies working toward his destruction. If the **dreamer is accused of being a traitor, or considers himself one**, he will not have much enjoyment.

Transfiguration — If the dreamer sees himself transfigured, he will enjoy the excellent opinion of people of honor and esteem.

Trap — If the **dreamer falls into a trap**, it indicates that he is a suspicious type, suspicious even of those who do not warrant it. If the **dreamer himself laid the trap**, it is a sign that he will soon lose a court case and will use sly means to implement his plans. **Being caught in a trap** means that his rivals will outsmart him. If the dreamer catches animals in a trap, he will enjoy professional success. An **empty trap** warns of an imminent mishap. A **worn or non-functional trap** is a sign of business setbacks and possible illness in the family.

Traveling — **Dreaming about traveling** is a sign of lucrative and enjoyable things. If the **dreamer is traveling through unfamiliar, harsh terrain**, he is warned of illness and foes. If **his travels take him over bald, rocky cliffs**, success will be followed immediately by disappointment. If the **terrain is green, hilly and gentle**, it is a sign of joy and prosperity. **Dreaming about traveling alone in an automobile** means that the dreamer might go on an exciting, but worrying trip. **Traveling in a crowded automobile** is a sign of new, amusing friends and good experiences.

Tray — **Seeing a tray in a dream** is the sign of stupidly squandered money and unpleasant surprises. **Trays containing valuable objects** mean that the dreamer will enjoy good surprises.

Treasure — **Dreaming about discovering treasure** means that the dreamer will be helped on his path to wealth by an unforeseen source of largesse. **Losing treasures** means bad business and unfaithful friends.

Trees — **Trees in bloom** are a sign of happiness in a new love. **Bare trees** indicate marital problems. **Dead trees** are a sign of grief and loss. **Climbing a tree** means promotion to higher positions. **Cutting down a tree**, or uprooting it, is a sign of energy and money frittered away. If **green trees are chopped down**, it means that joy and happy events will soon be replaced by sadness.

Trenches — **Seeing trenches in a dream** is a warning of betrayal. The dreamer must be careful when embarking upon new endeavors or making new acquaintances. If the **trenches have been filled**, it means an accumulation of worries.

Triangle — **Seeing a triangle** shows that there is a conflict in the dreamer's mind, usually connected with choosing a marriage partner. **Dreaming about a triangle** is a prediction of friendships ending in separation and lovers' quarrels.

Tripe — The **appearance of tripe** in a dream heralds disease and peril. **Eating tripe** means a bitter disappointment.

Triplets — **Seeing triplets** is a sign of success in an enterprise which seemed doomed to failure. If a **man dreams about his wife giving birth to triplets**, it indicates a positive outcome to some complicated matter. If the **dreamer hears newborn triplets crying**, there will be a quick and satisfactory solution to some argument. A **young woman**

who **dreams of having triplets** means that she will be wealthy, but will not have luck in love.

Trophy — **Seeing trophies** means that the dreamer will have luck or pleasure because of someone that he barely knows. If a **woman presents a trophy**, there is a hint of unsavory pleasures and doubtful gains.

Trout — **Dreaming about trout** is a symbol of prosperity. **Eating trout** means a comfortable life. **Catching a trout with a fishing-rod** means joy and a good living. If the **trout slips back into the water**, this will be short-lived. **Catching trout with a net** is a sign of unparalleled financial blooming. If the **trout are swimming in murky water**, the dreamer's triumph in love will turn bitter and sorrowful.

Trowel — A **dream about a trowel** is a sign that the dreamer will successfully overcome hardship. A **rusty or broken trowel** heralds inevitable bad fortune.

Trumpet — If a **trumpet is heard in a dream**, it signifies an unexpected change for the better. If the **dreamer himself is playing the trumpet**, it means he will succeed in overcoming difficulties that face him, and his wishes will come true.

Trunks — **Dreaming about trunks** is a prediction of trips and bad luck. **Packing a trunk** symbolizes a nice trip. If the **contents of a trunk are scattered about**, it means that there will be arguments and an unsatisfactory, hastily undertaken trip. **Empty trunks** indicate disappointment in love and marriage. A **young woman attempting unsuccessfully to open her trunk** means that she will fail to win the heart of a wealthy man. If **she is unable to lock her trunk**, she will not be able to go on a long-awaited journey.

Truss — This is a sign of bad luck and bad health.

Trusts — A **dream about trusts** is a sign of mediocre success in the legal profession or in business. If the **dreamer is a member of a trust**, he will experience phenomenal success in an undertaking.

Tub — A **tub full of water** is a sign of domestic harmony. An **empty tub** means financial wealth and distress. A **broken tub** is a prediction of domestic disputes.

Tumble — If the **dreamer tumbles off anything**, it is a sign that he is not as careful as he should be, and should be more meticulous in business. If the **dreamer sees other people tumble**, he will profit from their carelessness.

Tumult — See **Riot**.

Tunnel — **Going though a tunnel** is not a good sign for love and business. **Driving through a tunnel in a car** signifies a lack of confidence, as well as insufficient business and a lot of wearying traveling. If the **dreamer sees himself trapped in a tunnel**, it means that he is trying to shirk responsibility. A **train coming toward the dreamer** in a tunnel means illness and a switch of profession. A **collapsing tunnel** is a sign of malevolent enemies and failure.

Turf (race track)— A **dream about turf** means that the dreamer will lead a life of enjoyment and wealth, but his moral character will come under scrutiny by his closest friends. If **he sees a green turf**, something of interest will fascinate him.

Turkey — **Seeing turkeys** is a sign of flourishing business and good crops. **Turkeys prepared for sale** means better business. **Sick or dead turkeys** are a sign of difficulties.

Dreaming about eating turkey signals an imminent happy event. **Flying turkeys** means a meteoric rise to fame. **Shooting turkeys** signifies that the dreamer will accumulate wealth by immoral means.

Turkish Bath — **Taking a Turkish bath** means that the dreamer will spend time far away from those dear to him, but he will enjoy himself greatly. If **he sees others in a Turkish bath**, it means that he will enjoy congenial company.

Turnips — A **dream about turnips growing** means an improvement in the dreamer's chances in life which will make him very happy. **Eating turnips** is a sign of illness, while uprooting them means better opportunities in life. **Seeing turnip seed** has a similar meaning. If a **young woman sows turnip seed**, she will receive a good bequest and will find a good-looking husband.

Turpentine — Dreaming about turpentine indicates that in the immediate future the dreamer will have futile and worthless appointments.

Turquoise — A **dream about a turquoise** means that one of the dreamer's wishes will come true, much to the joy of his family. If a **woman has a turquoise stolen**, she will be thwarted in love. If **she comes by the turquoise dishonestly**, she will pay for making rash decisions in love.

Turtle — A **dream about turtles** predicts disappointment in one's love life. **Seeing turtles** means that an exceptional event will improve the dreamer's business and give him pleasure. **Eating turtle soup** means that the dreamer will thrive on some piquant affair.

TV Quiz Show — If the **dreamer participates in a TV**

quiz show, he will soon have to answer unpleasant questions. If **he wins the show**, his reputation will remain excellent. If **he loses the show**, his reputation will be jeopardized.

Tweezers — A dream about tweezers means that the dreamer will be harassed by unpleasant situations and the attacks of his friends.

Twine — Dreaming about twine is a warning that the dreamer's business is becoming embroiled in problems that will be difficult to solve.

Twins — **Seeing twins in a dream** is a prediction of secure business and domestic happiness. If the **twins are unhealthy**, it means that the dreamer will make a decision that will bring about nothing but disillusionment and sorrow.

Type — **Seeing type in a dream** is a prediction of disagreement with friends. **Typing without errors** is a sign of love and prosperity.

Typewriter — Dreaming about using a typewriter means that the dreamer will soon be catching up with a long-lost friend.

Typhoid — If the **dreamer is ill with typhoid,** he should take care of his health and watch out for enemies. If there is **a typhoid epidemic,** business and health will drop to a low ebb.

Ugliness — This does not signify good things for the dreamer.

Ugly — **Dreaming about being ugly** means problems in love and business. If a **young woman considers herself ugly**, she will behave badly toward her lover and no doubt cause a breakup. A **young person seeing an ugly face** is also a sign of problems in love, and **an old-looking lover** means a breakup.

Ulcer (stomach) — **Seeing an ulcer** means poor business, losing friends and a breakup with someone the dreamer loves. If the **dreamer has an ulcer**, it is an indication of the dreamer's friends' dissatisfaction with his asinine conduct.

Umbrella — An **open umbrella** symbolizes happiness, success and love of life. A **new umbrella** held in a shower is a sign of enjoyment and prosperity. **Carrying an umbrella** means hassles for the dreamer. **Others carrying umbrellas** means that the dreamer will be requested to make charitable donations. **Borrowing an umbrella** signals a possible disagreement with a good friend. **Lending an umbrella** means that false friends can cause the dreamer harm. **Losing an umbrella** means misunderstandings with someone whom the dreamer trusts. A **torn or broken umbrella** means that the dreamer will be slandered and misquoted. An **umbrella with holes in it** means that the dreamer will not feel kindly toward his lover or friends.

Uncle — This is a sign of bad news in the near future.

Underground — **Dreaming about living underground** means a threat of losing money and one's good name. **Seeing an underground railway** means that the dreamer will get involved in a strange deal that will cause him worry and stress.

Undressing — **Dreaming about undressing** presages the dreamer's involvement in a scandal. If a **woman dreams of her country's ruler undressed**, she will experience sadness because of threatened evil to those close to her. **Seeing others undressed** is a sign of immoral pleasures which will soon give way to sorrow.

Unfortunate — Dreaming about being unfortunate is a sign of bad luck and trouble for the dreamer and others.

Unicorn — **Dreaming about a unicorn** is a sign of good luck and a comfortable life. **Seeing this mythical animal** is connected to virginity and sexuality in the dreamer's life.

Uniform (clothing) — If a **uniform appears in a dream** (on condition that it is *not* the dreamer who is wearing the uniform), it signifies that the dreamer has been blessed with peace, tranquillity and true love by the people around him. **Seeing a uniform in a dream** signifies that the dreamer has powerful friends who will help him on the path to success. **Seeing people wearing foreign uniforms** warns of breakdowns of diplomatic relations with other countries, or disagreements in families. A **young woman who dreams about wearing a uniform** will fall in love with a man who will return her love. If **she discards the uniform**, she will lay herself open to slander and gossip because of her daring conduct. If the **dreamer sees someone he knows looking sad while dressed in uniform**, it is a sign of bad luck or prolonged separation.

United States Mailbox — Seeing a US mailbox in a dream means that the dreamer is about to get involved in deals which will be accused of being unlawful. If the **dreamer drops a letter into a US mailbox**, he will be held responsible for the transgressions of someone else.

University — This is a dream that bodes well: It indicates ambition and the desire for achievements, as well as a high level of success in all areas of life.

Unknown — Meeting unknown people is a sign of good luck if the people are good-looking, or bad luck if they are ugly or deformed. If the **dreamer feels that he is unknown**, he will have bad luck as a result of peculiar occurrences.

Unlucky — See **Unfortunate**.

Urgent — If the dreamer is championing some urgent cause, it means that he will become involved in a matter that will require serious financial backing in order for it to succeed.

Urinal — A dream about a urinal means a chaotic home.

Urine — Seeing urine in a dream means that the dreamer will be cranky with his friends as a result of ill health. **Dreaming about urinating** is a sign of bad luck and unsuccessful love.

Urn — Dreaming about an urn signifies a mixture of good and bad luck. **Broken urns** mean sorrow.

Usurer — If the **dreamer is a usurer**, it means that his colleagues will treat him coldly, and he will suffer alarming setbacks in business. If **other people are usurers**, the dreamer will drop a friend because of a betrayal.

Usurper — Dreaming about being a usurper means that the dreamer will have difficulty establishing his right to an estate. If **others try to usurp his rights**, he will have a battle with his rivals, but in the end he will win. For a **young woman to dream about usurpers** means that she will be involved in a rivalry in which she will ultimately prevail.

Vacation — This indicates that the dreamer's life is about to change for the better, becoming calmer and more peaceful.

Vaccinate — **Dreaming about being vaccinated** means that the dreamer's weakness for women will be heartlessly exploited. **Dreaming that others are vaccinated** means that the dreamer will fail in his quest for happiness, resulting in business losses. If a **young woman is vaccinated on her leg**, she will suffer as a result of other people's treacherous behavior.

Vacuum Cleaner — Dreaming about a vacuum cleaner means that the dreamer will soon have to reach some quick decisions about personal or professional associations, at the risk of complications and embroilment.

Vagina — See **Penis**.

Vagrant — **Dreaming about being a vagrant** is a prediction of poverty and wretchedness. **Seeing vagrants** is a sign of an epidemic in the dreamer's environment. **Giving to a vagrant** means that the dreamer's generosity will be acknowledged and approved of.

Valentines — **Dreaming about sending valentines** predicts that the dreamer will miss the opportunity of increasing his wealth. If a **young woman receives a valentine**, she will marry an eager but weak lover against the advice of other people.

Valley — **Dreaming about a valley** is a sign that there will be a change in place of residence. **Walking through a lovely green valley** is a sign of flourishing business and happy love. A **barren valley** is a sign of financial losses and unhappy love. If the **valley is marshy**, there could be illness and hassles.

Vampire — **Seeing a vampire** signifies the dreamer's lack of self-confidence. **Dreaming about a vampire** means that the dreamer should watch out for someone trying to hurt or exploit him. **Being bitten or attacked by a vampire** means that the dreamer should be alert for false friends. If the **dreamer is wrestling with a vampire or driving a stake through its heart** means that the dreamer will overcome his enemies. If an **acquaintance of the dreamer is a vampire**, the dreamer should beware of that person's actions and intentions.

Vapor Bath — **Dreaming about taking a vapor bath** means that the dreamer's friends will be complainers. **Dreaming about getting out of a vapor bath** means that his worries will pass.

Varnishing — **Dreaming about varnishing** something means that the dreamer will attempt to achieve fame by fraudulent methods. If **others are varnishing**, it is a warning to the dreamer that friends want to increase their wealth at his expense.

Vase — **Seeing a vase** indicates that the dreamer is egocentric and only cares about his own good, and that the dreamer must demonstrate a higher degree of empathy and sensitivity toward others. **Dreaming about a vase** is a sign of an extremely happy domestic life. **Drinking from a vase** predict the thrills of an illicit love affair. A **broken vase** means untimely sorrow. If a **young woman receives a vase**, her most fervent wish will soon come true.

Vat — This is a bad sign, predicting the dreamer's suffering at the hands of sadistic people who have gotten hold of him.

Vatican — **Dreaming about the Vatican** means that the dreamer will receive unexpected perks. If **he sees royal figures conversing with the Pope**, he will become acquainted with high-ranking people.

Vault — **Dreaming about a vault** is a sign of misfortune and death. **Seeing a vault for valuables** means that despite the dreamer's modest lifestyle, people will be amazed at his actual worth. If the **doors of a vault are open**, trusted people will betray and abandon him.

Vegetables — **Seeing vegetables** in a dream reflects the dreamer's careful nature: He does not like to take unnecessary risks. **Eating vegetables** predicts peculiar luck. At first, he will think that he has been very successful, but he will in fact have been deceived. **Rotten or withered vegetables** are a sign of grief and misery. If a **young woman prepares vegetables**, she will marry a good and faithful man.

Vegetation — Dreaming about green vegetation is a good sign: The dreamer can expect exciting surprises or good news.

Vehicle — **Driving in a vehicle** is a sign of loss or ill health. **Being thrown from a vehicle** means sudden bad news. A **broken-down vehicle** means failure in important undertakings. **Buying a vehicle** means recouping one's losses. **Selling a vehicle** means a reverse in business.

Veil — **Dreaming about a veil** means that the dreamer

will not be absolutely honest with his lover and will have to use little deceptions to keep her. If **others wear veils**, so-called friends will slander and malign him. An **old or torn veil** is a warning of deceit surrounding the dreamer. If a **young woman loses her veil**, her deceit will be discovered by her lover, who will retaliate in kind. **Seeing a bridal veil** predicts an imminent, positive and joyful change in the dreamer's life. If a **young woman wears a bridal veil**, she will be very successful and prosperous in some endeavor. If the **veil becomes loose**, or something happens to it, she will have pain and worries. **Discarding a veil** means separation or shame. **Seeing mourning veils** is a sign of sorrow and business losses.

Vein — If the **dreamer sees his veins**, and they are as they should be, it makes him immune to slander. If **his veins are bleeding**, inescapable grief awaits him. **Swollen veins** means a rapid rise to honor and positions of responsibility.

Velvet — **Touching velvet** signifies problems, arguments and domestic quarrels. **Dreaming about velvet** is a sign of success in business. **Wearing velvet** means that the dreamer will achieve a degree of fame and honor. **Old velvet** means that his prosperity will diminish because of his foolish pride. If a **young woman wears velvet**, she will receive favors and honors, as well as a choice of suitable lovers.

Veneer — If the dreamer is veneering, it means that he will deceive his friends as a matter of course. His business undertakings will be of a dubious nature.

Ventriloquist — **Dreaming about a ventriloquist** means that some treacherous matter is going to be harmful to the dreamer. If the **dreamer thinks he is a ventriloquist**, it means that his conduct toward people who trust him will not be honorable. If a **young woman is confused by a ventriloquist's voice**, it means that she will be conned into an illicit affair.

Veranda — **Dreaming about being on a veranda** means that a worrying affair will have a successful outcome. If a **young woman and her lover are sitting on a veranda**, it is a sign of an early and happy marriage. An **old veranda** means fading hopes, as well as disillusionment in love and business.

Vermin — **Seeing vermin crawling** is a sign of huge problems and illness. If the **dreamer can get rid of them**, he will enjoy average success, but if **he cannot**, death will threaten either him or a family member.

Vertigo — Dreaming about vertigo means that the dreamer's domestic happiness will decrease, and his business prospects will look dim.

Vessels — Dreaming about vessels is a sign of work and activity.

Vexed — **Being vexed** in one's dreams means that one will awake to many worries. If the **dreamer thinks that someone is vexed with him**, he will not settle a minor argument in the near future.

Vicar — **Dreaming about a vicar** means acting stupidly while in a fit of jealousy. If a **young woman marries a vicar**, she will suffer from unrequited love; either she will not marry, or she will marry for convenience.

Vice — If the **dreamer indulges in vice**, it means that he is succumbing to temptation which will cost him his good name. If **others are surrendering to a vice**, bad luck will strike one of the dreamer's relatives or acquaintances.

Victim — Dreaming about being the victim of some plot means that the dreamer will be devastated by his enemies, and there will be a lack of domestic harmony. If **others are victimized**, it means that the dreamer will make money in a disreputable fashion and indulge in immoral affairs — much to his relatives' chagrin.

Victory — Dreaming about winning a victory means overcoming enemies and success with women. **Claiming victory** is a warning against taking sides in an argument in which the dreamer has very little knowledge of the subject at hand.

Village — Dreaming about being in a village is a sign of good health and prosperity. If the **dreamer sees himself in the village of his childhood**, there will be positive changes in his life in the near future as well as good news from faraway friends. A **run-down village** means imminent worry and distress.

Vine — Seeing a vine with grapes indicates hard work that will result in prosperity and great success. **Dreaming about vines** is a sign of success and joy. Flowering vines signify good health. **Dead vines** are a warning of failure in an important undertaking. **Poisonous vines** means that the dreamer will be taken in by a clever scheme, and his health will suffer.

Vinegar — Any dream about vinegar symbolizes disharmony or jealousy: One of the dreamer's principal traits is jealousy, which may cause him suffering throughout his life. **Drinking vinegar** means that the dreamer will be bulldozed into agreeing to some meeting about which he has a very bad gut feeling. **Sprinkling vinegar on vegetables** means that existing troubles will become even more serious.

Vineyard — Dreaming about a vineyard signifies success in the economic field and particularly in the field of romance. **Visiting a badly maintained and stinking vineyard** means that the dreamer's hopes will be dashed brutally.

Violence — Dreaming about violence is an indication of pressure, anxiety or fear of the person or factor that the dreamer encounters in his dream. If the **dreamer is the victim of violence**, he will be defeated by his enemies. If **he is violent toward someone else**, he will lose his good name and people's admiration because of his unscrupulous business conduct.

Violets — Dreaming about violets indicates a love of the good life, hedonism and the pursuit of pleasure. **Seeing or gathering violets** means happy events which will cause an important person to favor the dreamer. If a **young woman picks violets**, she will soon meet the man she will marry. **Dry, withered violets** signify that her love will be spurned.

Violin — If one sees or hears a violin in a dream, it means the dreamer is becoming increasingly popular in social circles, and will enjoy domestic harmony and smooth financial affairs. If a **violin string snaps**, it signifies that the dreamer is a peace-maker. **Tuning a violin** indicates an imminent love affair. If a **young woman plays the violin**, she will earn respect and receive valuable gifts. If her performance is not well received, she will lose other people's approbation, and her hopes will never be realized. A broken violin is a sign of bereavement and separation.

Viper — Dreaming about a viper is a sign of impending catastrophes. If a multicolored viper attacks the dreamer, it means that his enemies are absolutely determined to ruin him.

Virgin — Dreaming about a virgin means fairly good business dealings. If a married woman dreams that she is a virgin, she will agonize over her past and lose all hope in the future. If a young girl dreams that she is no longer a virgin, she is warned of losing her good reputation by indiscreet behavior. If a man dreams about a wrongful, intimate relationship with a virgin, he will fail in some endeavor, and will be plagued by people's pleas for help. His hopes will be dashed because of keeping the wrong company.

Vision — Dreaming about seeing a peculiar vision means bad luck in business and ill health. If people appear to the dreamer in visions, there will be insurgence and strife in the country and the family. If the dreamer's friend is in a state of decadence in real life, the friend may appear suddenly in a vision, wearing white. Any kind of visions in dreams portend unusual developments in business and changes in the dreamer's private life — often temporarily for the worse, but ultimately improving.

Visit — If the dreamer visits someone, it is a sign of a pleasant event in the near future. If he does not enjoy the visit, his pleasure will be spoiled by the actions of spiteful people. If a friend visits the dreamer, good news will arrive soon. If the **friend arrives sad and weary**, the visit will not be an unmitigated success. If the **visitor is dressed in white or black, or looks livid**, it is a prediction of a serious disease or accident.

Vitriol (sulfuric acid) — **Seeing vitriol** means that someone is being unjustifiably reprimanded by the dreamer. **Throwing vitriol on people** means that the dreamer will behave ungratefully toward those that want to help him. If a **jealous rival throws vitriol in a young woman's face**, it means that she will be the innocent victim of someone's hatred. For a **businessman**, the dream signifies enemies and persecution.

Voices — **Hearing voices in a dream (without seeing their source)** means that the dreamer will soon experience feelings of distress, sadness or depression. **Dreaming about hearing calm, pleasant voices** means making up quarrels peacefully. If the voices are shrill and angry, unpleasant and disappointing situations will follow. **Weeping voices** predict that the dreamer will hurt a friend in a fit of anger. **Hearing the voice of God** means that the dreamer will endeavor to adopt higher moral standards, and will be admired by worthy people. If a **mother hears her child's voice**, it is a sign of misery and agonizing doubts. **Hearing a voice of distress or warning** means the dreamer's own bad luck or that of someone close. If **the voice is identified**, it could indicate an illness or an accident.

Volcano — **Seeing a volcano** means that the dreamer has an urgent need to control his emotions, especially during arguments, as his credibility and reliability are undermined.

If a **young woman sees a volcano**, it signifies that her egoism and hedonism will lead her into secret and complicated affairs.

Vomiting — Seeing vomiting reflects an uneasy conscience: The dreamer is tormented because his actions were not pure. If the **dreamer vomits**, it is a warning of a debilitating disease, or of involvement in a scandal. **Seeing other people vomiting**, the dreamer will become aware of the fact that the people who want his help are deceiving him. If the **dreamer vomits blood**, he will become ill suddenly, and this will lead to general depression and unhappiness at home.

Voting (at a polling station) — **Voting with a ballot** attests to the dreamer's need for social involvement and the desire to be influential. **Voting fraudulently** means that the dreamer's dishonesty will defeat his better nature.

Vote — If the **dreamer's vote is the deciding vote**, it signifies a lack of confidence, a low self-image, and an impractical nature. If **he casts a vote on any matter**, he will become embroiled in chaos, to the detriment of his surroundings.

Voucher — **Dreaming of vouchers** means that hard, constant work will prevent success being snatched away from the dreamer. **Signing a voucher** means that the dreamer is trusted by those around him, in spite of his enemies' endeavors to the contrary. **Losing a voucher** means that the dreamer will have to fight for his rights with his relatives.

Vow — **Dreaming about a vow** is a sign of an improvement in business and in one's financial situation.

Making or hearing vows means that the dreamer will be accused of dishonesty in business or love. **Taking clerical vows** means that the dreamer will display unwavering honesty throughout some difficult situation. **Breaking or ignoring a vow** means that disaster will strike the dreamer's business.

Voyage — Making a voyage means that the dreamer will receive an inheritance. A **catastrophic voyage** means false love and financial difficulties.

Vulture — Dreaming about a vulture (or any bird of prey) is a sign that a cold and ruthless enemy threatens the dreamer. If the **vulture is injured or dead**, the enemy will succeed. If a **woman dreams about a vulture**, she will be devastated by malicious, vicious slander.

Wading — **Wading in clear water** is a sign of wonderful but transient pleasures. **Wading in murky water** is a warning of illness and sorrow. **Seeing children wading in clear water** is a sign of good luck in business. If a **young woman wades in clear, bubbly water**, her dearest wish will soon come true.

Wafer — **Seeing wafers** is a sign of an imminent confrontation with enemies. **Eating wafers** is a sign of a decrease in revenue. If a **young woman bakes wafers**, it means that she is plagued by the fear of not marrying.

Wager — **Dreaming about making a wager** means that the dreamer will use crooked measures to promote his schemes. If **he loses a wager**, he will be harmed by association with people of a lower social standing. If **he wins a wager**, his fortune will be repaired. **Inability to put up a wager** means frustration and devastation by the blows dealt by fate.

Wages — **Receiving wages in a dream** indicates that without the dreamer's knowledge, someone is causing him harm and undermining him. **It also means** unexpected good luck in new endeavors. **Paying wages** is a sign of deep dissatisfaction. A **reduction in wages** is a warning of hostile actions against the dreamer. An **increase in wages** means unprecedented profits in a deal.

Wagon — **Dreaming about a wagon** means an unhappy marriage, and worries that will cause the dreamer to be old before his time. **Driving a wagon down a hill** is an indication of events that will cause anxiety and loss. **Driving a wagon uphill** indicates an improvement in business.

Driving a heavily loaded wagon means that the dreamer's sense of duty will keep him in check, although he longs to cast it off. **Driving a wagon into muddy water** is a terrible prediction of worry and unhappiness. A **covered wagon** implies subtle treachery which will sabotage the dreamer's progress. If a **young woman drives a wagon perilously close to the edge of an embankment**, she will be forced into an illicit embroilment, and she will be petrified of being discovered. If **she drives a wagon across clear water**, she will have an enjoyable, and not reprehensible, affair. A **run-down wagon** is a symbol of failure and trouble.

Waif — This is a sign of troubles of a personal nature and particular bad luck in business.

Wail — If the **dreamer hears a wail**, it predicts terrible news of catastrophes and misery. If a **young woman hears a wail**, she will be abandoned in her hour of need, and possibly in her shame.

Waist — Dreaming about a round, shapely **waist** means that the dreamer will come into a nice amount of money. A **small, distorted waist** means failure and accusatory quarrels.

Waiter / Waitress — Dreaming about a waiter means that the dreamer will be entertained agreeably by a friend. **Seeing a waiter** shows that the dreamer has an ambitious personality, and is striving to improve his financial situation. If a **waiter behaves inappropriately**, the dreamer will have unpleasant people taking advantage of his hospitality.

Wake — If the **dreamer attends a wake**, it means that he will forego an important appointment in order to go to an unsavory meeting. If a **young woman sees her lover at a wake**, it means that she will give in to some man's impassioned pleas, thus losing her honor.

Waking — If the dreamer dreams that he is being awakened from sleep, a close and beloved person is about to appear and bring him much joy.

Walking — **Walking along a long, unbroken path** indicates that the dreamer must cope with problems in his life. A **brisk, steady walk** means that he will overcome all the obstacles along his way. **Walking in nice places** is a sign of good fortune. **Walking along rough, thorny paths** symbolizes business embroilments and misunderstandings that will lead to the rejection of the dreamer. **Walking at night** means bad luck and the vain battle for happiness. A **young woman walking quickly** will inherit property, and will attain the object of her dreams.

Walking Stick — **Seeing a walking stick** means that the dreamer will strike deals without giving them their due consideration, and this will cause him hassles. If **he uses a walking stick** while walking, it means that he will depend on other people's counsel. If the **dreamer admires beautiful walking sticks**, he will entrust his business concerns to others, and they will be loyal.

Wall — If the **wall is solid and erect**, the dream represents a warning against danger. If the **wall is crumbling and falling**, it actually symbolizes protection, and the dreamer will not be harmed. **Finding a wall in one's path** means that the dreamer will be influenced negatively, and will jeopardize success in business. **Jumping over a wall**

means overcoming obstacles and having wishes come true. **Breaching a wall** means success by sheer will power and determination. **Demolishing a wall** means destroying enemies. **Building a wall** means carefully constructed and considered plans for consolidating the dreamer's assets, without a possibility of failure. **Jumping off a wall** means reckless wheeling and dealing, and disappointed love.

Wallet — If the **dreamer finds a wallet**, it indicates prosperity and financial success. The **loss of a wallet** predicts disappointment and frustration. **Seeing wallets** is a prediction of duties of an agreeable nature awaiting the dreamer. An **old, dirty wallet** means hard work culminating in poor results.

Walnut — **Dreaming about ripe walnuts** is an excellent sign. **Seeing walnuts** is a sign of marriage to a rich partner. **Eating walnuts** in a dream indicates that the dreamer is wasteful and extravagant. **Cracking a rotten walnut** means that the dreamer's hopes will be brutally dashed. If a **young woman's hands are stained with walnut juice**, her lover will leave her for someone else, and she will feel remorse for her past indiscretions.

Waltz — **Watching people waltzing** means a fun-filled friendship with a lively person. If a **young woman waltzes with her lover**, she will be greatly admired, but no one will want to marry her. If **she sees her lover waltzing with a rival**, she will use her wits to overcome obstacles. If **she waltzes with another woman**, she will be admired for her goodness and charm. If **she sees a wild whirling of waltzing people**, she will be so overcome with desire that she will not be able to resist any man who may want her.

Want — Dreaming about being in want means that the dreamer has behaved foolishly, ignoring the harsh realities of life, and is now afflicted with grief and trouble. If the **dreamer is satisfied with being in a state of want**, he will be stoic in the face of adversity, and his troubles will gradually disappear. **Relieving want** means that the dreamer will be admired for his generosity, but will derive no pleasure from doing good deeds.

War — Dreaming about war means business failures, and domestic chaos and disharmony. If the **dreamer declares war**, it signifies success in the areas of business and economics. If the **dreamer is a witness to war**, it means that he must avoid actions that might endanger him, and only act following careful consideration. If a **young woman's lover goes to war**, she will hear something bad about him. If the **dreamer's country is conquered in war**, there will be financial and political revolution which will affect his business. If **there is a victory in war**, business will improve, and domestic life will be harmonious.

Wardrobe — Dreaming about one's wardrobe means that the dreamer will risk his fortune in order to appear better off than he actually is. If the **dreamer has a limited wardrobe**, he will take risks.

Warehouse — Dreaming about a warehouse symbolizes prosperous business. An **empty warehouse** means that the dreamer will be cheated and thwarted in a well-thought-out plan.

Warrant — If a **warrant is served on the dreamer**, it means that he will be involved in an endeavor of such significance that he worries about it. If a **warrant is served on someone else**, the dreamer runs the risk of his actions causing serious disputes or misunderstandings.

Warts — If the **dreamer suffers from warts on his body**, he will not be able to prevent attacks on his good name. If the **warts disappear**, he will overcome the obstacles on the way to fortune. **Seeing warts on other people** signifies the presence of sworn enemies nearby. If the **dreamer treats the warts,** he will fight vigorously to avert danger to himself and his family.

Washboard — **Seeing a washboard in a dream** is a sign of embarrassment. **Seeing a woman using a washboard** means that women will drain the dreamer's fortune and energy. A **broken washboard** signifies the dreamer's downfall as a result of impure and decadent living.

Washbowl — **Dreaming about a washbowl** is an indication of new careers that will interest the dreamer. If the **dreamer washes his hands and face in a washbowl,** he will have a passionate and binding relationship with someone for whom he had not always felt passion. If the **washbowl is dirty or broken**, he will feel remorse for an illicit affair which gave him little pleasure, and hurt others badly.

Washerwoman — **Seeing a washerwoman in a dream** symbolizes infidelity and a peculiar occurrence. A **washerwoman** is a sign of flourishing business for the businessman, and of abundant crops for the farmer. If a woman dreams that she is a washerwoman, she will throw discretion to the winds in her attempts to hold onto an illicit relationship.

Washing — If the dreamer is washing himself, it means that he is proud of the large number of affairs he is having.

Wasp — If the dreamer sees a wasp, it means that bad news is on the way, in the form of spiteful and harmful enemies. If a wasp stings the dreamer, it symbolizes envy and hatred. Killing wasps means overcoming enemies and standing up for the dreamer's rights.

Waste — Dreaming about wandering through wasteland is a sign of failure and uncertainty instead of sure success. If the dreamer wastes his fortune, it means that he will be burdened with domestic responsibilities against his will.

Watch — Dreaming about a watch means that the dreamer will be successful as a result of well-planned business strategies. Looking at a watch to see the time means that rivals will overcome the dreamer. Breaking a watch predicts a threat of loss and trouble. If the glass falls out, it is a sign of carelessness or disagreeable associates. If a woman loses a watch, there will be domestic disharmony. Stealing a watch indicates a dangerous enemy who will slander the dreamer. Giving a watch as a gift means that the dreamer will neglect his most important interest in order to pursue trivial and worthless pastimes.

Water — Dreaming about clear water is a sign of prosperity and enjoyment. Muddy water is a prediction of danger and misery. Falling into muddy water predicts many bad mistakes with bitter consequences. **Drinking clear water** is a sign of success, happiness and abundance. **Drinking impure or muddy water** warns against health problems. **Dreaming about playing**  **in water** signifies that the dreamer receives a lot of love from those around him; he will also feel passion. If **water is sprayed on him**, his passion will be reciprocated. If **water rises in the dreamer's house,** he will have a battle against evil. Only if it subsides will he resist it. **Bailing water out,** feet wet, means distress, disease and misery which can be averted by the dreamer's alertness. This is the same if **muddy water rises in ships and boats. Stormy waters** indicate problems on the path to economic independence.

Water Carrier — Seeing water carriers in dreams means good luck in love and business. If the **dreamer is a water carrier,** he will go up the ladder of advancement.

Waterfall — Seeing a waterfall means that the dreamer's wildest dream will come true, and he will have a lot of luck. **Swimming under a waterfall** means that the great efforts that the dreamer has made will not bear fruit. If **another individual is swimming under the waterfall**, it means that the person is in danger.

Water Lily — Dreaming about a water lily, or seeing them growing, means that the dreamer will experience a combination of prosperity and grief.

Watermelon — This symbolizes superstition, and reflects hidden fears and concealed anxiety.

Waves — If the **waves are clear**, it means that the dreamer understands exactly what he has to do in a complicated matter. If the **waves are muddy or stormy**, he will make a fatal error.

Wax — This warns against wastefulness and extravagance.

Wax Taper — **Lighting wax tapers** means meeting long-lost friends at a pleasant event. **Blowing wax tapers out** is a sign of disappointment, and lost opportunities of meeting esteemed friends because of illness.

Way — If the dreamer loses his way, he can forget about successful deals unless he manages his business with the utmost care.

Wealth — If the **dreamer is very wealthy**, it means that he has the determination and drive to meet and solve life's problems. If **others are wealthy**, the dreamer's friends will bail him out of dangerous situations. If a **young woman dreams that she belongs to a circle of wealthy people**, she has lofty ambitions and will find someone who can help her realize them.

Weasel — If the **dreamer sees a weasel out hunting**, he should beware of making friends with erstwhile enemies, as they are waiting for an opportunity to destroy him. **Killing weasels** is a sign of defeating enemies.

Weather — **Dreaming about the weather** symbolizes changes in fortune — advancement is suddenly replaced by setbacks. **Hearing or reading the weather report** means moving house after a lot of deliberation, but it will be to the dreamer's advantage.

Weaving — **Dreaming about weaving** means that the dreamer will strenuously resist any attempt to keep him from accumulating wealth. **Seeing others weaving**

means that the dreamer's surroundings will be healthy and comfortable.

Web — **Dreaming about a web** warns that dishonest friends will try to cause the dreamer harm. If the **web is inflexible**, the dreamer will withstand the attacks of jealous people who want to exploit him.

Wedding — **Dreaming about a wedding** usually expresses the dreamer's wish. When a **bachelor dreams about his own wedding**, it means that unpleasant news is on its way. If a **bachelor dreams of another person's wedding**, it means that a period of happiness awaits him. If a **married person dreams about a stranger's wedding**, it means that he is jealous of his spouse. **Attending a wedding** predicts an event that will cause the dreamer bitterness and a postponement of success. If a **young woman dreams that her wedding is a secret**, it foretells her fall from favor. If **her match is approved of**, she will gain the respect of those around her, and her expectations will be realized. If **her parents disapprove**, her impending marriage will cause dissent among her family. If **she dreams that her lover marries someone else**, it means that she is worrying needlessly about her lover's fidelity. If **she dreams that a person dressed in mourning** attends her wedding, she will have an unhappy marriage. If **this mourner attends someone else's wedding**, she will be upset about a relative's misfortunes, and she may be threatened with ill health and unpleasant things.

Wedding Clothes — **Seeing wedding clothes** is a sign that the dreamer will participate in nice new things and make new friends. **Dirty or**

crumpled clothes mean that the dreamer will become estranged from a person whom he holds in high esteem.

Wedding Ring — If a **woman's wedding ring is bright and shiny**, it means that she will be protected from worries and infidelity. If **her ring breaks or gets lost**, she will have grief because of bereavement and incompatibility. **Seeing a wedding ring on someone else's finger** means that the dreamer will not respect his vows and will pursue immoral enjoyments.

Wedge — Dreaming about a wedge means that there will be a business dispute which will cause a break-off of relations with relatives — or even between lovers.

Wedlock — If the **dreamer is caught in an unhappy wedlock**, it means that he will become embroiled in an unfortunate matter. If a **young woman dreams that she is dissatisfied with wedlock**, it predicts that she will become involved in scandalous affairs. If a **married woman dreams about her wedding day**, it is a warning that she should muster her strength against grief, disillusionment, quarrels and jealousies. If a **woman dreams that she is happily and safely** married, this is a sign of good luck.

Weeding — **Dreaming about weeding** means that the dreamer will have trouble with a project which is supposed to bring him honor. **Seeing others weeding** means that the dreamer is afraid that enemies will spoil his plans.

Weeping — If the **dreamer is weeping**, it is a sign of bad news in the family. **Seeing others weeping** means a happy reunion after a period of separation. For a **young woman**, dreaming about weeping refers to lovers' quarrels which can only be resolved if she is prepared to make compromises.

Weevil — This is a sign of bad business and deception in love.

Weighing — **Dreaming about weighing** indicates an imminent period of prosperity — with dedication, the dreamer will accumulate a tidy sum. **Weighing others** means that the dreamer will manipulate other people to do as he wants. If a **young woman weighs her lover**, he will do whatever she wants at any time.

Welcome — **Dreaming about receiving a warm welcome into any society** means that the dreamer will acquire distinction and strangers will defer to him. His fortune will increase to the desired dimensions. If **others are welcomed**, it means that the dreamer's warm and cheerful character will be the key to his success and pleasure in life.

Well — **Falling into a well** is a sign of overwhelming despair. If a **well caves in**, the dreamer's enemies will get the better of him. **Drawing water from a well** signifies the fulfillment of urgent desires. If the **water is not pure**, bad things will follow. **Seeing an empty** well means that the dreamer will be mugged if he takes strangers into his confidence. **Seeing a well with a pump in it** predicts the advancement of the dreamer's prospects. **Dreaming about an artesian well** means that the dreamer's intelligence will allow him into the realms of knowledge and enjoyment. **Working in a well** means that the dreamer will have troubles because he is not focused on the correct things.

Welsh Rabbit — Dreaming about preparing or eating

Welsh Rabbit means that the dreamer's affairs will become complicated as a result of his being distracted by cunning women and superficial amusements.

Wet — Dreaming about being wet means that a certain pleasure might bring the dreamer loss and disease. He should beware of the temptations offered by apparently well-meaning people. If a **young woman dreams that she is soaking wet,** she will experience disgrace as a result of having an affair with a married man.

Wet Nurse — Dreaming about being a wet nurse means that the dreamer will either be widowed, or will have to take care of elderly people or small children. If a **woman dreams about being a wet nurse,** it means that she will have to support herself.

Whale — Seeing a whale is a sign that the dreamer is deprived of maternal love. If the **whale is approaching a ship,** the dreamer will have a conflict of interests with a threat of lost assets. If the **whale is killed,** the dreamer will be able to decide between what he wants and what he should do, and will be successful. If a **whale upends a ship,** it is a sign of catastrophes for the dreamer.

Whalebone — Seeing or working with whalebone is a prediction of a solid and beneficial alliance.

Wheat — Seeing large fields of growing wheat means that the dreamer's interests are taking on new, positive dimensions. If the **wheat is ripe,** it symbolizes abundance, success, material wealth and love. **Large grains of wheat running through the threshing machine** are a sign of prosperity. **Seeing wheat in barrels or sacks** means that the dreamers aspirations in business and love will be realized. If the **wheat gets wet because it was not well covered**, it means that the wealth accumulated by the dreamer was not properly secured, and it is going to decrease. **Rubbing wheat into one's hand and eating it** symbolizes working hard to succeed and ensure one's rights.

Wheels — **Seeing wheels revolving quickly** means that the dreamer will work hard and economically, and will enjoy a happy domestic life. **Stationary or broken wheels** are a sign of an absence or a death in the dreamer's household.

Whetstone — Dreaming about a whetstone tells the dreamer of pressing anxieties, and warns him to keep a close eye on his business affairs if he wants to stay out of trouble. He may have to undertake an unpleasant journey.

Whip — If the **dreamer whips an attacker**, it means that he will earn respect and wealth by diligence and courage. **Dreaming about a whip** symbolizes unfortunate disputes and unreliable friendships.

Whirlpool — Dreaming about a whirlpool is a sign of imminent great danger to the dreamer's business. He must take great care not to have his reputation ruined in some shameful affair.

Whirlwind — If the **dreamer is in the path of a whirlwind**, it means that he is facing a change which may be disastrous to him. If a **young woman is caught in a whirlwind and cannot control her skirts from flying up**, she will get involved in a clandestine affair which will become common knowledge and cause her to be ostracized.

Whisky — **Dreaming about whisky** is generally a sign of disappointment. If the **dream concerns whisky in bottles**, it means that the dreamer will protect his interests carefully, and as a result, they will increase. **Drinking whisky alone** means that the dreamer's egoism will drive his friends away. **Destroying whisky** is a sign of losing friends because of mean behavior. **Seeing or drinking whisky** means attempting to attain an objective after many setbacks. **Only seeing whisky** means that the objective will never be attained.

Whispering — **Dreaming about whispering** is a sign that the dreamer will be subjected to the vicious gossip of people nearby. If **he hears a whisper that is intended to warn him or give him advice**, it means that he needs to seek counsel.

Whistle — **Dreaming about whistling** means that ill-intentioned people are spreading malicious gossip about him. **Hearing a whistle in a dream** means that the dreamer will be appalled by some bad news, which will destroy his plans for something pleasant. If **he is whistling**, it is a prediction of a happy event in which he will be a central figure. For a young woman, **dreaming about whistling** predicts wild behavior and the failure to attain objectives.

White — See individual entries.

White Lead — Dreaming about white lead warns the dreamer that members of his family are in jeopardy because of his carelessness. Prosperity is also shaky at the moment.

Whitewash — If the **dreamer is whitewashing**, it signifies that he wants to regain his friends' approval by eschewing disgusting habits and objectionable companions. If a **young**

woman is whitewashing, it is a sign that she has designed a sophisticated strategy of deception to win back her lover.

Widow — If a **dreamer dreams about being widowed from his spouse**, this ensures a long life for his partner. **Dreaming about being a widow** predicts that vicious people will cause the dreamer many hassles. An **unmarried person who dreams about being widowed** may expect marriage in the future. If a **man dreams of marrying a widow**, it means that a project which is dear to his heart will collapse and fizzle out.

Wife — If the **dreamer dreams about his wife**, it is a sign of domestic strife. If **his wife is uncharacteristically amiable**, he will have good profits from trade. If a **wife dreams that her husband whips her**, it means that she will be harshly criticized for having been persuaded to do certain things, and chaos will follow.

Wig — **Dreaming about a wig** is a sign of a lack of confidence in one's love life, and a struggle in making choices in romance. **Wearing a wig** means that the dreamer will make an unlucky change. **Losing a wig** signifies that the dreamer's enemies will deride and despise him. **Seeing others wearing wigs** means that the dreamer is becoming embroiled in treachery.

Wild — **Dreaming about running about wildly** predicts a fall or accident for the dreamer. If **others are acting wild**, setbacks will make the dreamer anxious and agitated.

Wild Man — **Seeing a wild man** means that the dreamer's enemies will brazenly try to sabotage his endeavors. If the **dreamer is a wild man**, his plans will not go well.

Wildness / Raging — If the dreamer participates in a wild, unruly event causing him to panic, it predicts financial difficulties in the near future.

Will — **Writing a will in a dream** is actually a sign of a long and happy life. **Dreaming of making one's will** predicts problems. If a **wife or anyone else thinks that a will is disadvantageous to them**, it means that soon there will be dissent and turmoil in some event. **Failing to prove a will** means that the dreamer will run the risk of being slandered. **Losing a will** is a bad sign for business. **Destroying a will** warns the dreamer that he is about to be an accomplice in an act of treachery and fraud.

Willow — **Seeing a willow** has a painful significance: Mistakes made in the family context cannot be rectified. **Dreaming of willows** predicts a sad journey with consolation from good friends.

Wind — A **strong wind**, one that causes the dreamer anxiety, is a sign that he will find it difficult to cope with everyday life. If the **strong wind does not frighten him**, it shows that he will be able to cope with problems easily and successfully. **Dreaming about the wind blowing gently and sadly** means that the dreamer will become wealthy from bereavement. A **sighing wind** warns the dreamer of becoming estranged from someone who needs him. **Walking against a brisk wind** means that the dreamer will go after his goals with determination, resisting temptation on the way. If the **wind blows the dreamer in the wrong direction**, it is a sign of failure in business and love. If the **wind blows the dreamer in the**

right direction, the dreamer will suddenly find allies, and he will easily beat a rival.

Windmill — Seeing a windmill working means that the dreamer will be happy and wealthy. If a **windmill is stationary or non-operational**, troubles will take him by surprise.

Window — If the **dreamer is gazing out of a window**, it means that he will be reconciled with someone with whom he has quarreled. If **another person is looking at the dreamer through a window**, it warns of malicious gossip. **Seeing windows** means that the dreamer's hopes will be dashed, and his endeavors will fail. **Closed windows** mean abandonment. **Broken windows** mean that the dreamer will be plagued with suspicion of his loved ones' infidelity. **Sitting in a window** signifies that the dreamer will fall victim to another person's stupidity. If the **dreamer enters a house through the window**, it is a sign that he will be caught using dishonest means to achieve an honorable end. **Escaping through a window** indicates that the dreamer will become embroiled in a problem that will not release him easily. **Looking through a window and seeing peculiar objects** predicts failure in the dreamer's chosen profession, followed by the loss of the hard-earned respect of his colleagues.

Wine — The interpretation of wine in a dream depends on the particular culture: **some interpret wine** as a sign of abundance, while others see it as a symbol of drunkenness and failure. Usually **dreaming about wine** means that the dreamer can expect family celebrations. **Drinking wine** portends happiness and friendships. **Breaking bottles of wine** means that the dreamer's love and passion will almost be excessive. **Barrels of wine** are a symbol of luxury. **Pouring wine from one container to another** predicts a variety of pleasures and travels for the dreamer. If the **dreamer deals in wine**, his profession will be lucrative. If a **young woman dreams of drinking wine**, she will marry a rich and respectable man.

Wine Cellar — Dreaming about a wine cellar predicts wonderful times ahead for the dreamer.

Wineglass — Dreaming about a wineglass signifies that the dreamer will be deeply affected by a disappointment.

Wings — **Dreaming about having wings** indicates the dreamer's fear for the safety of someone who is traveling far away. **Seeing the wings of birds or fowl** signifies that the dreamer will eventually overcome all his problems and will achieve wealth and status.

Winter — **Wintry weather** indicates success in the near future. A **dream about winter** is sometimes interpreted as a sign of family problems, particularly parent-child relationships. It also indicates ill health and slow business.

Wire — **Dreaming about wire** means that the dreamer will make many short trips which will be to his disadvantage. **Old or rusty wire** means that the dreamer is bad-tempered, causing unpleasantness to those around him. If **he sees a wire fence**, it means that he will be defrauded in a deal.

Wisdom — If the **dreamer possesses wisdom in a dream**, it means that he will be courageous in difficult circumstances, overcoming them and elevating himself to a higher plane of living. If **he lacks wisdom**, it indicates that he is not exploiting his talents at all.

Witch — Generally speaking, a **dream about a witch** means that bad news can be anticipated. **Dreaming about witches** means that the dreamer and his cronies will embark upon lively and noisy adventures, which will eventually go humiliatingly wrong. If **witches approach the dreamer**, he will suffer setbacks in business and strife at home.

Witness — **Dreaming about bearing witness against other people** means that trivial incidents will cause the dreamer great distress. If **others bear witness against the dreamer**, he will have no choice but to refuse to help friends in order to preserve his own interests. If **he is a witness for someone who is guilty,** it is a sign that he will be implicated in some disgraceful matter.

Wizard — **Dreaming about a wizard** means that the dreamer will have a large family that will cause him displeasure and inconvenience. For **young people**, this dream is a prediction of loss and breakups.

Wolf — The **appearance of a wolf in any form in a dream** signifies bad news. The news will be even more awful if the **dream is about a pack of wolves. Dreaming about a wolf** indicates that one of the dreamer's employees is a thief and a traitor. **Killing a wolf** means that the dreamer will outwit enemies who wish to discredit him. **Hearing a wolf's howl** reveals to the dreamer the fact that there is a conspiracy to beat him in straightforward competition.

Woman — **Dreaming about a woman** represents a warning to think carefully before making an important or fateful decision. **Dreaming about women** is a prediction of intrigue. If the **dreamer argues with one,** he will be thwarted and defeated. A **dark-haired, blue-eyed woman** means that he will withdraw from some competitive situation which he had a good chance of winning. **Seeing a brown-eyed woman** means that he will be seduced into a risky deal. **Seeing an auburn-haired woman with brown eyes** means that he will have exacerbated confusion and worry. **Seeing a blonde woman** means pleasant events and enjoyments.

Wooden Shoe — Dreaming about a wooden shoe indicates solitary wandering and poverty. In **love,** it is a sign of infidelity.

Woodpile — Dreaming about a woodpile predicts problems in business and love.

Woods — Dreaming about woods is a sign of changes in the dreamer's affairs: If the **woods are green,** the change will be positive. If the **woods are dry and brown,** the change will be disastrous. If the **woods are on fire,** the dreamer's plans will reach fruition, and bring lucrative results. **Dealing in firewood** means that the dreamer's determined hard work will lead to wealth.

Wool — Dreaming about wool is a prediction of business expansion and prosperity. If the **wool is dirty or stained,** the dreamer will look for a job with people who abhor his beliefs.

Work — Dreaming about working hard means that the dreamer will be successful by concentrating his will and his energy on the desired goal. **Seeing others at work** means that there is an atmosphere of optimism surrounding the dreamer. **Looking for work** means that the dreamer will profit from some inexplicable event.

Workshop — Dreaming about a workshop indicates that the dreamer will be able to achieve all to which he aspires. Any task that he undertakes will be a success. **Seeing a workshop** means that the dreamer will resort to unbelievable stratagems to defeat his enemies.

Worm — Dreaming about worms means approximately the same as a dream about a snake, but to a lesser degree. (See **Snake**.) A **dream about worms** means that the dreamer will be bothered by the base schemes of unsavory people. If **worms crawl on a young woman**, it means that her aspirations are material. If **she kills the worms or discards them,** she will rise out of the basely material and reach a more spiritual and moral plane. **Using worms as bait** means that the dreamer will cleverly manipulate his enemies to his own advantage.

Wound — Dreaming about being wounded is a sign of distress and problems in business. If **others are wounded,** the dreamer will be judged unfairly by his friends. **Dressing a wound** means that soon the dreamer will be lucky.

Wreath — Dreaming about a wreath of fresh flowers means that soon the dreamer will have the chance to make a lot of money. A **dry wreath** is a sign of sickness and love problems. A **bridal wreath** means that uncertain things will sort themselves out positively.

Wreck — Seeing a wreck in a dream means that the dreamer will be plagued with worries about poverty and failure in business. **Dreaming about a railway wreck** in which the dreamer is not involved means that someone close to the dreamer will be in an accident, or he will have business problems.

Writing — **Dreaming about writing** means that the dreamer will make a mistake that will almost destroy him. **Seeing writing** means that he will be reprimanded for carelessness, and might be subjected to a lawsuit. **Attempting to read strange writing** means that the dreamer will avoid his enemies only if he makes no new deals after this dream. If the **dreamer is writing a letter**, it means that a letter will arrive. If **others are writing a letter**, it means that the dreamer will quarrel with a person who is close to him.

X-ray — **Dreaming about an X-ray** signifies fear of poor health or serious financial problems. **Dreaming about being X-rayed** means that some authority will try to reveal something that would be damaging to the dreamer and his family. The dreamer must find out what it is in order to protect himself.

Xylophone — **Dreaming about playing a xylophone** predicts a delightfully happy occasion. A **broken xylophone** means that the dreamer ignored advice and opportunities during times of trouble, and is advised not to do so again.

Yacht — **Seeing a yacht** signifies a holiday from work and worries. If a **yacht is grounded**, it means that various plans for fun will not materialize.

Yankee — Dreaming about a Yankee predicts that the dreamer will remain loyal and dutiful; if he is not careful, however, he will be cheated in some deal.

Yardstick — Dreaming about a yardstick indicates that although the dreamer's business will be unusually brisk, he will be overcome with worry.

Yarn — A **dream about yarn** predicts success in business and a diligent partner at home. If a **young woman dreams about working with yarn**, it means that she will find an excellent husband who will be proud of her.

Yawning — If the **dreamer yawns in his dreams**, he will not find happiness and health. **Seeing others yawning** means that the dreamer's friends will be wretched and ill, unable to work.

Yearning — **Dreaming about yearning for someone** means that the dreamer will soon receive good news from faraway friends. If a **young woman dreams that her lover is yearning for her**, she will soon receive a longed-for proposal. If **she tells her lover that she is yearning for him**, she will be abandoned.

Yeast — This indicates a good life, abundance and a satisfying economic situation.

Yellow Bird — If a **yellow bird darts around**, it means that the dreamer will be petrified of the future as a result of some momentous event. If the **yellow bird is sick or dead**, it means that the dreamer will suffer for another person's stupidity.

Yew Tree — **Dreaming about a yew tree** is a sign of disease and disillusionment. If a **yew tree is dead and bare**, it is a prediction of a tragic death in the dreamer's family, for which no material possessions can make up. If a **young woman sits under a yew tree**, she will be tormented with doubts about her lover's fidelity. If **her lover is standing near a yew tree**, she will hear that he is ill or unlucky. If **she admires a yew tree**, she will be ostracized by her family because of choosing the wrong man.

Yield — If the **dreamer yields to the will of someone else**, it is a sign that he will waste a wonderful opportunity of advancement because of weak vacillation. If **others yield to the dreamer**, he will be granted unique privileges and will be promoted above all his colleagues. If the **dreamer's hard work yields poorly**, worries and anxiety are in the offing.

Yoke — **Seeing a yoke** means that the dreamer will conform to the desires and customs of others against his will. **Yoking oxen** means that the dreamer's subordinates will accept and obey whatever he suggests or says. **Failing to yoke oxen** means that the dreamer will worry about a badly behaved friend.

Young — **Seeing young people** means patching up family quarrels and making plans for new business endeavors. **Dreaming about being young again** means that the dreamer will try in vain to retrieve lost opportunities. **Seeing young people at school** means that the dreamer will be prosperous.

Yule Log — Dreaming about a yule log means that the dreamer will attend happy and festive events that he looked forward to.

Zebra — **Dreaming about a zebra** means that the dreamer will take an interest in transient ideas. **Seeing a zebra** signifies that the dreamer will suffer from a severe illness or fatal accident in the future.

Zenith — Dreaming of a zenith means prosperity and the successful choice of a mate.

Zephyrs — **Dreaming about zephyrs** means that the dreamer will sacrifice wealth for love, and his love will be reciprocated. If a **young woman hears the gentle zephyr and feels sad**, she will miss her lover, who had to travel far from her.

Zinc — **Working with zinc or seeing it** means good progress and brisk business. **Dreaming about zinc ore** means forthcoming success.

Zodiac — **Dreaming about the zodiac** is a symbol of peace, prosperity and economic and social success, following a great deal of effort and hard work. A **peculiar zodiac** means that the dreamer will have to fight off some impending sorrow. **Studying the zodiac** means that the dreamer will become well-known because of his connection with strangers.

Zoological Gardens — **Visiting a zoo** is a sign of a good and successful future mixed with the odd conflict with enemies. **Seeing a zoo** also means that the dreamer will travel and live in foreign countries.

Without a doubt, dreams are among the most mysterious, mystical and incomprehensible phenomena experienced by a person during his lifetime. The existence of dreams is actually one of the few phenomena of its type that we find documented in every historical period and in every culture.

Dreams have inspired a veritable flood of articles, interpretations and references in every culture and in every tongue. While there is a surprising amount of common ground in attitudes toward dreams, major differences between various cultures and eras do exist. Even more unexpected is the discovery that, despite the fact that the dream is one of the most researched and investigated phenomena in the fields of psychology and mysticism, we actually know very little about dreams, their interpretation, and the reasons behind them. When it comes right down to it, we know more about the atmosphere on Mars – to give one example – than we do about dreams. What's more, this extraordinarily strange phenomenon occurs in tandem with another unexplained phenomenon that is also experienced by man on a daily basis – namely, sleep!

Sigmund Freud, who was known as the "Great Dreamer," published his exhaustive work on dream interpretation in 1899. Since then, in every subsequent edition of his book, there have been essential changes in its content. Freud himself claimed that each time he examined another drop from the great ocean of dreams, he encountered new principles to add to his theory.

In ancient Babylon – perhaps the earliest culture to

produce "codexes," or detailed guidebooks in various spheres of life – there were books dealing with dream interpretation. At the beginning of every such book was the warning: "Do not alter the contents of this book."

In China, books dealing with dream interpretation spread far and wide during the era of the Great Empire. Since each book differed in its interpretations, the Yellow Emperor commanded that an "official" book of dream interpretation be prepared.

Approximately one third of each day is taken up by sleep, so that cumulatively we spend about one third of our entire lifetime sleeping. (Exceptions to this "rule" include Sleeping Beauty, Rip Van Winkle and the Talmudic figure "Honi Hame'agel"; their sleep, of course, was not interrupted by dreams!) In order to grasp just how much time we devote to sleeping, consider that a woman who retires at the age of 60 has spent more years in sleep than the entire lifetime of her son who has just completed his college degree!

Approximately one quarter of our sleep time – some two hours out of each sleep sequence – is given over to dreaming. In other words, this same woman, by the time she reaches retirement age, has devoted at least five years of her life to dreaming – enough time to obtain a master's degree, or even a doctorate, from any university!

A dream is the greatest show of a person's life – the ultimate theater, which every one of us experiences. Where else can a person simultaneously be both spectator and participant in a play where the scenery changes from moment to moment, and real characters mix with heroes from the past, imaginary figures...and the dreamer himself, in his thousands of different roles? A play in which time has no meaning, and a moment can encompass a hundred years of history; a play which – though its impact on the dreamer may at times be too great to bear – is erased from his memory only moments after he has "emerged" from it.

We sometimes think that a dream is unreal, or "dreamlike," meaning that only the imagination is put to work while the dreamer's physical self plays no role at all. But this is not so.

We know very little about dreams, but we do know that there are physical phenomena that accompany them – erection or ejaculation, movement of the eyelids, perspiration, swallowing of saliva, reflex action of the intestines, tightening of the skin, hair that stands on end, and numerous other phenomena related to brain waves, and electrical and electromagnetic impulses in the body.

A dream contains a number of stages that are known to us and can be defined; however, the movement from one stage to another during sleep – like sleep and dreams as a whole – is not entirely clear to us in terms of the rate, the purpose and the nature of these transitions.

Sleep begins with a "clouding over" of the senses during which the brain, or thought process, relinquishes its grip on reality and sinks into a black whirlpool of "sensory deprivation"; it ends with the emergence from this state of darkness. Upon awakening, the individual is hardly aware of the fact that, during his eight hours of sleep, he passed through seven or eight dream cycles which have been almost totally wiped from his memory!

When a person sinks into sleep, he passes through a "hallucinatory" state (actually a hypnotic illusion). During this stage, which is like a "preamble" to the dream, he sees pictures before his eyes (like those that we see when we close our eyes tightly). These pictures, which he continues to see through the "eyes of the spirit," are attributed to stimuli that have been absorbed by, or transmitted to, the optic nerve ends; during the stage of hypnotic illusion, they pass into the brain, as if to "cleanse" the optic nerves.

During the hypnotic illusion, the brain, or thought process, sometimes tries to regain "control"; at such times, the body feels a tremor or an intense shaking, and the person generally moves or groans.

As with sleep and dreams, so too the hypnotic illusion at the onset of sleep, and the tremor that passes through the body before sleep takes over, lack a widely accepted explanation. If we become familiar with sleep and with dreams, which are our major interest here, perhaps we will also come to comprehend the phenomenon of the hypnotic illusion, which we have all encountered in our sleep.

Dream researchers now ask many and varied questions, which they address with the help of assorted research tools. What is a dream? Why do we dream? Which section of the brain engages in dreaming? To what extent do internal or external stimuli affect a dream? How many times do we dream in the course of ordinary sleep? Do we all dream? Do blind people dream? Is there a difference in the sensation of dreaming between men and women, young and old? Do newborns dream? Does the fetus dream inside his mother's womb? Do animals dream? And, most importantly, what is the meaning and significance of dreams to a person's physical and spiritual existence? Numerous other questions are involved in the study and interpretation of dreams, but we will limit ourselves to the principal ones.

A large part of the research tools in this field are those related to "physical" research. We examine phenomena that can be measured, quantified and represented graphically, such as perspiration, brain waves, and pulse rate during sleep, along with positions and changes in position.

We know that the brain is active – electrically and electromagnetically – during sleeping and dreaming, but not in the same way as it is during a state of wakefulness. From EEG devices, we have learned that rapid-frequency waves known as "alpha" waves are characteristic of the waking, conscious state, whereas the slower-frequency "delta" waves are typical of the sleeping brain.

Continuous monitoring during sleep shows that the waves being measured move gradually from alpha waves to delta waves - for reasons that are not exactly clear to us – and that this fluctuation is influenced by the physical and emotional health of the individual at the time in question.

It was only forty years ago that sleep researchers began to pay attention to eyeball movement (in infants, initially) during various stages of sleep. Observation, which today appears to us to be such an obvious tool, revealed that infants, people in general, and animals pass through several such series of eye movements during sleep. When these movements were monitored, it became clear that they resemble the movement of the eyes when a person is "tracking" events taking place in front of him – or is merely observing the theater of life! The discovery of these eye movements, known today as REMs (for "rapid eye movements"), represented a real breakthrough in the study of dreams. Dreams passed out of the realm of stories, historical testimonies, and psychological and psychiatric reports, and into sophisticated sleep labs which investigated the physical changes that a person experiences during the states of sleeping and dreaming.

Several very important conclusions have been drawn as a result of systematic research into REM:

* We all dream, even people who swear that they never do.

* Dreams take place in several distinct segments during sleep. No one dreams from the moment he falls asleep until he returns to a state of wakefulness (even if he says so!).

* What follows from this is that during sleep, there are periods of "dream sleep" and periods of dreamless sleep.

* During the dream, we can distinguish REMs.

* Some 5 to 8 dreams take place during a given night, with intervals of about one hour between them.

With REMs allowing us to determine when a dream is taking place, we can also discern physiological changes that accompany the dream state: breathing becomes more rapid, and loses the deep, uniform rhythm of dreamless sleep; blood pressure rises; the body as a whole does not move during the dream itself; snoring ceases; the limbs and face move. Infants tend to make sucking noises while dreaming; children generally smile; men experience an erection; and women rub their thighs together.

In addition, researchers have found that, when a person

wakes up soon after an REM state, he is able to clearly recall his dream, since it is still fresh in his memory.

Following a sleep segment characterized by REMs, there is a segment where eye movement does not take place (known as NREM sleep, for "non-rapid eye movement"). This segment lasts about half an hour, during which time the person moves, changes position and, in effect, tries to get his bearings. REM sleep is a light sleep, whercas NREM sleep is heavy. Between these two states, there is always a brief transition period, lasting several minutes. REM sleep changes with age. Children spend about half of their sleep time in this state, while adults are in an REM statc for about one third of their sleeping hours.

Obviously, research into sleep, REM states and NREM states, is only the first stage in the study of dreams. For our purposes, the dreamer would actually need to awaken from a dream state and relate what he saw in his dream. We are aware that newborns, fetuses and animals pass through REM stages, but this knowledge does not aid us in the study of dreams, since we cannot hear what they saw in their dreams.

Physiological research has provided us with an opportunity to understand sleep better, and to mark the beginning and end of a dream state; now we must move on to psychological/historical, and perhaps spiritual research in order to understand dreams and their interpretation.

The time factor is one of the mysteries of the dream state. We live in a world where time is a fixed factor of great significance, affecting the lives of us all. We know that when we wish to calculate the speed of a ray of light, for example, we can measure the time it takes the ray to pass between two points. We know that there are nine months between conception and birth, that a person lives about 70 years, and many other facts – all related to time – that shape our lives and cultures.

In a dream, time operates on a different plane. We can pass through decades in a matter of minutes. Months or years of actual activity can be compressed into a few "dream moments." Records of dreams shows that many events which the dreamer experienced from beginning to end in his dream, actually took place over many years.

In other words, time in a dream is an "imaginary" or "illusory" measure. In Eastern mysticism, this form of time is known as maya; it is defined as a state in which the gods place a screen over a person's eyes, making an "impossible" time frame appear realistic to him. Put another way, everything happens at the same time!

The time that we live by is a false reality – only Brahma knows the true time!

Many religions – as well as books dealing with religious mysticism in Islam, Christianity and Judaism – contain legends of journeys undertaken with the aid of an angel. In these journeys, the traveller "passes through time"; although he experiences the passage of years and generations, when he returns to the world of reality, only a moment has passed from when he embarked on his journey.

This leads to the question: To what extent does a dream have a basis in reality? Or, put another way: To what extent does a dream have a reality of its own?

We know that primitive tribes on the one hand, and spiritually enlightened individuals on the other, relate to dreams as if they are reality – and a reality more exalted than that of their everyday lives. In some cases, they are unable to distinguish between dream reality and actual reality. In many tribes, a person who dreams that he ate a poisoned fruit will exhibit all the symptoms of poisoning and receive treatment accordingly.

A young girl who dreams that a strange man raped her can go to the tribal elder, and the man will be punished as if he had actually committed the action. A man who has experienced nocturnal ejaculation must find and compensate the woman he was thinking of. No distinction is drawn between objective reality and dream reality.

Children display the same trait, often leaving us unable to distinguish, from the child's recounting, between actual reality, and the reality (and illusion) of his dream. But we should not relate to this as "foolishness" or a childhood prank. "In dreams, everyone sees his true nature," wrote the Greek philosopher Heraclitus. Then too, there is the well-known story of the Chinese philosopher Tachao, who asked himself upon awakening: "Am I the Chinese philosopher Tachao who dreamed that he was a butterfly, or am I a butterfly who dreamed that he was the Chinese philosopher Tachao?"

Many European philosophers, among them Descartes and Schopenhauer, asked themselves whether there really is a criterion that can be used to distinguish between dreams and reality. In the wake of their theories, a mystic philosophy emerged (typified by Gordayev and his followers), which argued that for most people, life is actually the true dream, and they are unable to escape from the clutches of the dream reality. Most of humanity is in a "living dream" state, reminiscent of the living dead, and the role of the philosopher is to awaken the living dreamer from his dream and reveal true reality to him!

Such philosophical debates are necessary in order to bring us closer to the central question: What is the meaning of dreams? What is their interpretation? What is each of us supposed to learn from his dreams?

The questions relating to dreams are practically endless: Is what we dream correct? Do dreams reveal secrets from the past? Perhaps they reveal to us the secrets of the future? We know that prophetic dreams do exist. Is a dream a glimpse, through a time telescope, of the mist-enshrouded future?

Or perhaps a dream is a telepathic "tuning in" to scenes that someone is sending to the brain, which has temporarily abandoned its conscious role?

Whatever the answers, man has always searched for meaning in his dreams. In every culture, we encounter the phenomenon of dream interpretation. "A dream that has not been interpreted is like an unread letter!" was written nearly 2,000 years ago. And that is precisely the approach today: a dream is a letter which must be read if we are to know its contents!

Dream interpretation has worn two faces over the centuries. On the one hand stood the explicit dreams: If you dreamed that you would break your leg during tomorrow's hunting expedition, this was a direct warning to you from your guardian spirit or some other mystic source. If you dreamed that God commanded you to erect a temple, or a statue, you had better do so, because this was a direct order from God. If you were sick and wanted God to heal you, you went to sleep in the shade of his temple, and he would relay his healing powers to you by way of a dream.

But the second aspect, which relates to dreams whose message is hidden or merely hinted at, is even more fascinating. Only correct interpretation – which is sometimes beyond the ability of the "lay" dreamer – will elicit its true meaning.

Books on dream interpretation are to be found in every culture and in every era. A list of dream interpretation books that contain one hundred or more explanations of various dreams would encompass some 80,000 publications. Outstanding among the oldest dream interpretation books still extant are those of China, ancient Egypt, Babylon and other cultures.

A figure in a dream, or the overall dream scenario, does not always carry the same meaning in every culture. While there is a tendency to encounter similar imagery – a pillar signifies the penis; a bowl, the vulva; waves crashing repeatedly against the shore symbolize intercourse, in the view of Freud, Jung and their disciples – this is not necessarily the case. A snake can indicate danger in one culture, and be a sign of good tidings in another. An eagle can foretell death, or unexpected salvation.

Every dream should be interpreted through a book suited to the dreamer's culture, and every dream interpretation must be adapted to the time and place of the dreamer. It is simple enough to take a book of dream interpretations and translate or rework it; it is a lot harder to track cultural and spiritual currents and produce an interpretation of dreams that is relevant to the place and time in which we live.

If we wake a person every time we note the beginning of an REM state, we will actually be preventing him from dreaming. What would happen then? In most cases, the person would start to daydream, to see dreams or illusions while in a waking state. Dreaming, like sleep, is a physical and emotional necessity. The interpretation of dreams – even for the person who does not believe in mysticism – is a universal and deep-seated need. And just as a person who is prevented from dreaming will function poorly the next day, so too a person who refrains from having his dream interpreted will have a less than complete view of the reality in which he lives.